T0314945

Media Nation

POLITICS AND CULTURE IN MODERN AMERICA

Series Editors
Margot Canaday, Glenda Gilmore,
Michael Kazin, Stephen Pitti, Thomas J. Sugrue

Volumes in the series narrate and analyze political and
social change in the broadest dimensions from 1865 to
the present, including ideas about the ways people have
sought and wielded power in the public sphere and the
language and institutions of politics at all levels—local,
national, and transnational. The series is motivated by
a desire to reverse the fragmentation of modern U.S.
history and to encourage synthetic perspectives on social
movements and the state, on gender, race, and labor, and
on intellectual history and popular culture.

MEDIA NATION

The Political History of News in Modern America

Edited by

Bruce J. Schulman

and

Julian E. Zelizer

PENN

UNIVERSITY OF PENNSYLVANIA PRESS

PHILADELPHIA

Published by
University of Pennsylvania Press
Philadelphia, Pennsylvania 19104-4112
www.upenn.edu/pennpress

Printed in the United States of America
on acid-free paper

10 9 8 7 6 5 4 3 2 1

A Cataloging-in-Publication record is available from the Library
of Congress

ISBN 978-0-8122-4888-3

CONTENTS

Introduction
  Bruce J. Schulman and Julian E. Zelizer   1

1. Proprietary Interest: Merchants, Journalists, and Antimonopoly
   in the 1880s
   Richard R. John   10

2. Progressive Political Culture and the Widening Scope of
   Local Newspapers, 1880–1930
   Julia Guarneri   36

3. The Ominous Clang: Fears of Propaganda from World War I
   to World War II
   David Greenberg   50

4. When the "Mainstream Media" Was Conservative:
   Media Criticism in the Age of Reform
   Sam Lebovic   63

5. "We're All in This Thing Together": Cold War Consensus
   in the Exclusive Social World of Washington Reporters
   Kathryn McGarr   77

6. Objectivity and Its Discontents: The Struggle for the Soul
   of American Journalism in the 1960s and 1970s
   Matthew Pressman   96

7. "No on 14": Hollywood Celebrities, the Civil Rights Movement, and the California Open Housing Debate
   Emilie Raymond   114

8. From "Faith in Facts" to "Fair and Balanced": Conservative Media, Liberal Bias, and the Origins of Balance
   Nicole Hemmer   126

9. Abe Rosenthal's Project X: The Editorial Process Leading to Publication of the Pentagon Papers
   Kevin Lerner   144

10. "Ideological Plugola," "Elitist Gossip," and the Need for Cable Television
   Kathryn Cramer Brownell   160

11. How Washington Helped Create the Contemporary Media: Ending the Fairness Doctrine in 1987
   Julian E. Zelizer   176

12. The Multiple Political Roles of American Journalism
   Michael Schudson   190

Notes   207

List of Contributors   247

Index   249

Introduction

Bruce J. Schulman and Julian E. Zelizer

In the middle of 1966 the United States sank deeper and deeper into Vietnam. Although television had become the dominant medium by that time, the three major networks—CBS, ABC, and NBC—remained reluctant to devote coverage to political issues outside of the half-hour nightly newscasts. These commercial enterprises and their executives hesitated to interrupt shows that could generate advertising revenue.

When Senator J. William Fulbright, a Democratic internationalist from Arkansas and former ally of President Lyndon B. Johnson, held hearings about the Vietnam War, the networks initially limited their coverage to brief excerpts. After watching the first few days of testimony, with Fulbright grilling administration officials about what they had done, CBS News chief Fred Friendly decided that Americans needed to see what was going on. Imploring his colleagues to approve live broadcasts, especially since rival NBC had preempted regular programming on the morning a top-level administration official was going to appear, CBS executives agreed to show half an hour of testimony, canceling the popular children's show *Captain Kangaroo*. With double the morning audience of NBC, CBS President Frank Stanton balked at giving up any more time.

But as the hearings became even more dramatic, with the legislators directly assailing the entire rationale behind the war, CBS stayed with the live broadcast, preempting lucrative reruns of *I Love Lucy*, *The McCoys*, and *The Dick Van Dyke Daytime Show*. Friendly persuaded his colleagues to continue into the afternoon, which meant calling off the soap operas and game shows that earned huge ratings.

The decision did not please the network brass. CBS also came under pressure from the White House. Concerned about the impact the hearings were having, President Johnson telephoned Stanton and asked him to end the broadcast. When Vice President for Broadcasting John Schneider pulled the plug on the committee's interrogation of diplomat George Kennan on the grounds that housewives were not interested, Friendly resigned. He was furious about the decision. "TV is bigger than any story it reports," Friendly insisted. "It's the greatest teaching tool since the printing press. It will determine nothing less than what kind of people we are. So if TV exists now only for the sake of a buck, somebody's going to have to change that."

This story about Friendly, CBS, and the Fulbright hearings forms but one small chapter in the long and complex history of the news media in American politics. It highlights a number of enduring questions that this volume investigates: how does the overwhelmingly commercial nature of American mass media—the fact that journalism and even artistic production take place predominately within for-profit enterprises—shape the flow of information in modern America? How have government regulation and the exigencies of democratic competition affected the evolution of the mass media? How have media in turn reshaped both policy and politics? Friendly's outrage and Schneider's insouciance about the needs of housewives also point up the myriad, often incestuous ways that information and entertainment, profits and politics have interacted in shaping the modern American political landscape.

In the twenty-first-century era of the 24/7 news cycle, the Hollywood fund-raiser, and the presidential Twitter feed, it has become abundantly clear that the media play—and have long played—an enormous role in American politics. In many ways, the central problem of modern U.S. political history remains the shift from a politics of parties to a politics of interests, from the era of the machine to the era of the consultant. Nearly every serious analyst of recent American politics concedes that the relationship between political actors and the mass media is central to understanding the political history of the last century. Yet aside from some suggestive work by historical sociologists and emerging scholarship by historians like those whose work is collected here, these crucial transformations remain little understood.[1] In particular, American political history possesses little empirical research, based on archival resources, into the ways that policymakers reacted to the shifting media landscape, how they appropriated the new tools of public relations and new management, and how the press adjusted to both the greater influence it wielded and the greater scrutiny it received. As managing the story and news cycle became central features of political life and the broader culture of celebrity and mass consumption reshaped policymaking and electoral politics, major media outlets reconstituted themselves and their relationship to the political system. In so doing they altered the very nature of political competition in the United States.

Political historians have often relegated the mass media to supporting roles—using newspapers and advertisements as sources without studying their history, retailing well-worn stories about FDR's fireside chats or the Kennedy–Nixon debates, analyzing media outlets in exclusively partisan or ideological terms. To be sure, there have long been some notable exceptions, such as the work of the historical sociologist Michael Schudson (a contributor to this volume), who has produced outstanding historical work on the professional history of news journalism. There have also been important works that considered the media strategies of specific presidents, such as William McKinley's press operation, Calvin Coolidge's pioneering use of public relations professionals, Franklin D. Roosevelt's deployment of radio and alliances with Hollywood, Dwight Eisenhower and John F. Kennedy's mastery of television, and the ways in which Ronald Reagan's team choreographed each day to frame a media narrative about his presidency.

Still, as a field, historians have long found it difficult to avoid a simplistic technological determinism. A new medium—cheap newspapers, nationally circulated print advertising, radio, television, social media—appears as if out of nowhere, as an exogenous force that determines political behavior rather than as a product of complex interchanges among a variety of institutions, policy frameworks, and political and economic actors that not only shifted the content of political debate but reshaped the institutional matrix in which politics and policy take shape.

But if American political historians have often taken the mass media for granted, scholars of media studies and journalism historians have lamented the isolation of their field from mainstream historical research. Over the past two decades, the leading journals in those disciplines have repeatedly published state-of-the-field essays, often by eminent senior scholars, calling for the fuller integration of media studies. In 2002, for example, Schudson asserted that media specialists pronounce their object of study to be "the 'sense-making practice of modernity,' but most humanities scholars have paid no heed."[2] Seven years later, Boston University journalism historian Chris Daly concluded that his specialty remained intellectually isolated and that "other American historians rarely venture" into it.[3] More recently, John Nerone, professor of communications research and media and cinema studies at the University of Illinois at Urbana–Champaign, echoed this assessment.

Scholars in his field "worry that their work doesn't matter," Nerone asserts. They complain that it "does not find a broader audience among historians."[4]

These jeremiads apply not only to histories of the news business. For more than a generation, studies of other mass media like film, sound recording, and television have been dominated largely by theoretical arguments about the ways in which the media operates and how their output is consumed. Informed by postmodernism, there have been vigorous debates about how far the media goes in shaping what people think, and how much consumers have the ability to interpret media products and appropriate them for their own purposes. But until very recently, media scholars have for the most part avoided empirical analysis of the relationships between media and politics in modern American life. In his summary of the history of broadcasting, for example, University of Wisconsin scholar Robert McChesney bemoaned the "triviality" of the field and called for more rigorous engagement with issues of political economy and for locating broadcasting history in the broader context of the U.S. economy, polity, and society.[5]

Recently, an emerging generation of scholars in both history and media studies have taken up these calls to integrate mass media more thoroughly into the master narratives of modern American political development. This work focuses not only on long-standing areas of interest for students of mass culture, such as production—analyses of media content and the motives of content producers—and consumption—studies of audience reception, grassroots mobilization, and voting behavior; it increasingly engages with issues of ownership, subsidy, and regulation—the recognition that mass media not only influence political competition and shape the electoral and governing strategies of political actors, but also operate in environments structured by government and politics.

This new literature has developed several important themes. First, scholars have devoted increasing attention to the institutional and economic history of the mass media. Keynoted by contributor Richard R. John's histories of the Post Office and the telephone-and-telegraph business, this attention to "media industries" has generated suggestive work on the political economy of American media from scholars in journalism history, sociology, history, and media studies.[6]

Second, studies of political communication have proliferated. These include the seminal work of Kathleen Hall Jamieson on the changing nature of campaigns and the development of political advertising. In recent years, however, a new generation of scholarship has emerged. Documenting the operations of newspapers, film studios, and radio and television networks as well as the strategies of public officials, party leaders, and grassroots lobbying organizations, this work is defined by immersion in a wide variety of archival sources, attentiveness to the interactions between state managers and a range of societal actors, and detailed explication of the changing practice of politics in the twentieth-century United States.

A third body of current research focuses around the origins, development, and impact of self-consciously conservative media over the past seventy-five years. Growing out of the wide-ranging scholarship on the rise of the right that has been the most vibrant subfield in American political history, this work explores the ways conservatives built media operations, used them to mobilize supporters—often among people who had previously been politically quiescent—and, in the process, reshaped the national political landscape.

Many of the contributors to *Media Nation* are making signal contributions to this innovative scholarship. This book assembles some of the most exciting voices in the field of media and political history. The volume collects revealing case studies of the evolution of the media from the late nineteenth century through the era of television and the Internet. While the essays do not attempt a comprehensive history, each author presents a fresh perspective on key questions ranging from the creation of newspapers with national reach in the late nineteenth century, to battles over press freedom in the early twentieth century, to the social and cultural history of news reporters at the height of the Cold War, to the internal editorial struggles in the *New York Times* over the Pentagon Papers, to how the government abandoned the Fairness Doctrine and the impact that had on news productions.

The first four chapters of this book focus on the late nineteenth and early twentieth centuries—the six formative decades between the 1880s and the end of World War II, which witnessed the professionalization of journalism, the construction of truly national mass media, and the foundations of the modern American state. Richard John highlights the pivotal contributions of urban newspapers to the antimonopoly crusade that structured late nineteenth-century political debate. Directing attention away from the farmer and labor groups that dominate interpretations of this movement, John shows how journalists and cartoonists deployed innovations in publishing and illustration to publicize the grievances of shippers and wholesalers and to create the political environment for antitrust legislation.

If John's investigation of the antimonopoly press forces historians to rethink Gilded Age politics, Julia Guarneri's study of the shifting content of local newspapers offers a bracing reinterpretation of the rise and fall of Progressivism. Looking at newspapers across all regions of the United States, Guarneri analyzes a wide range of local news: coverage of elections and governance, to be sure, but also crime stories, sports pages, advice columns, theater reviews, and wedding announcements. In so doing, she charts the ways local news coverage defined Americans' sense of community and political community, and how the gradual replacement of truly local reporting with mass-produced news and national coverage helped dissipate Progressive political culture.

By the 1920s, new modes of political communication, like those explored by John and Guarneri, as well as the development of the public presidency, the rise of the public relations industry, and the sophisticated propaganda of the warring powers in World War I, had transformed the conduct of public life. The changes seemed so novel and thoroughgoing that they prompted backlash—concern over the ways the powerful could mold and manipulate public opinion. In this setting, a group of politicians and public intellectuals developed a critique of propaganda. David Greenberg explicates this emerging debate over the effects of mass media. In the decade after U.S. entry into World War I, Greenberg concludes, a "new culture of suspicion produced a cottage industry of anti-propaganda tracts that cemented a lasting distrust of publicity, especially from the government."

Sam Lebovic also considers media critics—in this case, liberal and leftist critiques of the conservative dominance of the mainstream press during the first half of the twentieth century. Recovering the lost history of these academics, popular writers, and political activists—figures ranging from California socialist Upton Sinclair to journalist George Seldes to New Dealer Harold Ickes—Lebovic shows how this antimedia populism in many ways anticipated later right-wing attacks on liberal bias in the media. But unlike contemporary conservative contempt for the "lame-stream media," earlier critics grounded their fears of press influence in a structural critique of capitalism. Lebovic's investigation of "media politics" thus widens the scope of the volume to include the politics of media ownership.

The remaining seven essays develop many of these themes and extend the analysis to the period after World War II, the era in which mass media clearly supplanted party organizations, and even interest groups, as the principal intermediaries between politicians and citizens. Kathryn McGarr reconstructs the social world of Washington reporters during the early postwar era to offer a highly original interpretation of how the Cold War consensus actually functioned. Acknowledging the limits of that consensus, the way it sometimes remained aspirational rather than reality, McGarr's essay nonetheless probes the ways that the manners and morals of the national press enforced conformity. "The daily working lives of Washington reporters," McGarr explains, "included a widespread, institutionalized blurring of the social and the professional that made dissent, especially on issues of foreign policy and national security, all but unthinkable."

In the following chapter, Matthew Pressman shifts perspective from the social and intellectual norms to the professional culture that shaped political reporting in the postwar era. Pressman explicates the external attacks and internal, institutional pressures that forced journalists to rethink their earlier commitment to objectivity as well as their long-standing deference to public officials, business leaders, and prominent citizens. Offering nuanced case studies of the *New York Times* and *Los Angeles Times*, Pressman shows how an emerging generation of editors and reporters, many with different backgrounds and training than their predecessors, responded to criticism of ideological bias and how they recast prevailing understandings of "objectivity."

Emilie Raymond also takes on the pivotal developments of the 1950s and 1960s, investigating a realm of media politics outside questions about coverage of public officials in daily newspapers and broadcasts. Exploring the role of Hollywood celebrities in the civil rights movement, Raymond recovers the myriad ways entertainers used a variety of media platforms to draw attention to an issue that they believed journalists had neglected. By drawing attention to the film and music industries, this essay analyzes a crucial transformation in the conduct of national politics. As entertainment became an increasingly important component of political leadership, Hollywood celebrities (and the venues in which they appeared), came to play a crucial role in mediating the communication between policymakers and public opinion. And yet, as Raymond concludes, celebrity activism could sometimes backfire; it helped create the controversial stereotype of the Hollywood Left that finds resonance in contemporary political debate.

Elucidating the origins and development of the conservative media establishment, Nicole Hemmer investigates the ways that politicians and journalists on the American right navigated many of the same controversies over objectivity, advocacy and relations with the powerful that vexed the mainstream press and left-leaning journalists after World War II. Hemmer shows how conservatives both created an explicitly ideological media, guided by a different set of standards, and simultaneously undermined the authority and challenged the standards of the journalism profession. In so doing, the Right reshaped the national media landscape. Kevin Lerner follows Hemmer's wide-ranging essay with a detailed, richly textured analysis of a key individual and a pivotal moment in the postwar transformation of the relations between media and government: *New York Times* editor Abe Rosenthal and the publication of the Pentagon Papers. Lerner's essay offers an engaging new perspective on a well-told story. Beyond reconstructing the path to and consequences of the momentous decision to publish, Lerner also situates the *Times* newsroom in its broader context, explaining how the generally conservative leadership of the *Times* adapted the paper to the challenges of the counterculture and the antiwar movement.

Kathryn Brownell isolates the same late 1960s–early 1970s watershed, but her subject is the emerging new medium of cable television, and her focus is public policy. Recalling some of the debates over media ownership in the 1930s that Lebovic investigated, Brownell emphasizes that the American system of commercial broadcasting has always involved policy choices, negotiation between public and private interests, and political calculation. Reinterpreting the origins of cable, Brownell reveals that the Nixon administration's antipathy toward what it believed to be a "liberal media" fueled an effort to restructure the broadcasting system in the United States. While Vice President Spiro Agnew publicly denounced the "nattering nabobs of negativism" in the press, Nixon used the administrative realm to "shape the future of the media landscape." Recovering this all-but-forgotten moment in recent history, Brownell also incorporates the perspectives of liberal reformers who in their own way shared Nixon's hope that cable television might expand of the variety of viewpoints represented in the mass media.

Julian E. Zelizer extends this attention to the intersections among politics, administration, and broadcasting into the 1980s. Explicating the 1987 decision of the Federal Communications Commission to terminate the Fairness Doctrine—a decision taken with enthusiastic support from the Ronald Reagan administration and congressional Republicans—Zelizer makes clear the pivotal role of public policy in shaping the contemporary media environment. In place since 1949, with roots stretching back to the radio era, the Fairness Doctrine had functioned as the policy foundation for the norm of objectivity that governed the news media through most of the post–World War II era. Without that restraint, Zelizer argues, and with more and more unfettered access to broadcasting by interests without commitments to traditional journalistic standards, little could hold back the move toward the contemporary era of polarized news and contentious, self-consciously ideological reporting.

Michael Schudson concludes the volume with an incisive overview of the multiple political roles of American journalism. Looking back across the entire post–World War II period, Schudson identifies a wide range of political roles that the press has played: as advocate, lobbyist, national security executive, government insider, and as "medium for the formation of political culture." Drawing on a number of telling examples, he shows how the news media not only reported the political process but also participated in it—in his words, "shaping, constituting, coordinating, and legitimating specific ways of doing politics and specific ways of thinking about politics."

It has long been a truism that the mass media form a crucial component of modern U.S. political history. Based on original research involving a wide range of sources, the contributors to this volume explain how and why this political landscape took shape: the ways that mass media have been vehicles for, participants in, and subjects of political debate and policy formation. Together, the essays in this book offer a field-shaping work that we hope will bring the media back to the center of scholarship on the history of the United States since the late nineteenth century.

CHAPTER 1

Proprietary Interest: Merchants, Journalists, and Antimonopoly in the 1880s

Richard R. John

"Many good people have imagined a bogey monster that doesn't exist. They have accepted as facts the fancies of sensational journalism." So declared business lobbyist Francis B. Thurber in December 1899 in the *Journal of Social Science*, in deploring popular hostility toward Standard Oil, the American Sugar Refining Company, and other corporate behemoths.[1] Journalists were wrong to demonize these giant organizations, Thurber warned, by conjuring up the "bogey monster" of monopoly. In fact, these giant organizations had a "right to combine"—subject to a "due regard to the rights of others"—since, as history demonstrated, economic consolidation would lower prices and increase output, making it a boon for the consumer.[2]

Thurber's exasperation with the popular press was rooted in his conviction that irresponsible journalists were fueling a wrongheaded legal crusade to criminalize the economically sound, well-intentioned, and morally praiseworthy mergers and acquisitions that had been undertaken recently by some of the country's largest and most powerful corporations. To check corporate abuse, Congress had in 1890 enacted a brief but sweeping law, known as the Sherman Act, which had made it a felony for anyone to monopolize, or even to "attempt to monopolize," any trade or form of commerce "among the several States, or with foreign nations."[3] From Thurber's perspective, the Sherman Act was a travesty of justice that had plainly been inspired by a "wave of radical public opinion" that had originated among economically illiterate farmers and workers and that would be amplified by demagogic politicians and a scurrilous "penny journalism." Even "our popular president" Theodore Roosevelt, Thurber elaborated in 1905, was "liable to err in his impulses unless he studies this subject more deeply than he has as yet."[4]

Thurber's lament is a pointed reminder of the complex tangle of interests and ideology that shaped the late nineteenth-century media campaign to regulate the conduct of large and powerful corporations. This media campaign would reach its apotheosis in the decade immediately preceding the enactment of the Sherman Act and has come to be known to contemporaries and historians alike as "antimonopoly." This story is familiar to historians of the period, yet it has only rarely been subjected to critical scrutiny. This essay tries to set the record straight.

It has long been conventional for historians—following, if unwittingly, obviously partisan corporate apologists like Thurber—to trace the late nineteenth-century antimonopoly movement to the grievances of farmers and laborers outraged by the excesses of big business, making it, as it were, the latest installment in a perennial contest between the many and the few. This oft-told story is not entirely mistaken. Farm and labor publications had lambasted railroad corporations since at least the 1870s. Yet it is oversimplified and in certain factual details misleading. In fact, the antimonopoly movement that crested in the 1880s—the decade in which it loomed largest in public life—received its primary impetus *not* from farmers and workers, but rather from some of the country's wealthiest and most influential merchants—the most vocal of whom were based in New York, Brooklyn, Chicago, and San Francisco—whose anticorporate, pro-proprietary worldview was powerfully amplified by a small but influential cadre of reform-minded journalists. These merchants popularized a critique of corporate power that would shape American public life for decades to come.

The wealthiest and most powerful merchants in the 1880s were not retailers (Sears would not build its first retail store until the 1920s), but, instead, wholesalers and shippers. Most merchants, including some of the wealthiest and most powerful, did not operate their businesses as state-chartered corporations that managed other people's money. Instead, their businesses took the form of wholly owned proprietorships—often partnerships with two or more principals—that had been organized under the common law. Historians sometimes assume that "big business" vanquished all comers in late nineteenth-century America. In reality, the "incorporation" of America was slow and halting. Even Andrew Carnegie's vast steel empire was organized not as a corporation but as a proprietorship. The phrase "big business" itself would not gain widespread currency until the twentieth century.[5] The economic and moral superiority of the proprietorship over the corporation was a truism for well-educated Americans who reasoned, not implausibly, that proprietorships fostered autonomy while corporations bred dependency. This truism was also an article of faith for big-city merchants, who remained in the 1880s one of the nation's most tightly organized political blocs. Corporations were obviously powerful, yet few assumed that their ascendancy was inevitable, while the proprietary-corporate moral equation would not shift in a decisive way until World War I.

While proprietorships and corporations were each capitalistic, they differed fundamentally in one key dimension. Corporations had been granted under state law unlimited liability for the losses they incurred; proprietorships had not. Since the wealth of almost every merchant was tied up in his business, this meant that, should he fail—as thousands would during the Panic of 1893—he was ruined.[6]

The vulnerability of merchants to financial collapse best explains why the antimonopoly movement found such a sympathetic reception in the press. It was not outsiders, but insiders, who fanned the flames. The corporations that New York City antimonopolists inveighed against with the greatest fervor in the 1880s were localized in one of three sectors: transportation (the New York & Hudson River Railroad), communications (Western Union), and energy (Standard Oil). Each threatened the economic interests of the city's merchants, though in different ways. The New York & Hudson Railroad and Western Union had it in their power to alter the terms of trade, cutting the merchants' margins to the bone. The threat posed by Standard Oil was less existential, though no less real: the noxious fumes that spewed forth from the East River refinery that it operated just north of Brooklyn fouled the air, imperiled property values, and undermined confidence in the self-regulating mechanisms of the market economy.

Journalists recognized the merchants' predicament and responded accordingly. The editorial positions of most influential big-city newspapers in the late nineteenth century, as in most periods of American history, remained closely aligned with the country's commercial elite, which in the 1880s continued to be dominated not by corporations, but by merchants. For this reason alone, it is thus not surprising that the antimonopoly movement found support in several of the nation's most influential newspapers, including the *Chicago Tribune* and the *New York World*.[7]

Thurber's relationship to the antimonopoly movement is especially suggestive. For several decades prior to 1893, he had been a proprietor of Thurber, Whyland & Company, a large and successful Manhattan-based grocery wholesaler that had acquired an enviable reputation as one of country's largest importers of coffee and tea. Thurber would fail in the Panic of 1893, ending his business career. Financially ruined, Thurber retrained as a lawyer, an unusual decision in an age in which midlife career changes remained uncommon.

Thurber's legal expertise provided him with the necessary credentials to hang out a shingle as a business lobbyist. Thurber also had an additional, perhaps even more important, qualification for his new job. For in the years prior to his bankruptcy, Thurber *himself* had been one of the very antimonopoly agitators he now cautioned the public against. The primary impetus for the antimonopoly movement that he now inveighed against, Thurber knew well, lay neither on the farm nor in the factory. Rather, it had been the brainchild of big-city proprietary capitalists like himself—that is, before he had gone bankrupt—an inconvenient fact now that he had switched sides, yet one that reveals much about media politics in the 1880s, the decade in which the antimonopoly movement would exert its greatest influence over the public imagination.

Much of the historical writing on the late nineteenth-century antimonopoly movement has viewed it through the lens of the Sherman Act, which is unsurprising, since for much of the twentieth century this law remained a cornerstone of U.S. economic policy. This essay approaches the topic from a different angle. Instead of treating the Sherman Act as the first chapter in a twentieth-century grand narrative of business challenge and government response, it casts a spotlight on the world out of which this law emerged. In this world, the most influential actors were neither farmers nor workers, but merchants and the journalists who publicized their grievances—voices often marginalized in standard accounts of late nineteenth-century public life.

Farmers and workers, to be sure, had good reason to oppose economic consolidation. Yet it would be an exaggeration to put them at the center of the antimonopoly movement of the 1880s. Other voices were far more influential, especially in the big-city press, which was where the movement found its most enduring expression. The antimonopoly movement of the 1880s did not begin on the periphery and move to the center. On the contrary, it originated in the nation's commercial centers and only later migrated to the agricultural hinterland.[8] Many ideas and images that originated in the big-city press would eventually find their way into farm and labor publications. Yet it would be a mistake to overlook their metropolitan-mercantile pedigree. The ubiquitous "robber baron" metaphor, for example, long an antimonopoly rallying cry, had its roots in historical accounts of medieval German commerce, and was initially popularized by well-to-do East Coast merchants and their journalistic devotees.[9] It should, similarly, come as no surprise that the antimonopoly rationale for government ownership of the telegraph had been widely discussed by merchants and journalists in the big-city press for several decades before it would find its way onto the Populist Party platforms in 1892 and 1896.[10]

Antimonopoly is easily misunderstood. In the main, its supporters were neither nostalgic defenders of a small-scale, agrarian society of self-sufficient husbandmen, nor anticapitalistic proponents of a workers' utopia. Contrary to what is sometimes assumed, they did not necessarily oppose economic consolidation. In fact, many antimonopolists deplored "cutthroat" competition—a presumption widely shared by the populists, as Charles Postel has recently demonstrated—and more than a few actually regarded the existing degree of economic consolidation as too low.[11] The problem with giant organizations for these antimonopolists was not that they were too large, but that they were too small: economic consolidation, if properly regulated, could foster economies of scale that could benefit the many as well as the few. At its core, antimonopoly was less about economics than morality: corporations were dangerous not because they were too *big*, but rather because they had become too *powerful* to operate unrestrained by law—and, in particular, too independent of the salutary regulatory mechanism of market competition.

"Antimonopoly" in the 1880s was a capacious term that could refer to one of three related yet distinct responses to economic consolidation. Open-access antimonopolists derided economic consolidation as the unnatural by-product of political collusion and tried to reverse it; consolidationists regarded economic consolidation as irreversible and tried to minimize its ill effects; nationalists lauded economic consolidation as a first step on the path toward government ownership. Each built on the worldview of the wealthy and powerful merchants who in the 1880s remained highly respected moral arbiters with considerable influence in the press. No antimonopolist viewed with equanimity the possibility that the common-law proprietorship might one day be supplanted by the state-chartered corporation as the country's dominant economic institution, or, for that matter, that corporate publicists would one day identify big business with the country's most cherished civic ideals. The valorization of managerial capitalism and the idealization of "free enterprise" remained in the future. And while not all antimonopolists were nationalists, most regarded government ownership of certain large-scale enterprises with relative equanimity: not until World War I, it is worth recalling, would government ownership of the railroad and the telegraph slip off the national political agenda.[12] This essay does not chart the rise of managerial capitalism, which would receive a vital impetus during the opening decades of the twentieth century and would be largely complete by 1940.[13] Instead, it surveys how an earlier generation of Americans thought about monopoly, what it proposed to do about it, and why its assault upon big business took the form that it did.

*   *   *

The oldest and in some ways the most enduring antimonopoly appeal regarded economic consolidation as the unnatural by-product of political collusion. Open access was its byword, barriers to entry its bête noire. The best kind of regulation was competition, and if lawmakers could be persuaded to eliminate the restraints that impeded the free flow of commerce, market forces would do the rest.

Open-access antimonopolism had broad support among wholesalers and shippers eager to lower prices on the movement of goods and services. It was also a favorite of insurgent promoters eager to challenge entrenched incumbents. It was for this reason that, not entirely implausibly, it proved appealing for a brief period in the 1870s to the notorious financier Jay Gould. Gould had invested in an insurgent telegraph network provider to challenge the incumbent, Western Union, and proclaimed himself an antimonopolist to rally support. Open-access antimonopolism also had many champions in the press—sometimes in earnest, yet more than occasionally as a feint to bamboozle unwary investors.[14]

The presumption that monopoly was unnatural was taken for granted by many critics of the railroad and the telegraph, two of the central pillars of the emerging corporate order. To make their case, these critics pointed to the raft of special privileges that Congress had bestowed on continent-spanning railroads, mostly in the form of generous land grants—subsidies that critics then and now contended had prematurely hastened railroad expansion.[15] Further proof that the market was rigged was the consolidation in 1866 of

Western Union as the country's dominant telegraph network provider. Whether or not the telegraph market could have been credibly contested after 1866 is beside the point. The fact remains that, in the thirty-six-year period between the opening of the first fee-for-service telegraph line in April 1845 and the takeover of Western Union by financier Jay Gould in January 1881, many of Western Union's critics assumed that the telegraph market would have been open to new entrants had Western Union not unfairly lobbied Congress and manipulated the press.[16]

Among the many journalists to find open access compelling was Frank Bellew, a talented illustrator who is best remembered today as one of the first cartoonists to render the American folk icon "Uncle Sam" in visual form.[17] The special privileges that lawmakers had lavished on the railroad, Bellew maintained in a series of hard-hitting front-page antimonopoly cartoons that ran in the New York *Daily Graphic* in the 1870s, were a direct assault on everything the country stood for.

While the *Daily Graphic* is largely forgotten today, it had the distinction of being the first daily newspaper in the United States to run illustrations in every issue, an innovation that obliged its editors to search far and wide for suitable content. The ancestor of the modern tabloid, it appealed primarily to novelty-seeking New Yorkers, who were joined by a sprinkling of curious outsiders who subscribed to a weekly edition that they received in the mail. In their quest for new material, the *Daily Graphic*'s illustrators invented much of the visual iconography that would later become a ubiquitous feature of the popular press. Its cartoons were, quite literally, *cartoonish*: vivid, hard-hitting, and unsubtle, they helped establish a gallery of viscerally appealing archetypes—the "octopus," the "robber baron," "the politico"—that would long remain a fixture in the iconography of political reform.[18]

It is, of course, hard to know how many Americans saw Bellew's anti-monopoly cartoons, let alone how they reacted. Yet there can be no question but that the iconography that he pioneered would be refined and elaborated by his successors for many decades, before it would be repurposed as a teaching tool in the U.S. history classroom at both high school and college levels—and also, most recently, as an educational resource on the web.[19]

The most arresting of Bellew's antimonopoly cartoons built on the conceit that the manipulation of the political process by corporate lobby-ists had transmogrified the railroad—exhibit A of the perils of economic consolidation—into a rampaging monster. Emboldened by its nefarious legislative triumphs, the railroad-monster set its sights on the levers of power.

The monster Bellew had in mind had a distinctly European, high-culture pedigree. This should come as no surprise: few antimonopoly icons were born in the United States. Bellew was an English immigrant, and, prior to his arrival in the United States, had served an apprenticeship in London drawing satirical sketches for the English comic magazine *Punch*. When Bellew depicted the railroad as an octopus, for example—a convention that he may well have invented—he drew for inspiration on Victor Hugo's 1866 novel *Toilers of the Sea*. Bellew's monster, like Hugo's, ensnared an innocent person in its tentacles. For Hugo, the victim was a fisherman; for Bellew, a young woman who symbolized "Columbia," a personification of the republic's civic ideals. Wrapped in the American flag, Columbia struggled to keep the Constitution out of the clutches of the voracious monster, which had already devoured "congressional honor" (Figure 1.1).[20]

The most celebrated of Bellew's antimonopoly cartoons took its inspiration from another literary monster, the malformed giant in Mary Shelley's *Frankenstein* (1818). For Bellew, the railroad became the vicious creature that Shelley's mad scientist brought to life. In the earliest of Bellew's *Frankenstein*-inspired cartoons, the mad scientist, outfitted as Uncle Sam, looked on in horror as the smoke-belching railroad-monster—nourished at the trough of "public lands" and trussed with a belt marked "R.R. monopoly"—sprang to life, crumpling the Constitution in his metallic hand.[21] In a later and better-known version of this cartoon, the railroad-monster, having escaped from the scientist's laboratory, terrorized a prostrate country. In one hand the monster wielded a club marked "capital"; in the other, he waved aloft the torn mantle of "judicial ermine." "Agriculture, Commerce and Manufacture Are All in My Power," the monster exulted, adding ominously that his ultimate "Interest" was the "Higher Law of American Politics."[22]

High-culture iconography also featured prominently in Bellew's "Modern Laocoön," another railroad-monster antimonopoly cartoon that drew its inspiration from European art. In this cartoon, Bellew reinterpreted the celebrated classical sculpture of the doomed Trojan prophet Laocoön by casting the prophet as "Agriculture," his two sons as "Manufacturing" and "Commerce," and the death-dealing snake that strangled them the "Railroad Monopoly."[23]

Open-access antimonopolism presumed that—in the absence of some kind of unfair, immoral, or even illegal special privilege—economic consolidation would be significantly forestalled. While not necessarily noninterventionist, it had certain affinities with the classical nineteenth-century

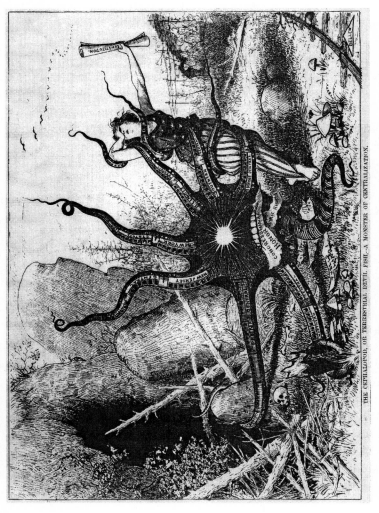

THE CEPHALOPOD, OR TERRESTRIAL DEVIL FISH—A MONSTER OF CENTRALIZATION.

Figure 1.1. This melodramatic 1873 Frank Bellew cartoon took its inspiration from a recently published novel by the French writer Victor Hugo. Outraged by the tight relationship between lawmakers and the land-grant railroads, Bellew depicted the railroads as the tentacles of a sea monster that had recently escaped from an underwater cave. This cartoon was almost certainly the first visual rendering of big business as an octopus, a convention that would prove remarkably enduring. Frank Bellew, "The Cephalopod, or Terrestrial Devil Fish—A Monster of Centralization," *Daily Graphic*, March 4, 1873.

liberal doctrine that its detractors would stigmatize as "laissez-faire." Each placed more faith in market forces than lawmakers and each feared the propensity of regulatory initiatives to strengthen incumbents and weaken insurgents. Its most celebrated journalistic monument was Ida M. Tarbell's searing exposé of John D. Rockefeller's Standard Oil Company, which she serialized in *McClure's Magazine* beginning in 1902 and published as a book two years later. Tarbell's father had been an independent oilman, and, like the pre-1881 critics of Western Union, Tarbell took it for granted that, had Rockefeller not been a beneficiary of special privilege, a salutary competition would have prevailed. To illustrate her thesis, Tarbell described in numbing detail the inner history of a thirty-year-old intra-industry set-to involving railroad rebates that she had learned about from her father and read about in the press.[24]

The open-access antimonopolism of Bellew and Tarbell was long on moralism and short on practicality. A related, yet in some ways markedly different, response to economic consolidation treated the rise of big business as inevitable and advocated permanent government regulation to align the emerging corporate order with the public good.

Among the most celebrated of the consolidationists were the journalists Henry George and Henry Demarest Lloyd. Though each had a well-deserved reputation as a radical, neither was an outsider to the world of proprietary capitalism. Both were urbanites who spent much of their adult lives in big cities—New York City for George, Chicago for Lloyd—and each spent many years reporting for big-city newspapers on the challenges that proprietary capitalists confronted in a world in which they remained a powerful political bloc.

Henry George's antimonopolism grew directly out of his firsthand experience as a journalist at a San Francisco daily. To try to obtain for his newspaper a telegraphic news feed, George journeyed in 1869 to New York City—the same year in which the transcontinental railroad had been completed. Following an unsuccessful meeting at Western Union headquarters, George concluded, correctly, that the news feed would not be forthcoming because Western Union had entered into a collusive relationship with the country's most important news broker, the New York Associated Press. This discovery led George to an epiphany that would give shape to his life's work. Technological innovation, George now understood, could be a curse as well as a blessing—or, as he put it, "progress" for the few could coexist with "poverty" for the many. Having reached this sobering conclusion, George turned his attention to the injustice of private land ownership, a monopoly that he regarded as even more pernicious than the collusive relationship between Western Union and the Associated Press.[25]

Lloyd's antimonopolism, like Henry George's, was nurtured during his years as a big-city newspaper journalist. George discovered his life's work in a single blinding flash; for Lloyd, in contrast, his ideas evolved gradually as he climbed the journalistic ladder. Starting out as literary editor for the *Chicago Tribune*, Lloyd rose through the ranks to become financial editor and then chief editorial writer. Following a quarrel with one of the newspaper's owners—who, as it happens, was Lloyd's father-in-law—he left the paper to become a freelancer. Lloyd lived well. Having learned a good deal about Chicago real estate during his years as a journalist, he astutely parlayed this knowledge into a substantial fortune. In making the case against monopoly power, Lloyd combined firsthand reporting with analytical insights gleaned from state-of-the-art European social science. As a journalist, Lloyd reported dutifully on political scandals, legal entanglements, and legislative infighting—setting the pattern for much of the antimonopoly journalism to follow. As a social-science popularizer, he built on the Victorian reassessment of the classical economics of Adam Smith. The fruits of Lloyd's labors appeared in countless newspaper and magazine articles, as well as in his masterpiece, *Wealth Against Commonwealth* (1894), an impassioned exposé of the business practices of John D. Rockefeller's Standard Oil.

Like Ida M. Tarbell, who had drawn extensively on Lloyd's reporting in her Standard Oil exposé, Lloyd found much to deplore. Yet unlike Tarbell, Lloyd regarded economic consolidation not as a perverse aberration, but rather as an irreversible social fact. By documenting the rise of the corporate order, Lloyd hoped to hasten the day when Americans would "save the liberties they have inherited" by "winning new ones to bequeath": "Monopoly is business at the end of its journey. It has got there. The irrepressible conflict is now as distinctly with business as the issue so lately met was with slavery."[26] Lloyd's task was to craft a narrative so compelling that it would raise the consciousness of his readers to such a pitch that they, too, would share his moral indignation at the injustice that he had revealed: "When it comes to know the facts the human heart can no more endure monopoly than American slavery or Roman empire. The first step to a remedy is that the people care. If they know, they will care. To help them to know and care; to stimulate new hatred of evil, new love of the good, new sympathy for the victims of power, and, by enlarging its science, to quicken the old into a new conscience, this compilation of fact has been made."[27]

The crux of Lloyd's argument was not economic but moral. Lloyd is justly remembered today as his generation's leading journalistic popularizer of social scientific ideas. The fact-value distinction was not among them. That "science" was the "substance" of the word "conscience" was no mere "verbal accident," Lloyd reminded his readers in the closing paragraph of *Wealth Against Commonwealth*: "We must know the right before we can do the right."[28] Monopoly was objectionable—like slavery—not because it was economically inefficient, but because it was morally pernicious. Its evils had nothing to do with size: mere bigness was not bad. If anything, the vast organizations that dominated the transportation and communications sectors rested on a foundation that was unnecessarily narrow.

The ultimate source of the moral iniquity of monopoly lay in the baleful moral philosophy of which it was the consummate expression. The widespread embrace of the ethically threadbare utilitarianism of the English moral philosopher Jeremy Bentham—who had the temerity to proclaim the tired shibboleth "the greatest happiness of the greatest number" to be a worthy civic ideal—had led, in an age of rapid technological innovation, to the accumulation of vast reservoirs of unregulated power by the supremely selfish individuals who ran the nation's corporations.[29] To respond, as many antimonopolists did, that the challenge of utilitarianism could be met by harnessing self-interest to the public good through the enactment of legislation establishing regulatory agencies to constrain self-interest, was an unrealistic "dream": "It is to accept the principle of the sovereignty of the self-interest of the individual and apply constitutional checks to it."[30] For this reason, Lloyd's *Wealth Against Commonwealth* can be read as a five-hundred-page meditation on the "discovery" that business corrupts politics—an insight that is typically associated not with the late nineteenth-century antimonopolists, but rather with the early twentieth-century muckrakers whose conclusions they did so much to prefigure.[31]

A devout Christian socialist, Lloyd urged Americans to renounce self-interest and embrace the "greatest happiness of all."[32] To reach the promised land, Lloyd looked to the past. In his search for templates for the good society, Lloyd commended two of the nation's oldest and most venerable institutions: the public school and the Post Office Department. While obviously different, each of these institutions shared a common DNA rooted in a civic mandate that transcended the utilitarian pursuit of self-interest: "We are to apply the co-operative methods of the post-office and the public school to many other common toils, to all toils in which private sovereignty has become through monopoly a despotism over the public, and to all in which the association of the people and the organization of processes have been so far developed that the profit-hunting Captain of Industry may be replaced by the public-serving Captain of Industry."[33]

Journalists provided the antimonopoly movement with its most enduring literary testaments: Henry George's *Progress and Poverty* (1879), Edward Bellamy's *Looking Backward* (1888), and Lloyd's *Wealth Against Commonwealth* (1894). Yet antimonopoly was by no means confined to the press. Among its nonjournalistic champions were the legion of wholesalers and shippers who relied on the railroad and the telegraph to buy and sell. Merchants had nothing against wealth. Yet they resented the accumulation of vast fortunes by corporate moguls who were seemingly unconstrained by market forces.

Among the most earnest of the merchant antimonopolists was Francis B. Thurber, the same individual who, following his bankruptcy, would rail against the antimonopolists for their supposed indifference to the iron laws of economics. Thurber was not a deep thinker, and his antimonopolism lacked subtlety. Even so, it was not without a certain unassailable cogency. Recent improvements in the forces of production, Thurber believed, of which the most important were the railroad and the telegraph, had enormously increased the ability of certain powerful men to perform useful labor. Unfortunately, the fruits of innovation remained inaccessible to the rest of the population, having been monopolized by soulless corporations whose owners reaped vast profits by manipulating the terms of trade. To remedy this evil, civic-minded citizens such as Thurber had an obligation to bring it to the attention of the middle and upper classes, since, in his view, the injustices that the railroad and telegraph were daily perpetrating were too abstract and arcane to be fully appreciated by the poor.[34] To assume that the lower orders could fully comprehend the full magnitude of the depredations that were being wrought by railroad and telegraph corporations defied common sense. After all, or so Thurber sanctimoniously assumed, only a cosmopolitan merchant like Thurber himself could possibly understand how the system really worked.

Thurber embraced the nineteenth-century liberal commonplace that human labor was the ultimate source of value. Yet he readily conceded that recent technological innovations had fundamentally altered the relationship between work, power, and wealth. With the advent of steam power, a new, nonhuman agency had unexpectedly become the world's greatest labor saver, making it the "greatest creator of wealth in existence." The harnessing of electricity raised an analogous conundrum: could the energy generated by steam and electricity be privately owned? Thurber's answer was an emphatic no. Human beings had the right to own their own labor, but not the energy generated by steam or electricity. This was because these new forms of power were gifts from God: "Like light, or air, or water, they are God's gifts to the human race, and should be possessed and enjoyed by everyone." Tragically, however, the "great middle class" had been largely shut off from the benefits of this new form of power, while the poor found themselves confronted for the first time by employers who, having harnessed the power of steam and electricity, had become "independent" of their exertions.[35]

To draw public attention to the injustices that were being daily perpetrated by the railroad and the telegraph, Thurber organized the National Anti-Monopoly League in 1881. The immediate catalyst for its establishment was the frustration of an influential cohort of New York City–based merchants at the reluctance of Republican state lawmakers to establish a state railroad commission. Though the league aspired to be a "national" organization, it was in fact headquartered in New York City, and during its brief heyday in the 1880s remained a mouthpiece for the city's proprietary capitalists, who, in this period, counted among their ranks some of the city's wealthiest and most highly respected men. Farmers played no role in the league's founding, and workers were important only as an audience for its appeals. Instead, the league was a publicity machine that had been organized by some of the city's wealthiest merchants to win votes and build a political constituency to regulate the emerging corporate order.

The league attained one of its primary goals in 1882 when the New York state legislature established a railroad commission. Flush with victory, its organizers broadened their agenda to embrace the monopoly question in all of its dimensions. To get their message across, they turned to the press. How else would it be possible to persuade a broad cross section of the electorate of the daily injustices that were being perpetuated by corporations? Central to the league-sponsored media campaign was the launching in 1882 of *Justice*, a weekly newspaper devoted to "Anti-Monopoly Principles" from the standpoint of the "Rights of the Many as Against the Privileges for the Few."[36]

In the next few years, *Justice* ran hundreds of fact-studded articles detailing corporate abuses, which it supplemented with a sprinkling of antimonopoly cartoons. Among these cartoons was yet another by Frank Bellew. Dubbed "Comparative Bigness" in the explanatory article that accompanied it in the magazine in which it originally appeared, Bellew's cartoon was re-titled "Upon What Meat" by the editors of *Justice*, a high-toned reference to a line from Shakespeare's "Julius Caesar." In this cartoon, which occupied the entire top right column of the newspaper's first page, Bellew compared the "relative proportions" of railroad tycoon William H. Vanderbilt, who at the time was worth $100 million, with that of a wealthy man worth $1 million—an impressive total even for the most successful proprietary capitalist—and a worker, defined as "small capital and labor," who made ten dollars a week. To make this comparison visually arresting, Bellew hit upon an ingenious conceit: he portrayed Vanderbilt, the millionaire, and the worker as if their wealth were proportional to their height. In such a rendering, Vanderbilt filled the newspaper's column from top to bottom, the millionaire was over-shadowed by Vanderbilt's shoe, and the worker was buried at the bottom of an enormous pit so deep that the full length of its shaft could not be fully displayed on the page.[37] "Is it any wonder," the editor added, with a palpable sense of frustration at the indifference of his readership toward the injustice that Bellew had depicted, "that the people stand evils without general protest even, that the great man has a supreme contempt for them and says, 'The public be damned?'" (Figure 1.2.)[38]

It is hard to know how many articles Thurber himself may have contributed to *Justice*, or even if he wrote for it at all. Most *Justice* articles were unsigned, and many appear to have been recycled from other publications. Yet there can no doubt that Thurber fully shared Bellew's outrage at economic inequality, and, in particular, the rapidly growing wealth gap between the rich and poor. We are "fast becoming a nation of millionaires and tramps," Thurber declared in a public address on "Democracy and Anti-Monopoly" that he delivered in 1883. Such an inegalitarian, class-divided society was most emphatically not what the founders of the republic had had in mind when they had tried to level the playing field for future generations by abolishing primogeniture and entail: "Could they have foreseen the invention of steam and electricity and the consequent enormous development and power of corporate life, can it be doubted that they would have placed adequate checks and limitations thereto?"[39]

Figure 1.2. The enormous wealth gap between railroad magnate William H. Vanderbilt and the rest of the population furnished the theme for this ingenious Frank Bellew antimonopoly cartoon, entitled "Comparative Bigness," in an accompanying article by the editors of the comic magazine in which it originally appeared. By translating wealth into height, Bellew depicted Vanderbilt—whose personal wealth in 1882 hovered around $100 million—as an overgrown giant who towered over not only ordinary workers—who, crushed by corporate rapacity, were rapidly being suffocated in a pit much too deep to be visually rendered on the printed page—but also the ordinary millionaire, a midget dwarfed in height by Vanderbilt's right foot. *Canard*, October 28, 1882, p. 4. Collection of the New York Historical Society.

Thurber aimed his barbs not only at corporations, but also at the corrupt and corrupting influence of corporate-based financial speculation on the press. Like many New Yorkers who read the newspapers or perused *Puck's* gallery of antimonopoly cartoons, Thurber was deeply troubled by the quality of the financial information upon which every merchant relied. Every well-informed New Yorker understood that speculative high-flyers like Jay Gould routinely planted fake news stories in big-city newspapers that had been designed to trick gullible investors into making foolish investment decisions.[40] It was by no means unheard of, Lloyd sardonically reported in *Wealth Against Commonwealth*, for corporate lobbyists to persuade journalists to intentionally misreport antimonopoly speeches.[41] In such a house of mirrors, Thurber believed, it had become a civic obligation for right-thinking Americans to help subsidize an independent newspaper like *Justice*. "Subscribe for *Justice*"—or so ran a solicitation that appeared frequently in its pages—"a Paper whose Opinions are Not for Sale."[42]

Thurber shared Lloyd's conviction that the perils of monopoly were better understood by the few than the many, and, thus, that insiders like himself had a special obligation to publicize the immorality of business practices that the many were regrettably prone to ignore: "The masses do not appreciate how great, many and dangerous have been the attacks made by corporate monopolies upon our free institutions. Time will not permit me to enumerate many of them, but the following . . ."[43]

The "checks and limitations" on corporate power that Thurber envisioned were regulatory. Confident that lawmakers could set matters right, Thurber had little patience with Lloyd's conviction that government regulation was futile, since it would inevitably become a tool for the few. If the "centralization" of power could be checked, Thurber favored local control. Yet that time had passed: "I am opposed to the centralization of power either in the hands of Government or of corporations, but centralization is a *fact* staring us in the face and we must see if we cannot make one form of centralization neutralize the other."[44] The only alternative to the countervailing power of government regulation, Thurber declared, was an "anarchy" dominated by men whose "individuality" had become so submerged in a "corporate organization" that it had rendered them "as hard as steel, as pitiless as the storm."[45]

Antimonopolists like Thurber and Lloyd spilled a great deal of ink in the 1880s on the perils of economic consolidation. In pamphlet after pamphlet, newspaper article after newspaper article, and government investigation after government investigation (mostly at the state level), they mounted a searing assault on the corrupt and corrupting business practices that would long echo and reecho in the press. Their indictment was fact-laden, indignant, and morally charged. They aspired not only to change minds, but also to open hearts. Corporate magnates like William H. Vanderbilt, Jay Gould, and John D. Rockefeller had not only clogged the channels of trade; they were conspiring to destroy the republic.[46]

Cartoonists proved adept at translating the antimonopoly appeal into a visually arresting form. The disclosure that Standard Oil had colluded with the railroads to cut costs might not stir the blood. Yet if the oil refiner were transmogrified into an octopus, it became much easier to render legible the consequences of phenomena that were otherwise not easily grasped.[47] The ecological devastation wrought by Standard Oil's archipelago of big-city refineries was an especially compelling target. After all, the link between its business practices and the noxious fumes that belched forth from its East River refinery just north of Brooklyn was plain for all to see—or, more precisely, to smell. Standard Oil was a "horrible monster," screamed the caption of a haunting antimonopoly cartoon illustrating these hazards that ran in the *Daily Graphic* in 1880 (Figure 1.3).[48]

The oil-refinery monster conceit was reminiscent of, and was very probably indebted to, the railroad-monsters that Frank Bellew had drawn for the *Daily Graphic*. Yet its victims were different. No longer had the corporation set its sights on the government, as had Bellew's railroad-monster. Rather, its victim was the multitude of urbanites—including many who the cartoonist plainly depicted as well-to-do—whose air had been poisoned by the foul odors emanating daily from Standard Oil's refinery, a hazard that the cartoonist rendered visually arresting by depicting the source of the malodorous stink that was spreading "poverty, death, and disease" as the outstretched "tentacles" of the oil refinery-monster insidiously extended its reach.[49]

The iconography of antimonopoly entered a new and more expansive phase following Jay Gould's takeover of Western Union in January 1881. Nowhere was this more evident than in the New York City–based humor magazines *Puck* and *Judge*. Like the *Daily Graphic*, these magazines appealed to an upscale audience of worldly New Yorkers who reveled in their inside-dopester political satire and admired the multicolor chromolithographs that were featured in every issue.

For Joseph Keppler, one of the ablest cartoonists of this or any age, Gould's takeover provided the inspiration for a gallery of stunning antimonopoly cartoons. The first, which appeared within days of Gould's takeover,

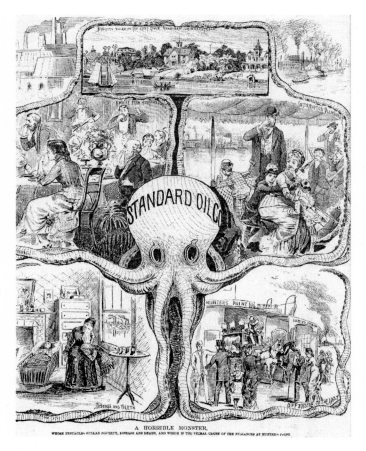

A HORRIBLE MONSTER,
WHOSE TENTACLES SPREAD POVERTY, DISEASE AND DEATH, AND WHICH IS THE PRIMAL CAUSE OF THE NUISANCES AT HUNTER'S POINT.

Figure 1.3. The ecological devastation wrought by a Standard Oil refinery just north of Brooklyn inspired this haunting antimonopoly cartoon, in which the corporation became a "horrible monster" whose tentacles had become noxious fumes that polluted the air, fouled middle-class parlors, and rendered genteel waterside villas uninhabitable. In contrast to Frank Bellew's railroad-monster, the oil refinery-monster had fixed its tentacles not on the government but on the environment. "Hooper," "A Horrible Monster," *Daily Graphic*, July 19, 1880.

was entitled, fittingly enough, "Consolidated." In the background, telegraph poles bearing the names of telegraph companies that Gould had recently acquired stretched across the land. In the foreground, a gleeful Gould perched comfortably on a playground swing (the "telegraph monopoly") tethered by telegraph wire to statues representing "commerce" and "the press." As Gould glided back and forth, the wires tightened around the statues' necks, strangling them to death.[50]

The republic was "In Danger," screamed the caption for another Keppler cartoon that ran in *Puck* the following month. This time the threat lay in the corrupt nexus of lawmakers and business interests that Keppler depicted as a snake (labeled "monopoly") that had slithered out of the Capitol, whose alternating stripes bore the names of lawmakers and corporations ("Standard Oil," "Pennsylvania Central Railroad") as well as notorious corruption scandals ("Alaska"). The intended victim of this corrupt nexus-monster was, as it had been so often for Bellew, the country's vaunted civic ideals, as personified by a flag-clad matron whose Phrygian cap, a venerable symbol of freedom, bore the word "Liberty" across its front. Whether or not the republic could be saved remained an open question. "What are you going to do about it?" *Puck*'s mascot asked Uncle Sam, whom Keppler rendered as a kindly yet ineffectual bystander who had yet to make up his mind to take a decisive stand against corruption.[51]

For cartoonists, the answer to the mascot's question depended on one's politics. For Keppler, publicity held the key. Keppler's cartoon "The Monster Monopoly" made this point with particular force. Once again, the grasping corporation took the form of a creature from the deep. This time, however, the monster was not an octopus, but a whale. The whale—which sported Gould's face on its head, and the faces of Gould's collaborators William H. Vanderbilt and Cyrus Field on its tail fins—spouted "monopoly" as it flipped its tail fins to upend a flimsy rowboat ("business"). To the rescue came the press in a sturdy little craft (the "Dauntless") manned by skillful rowers whom the cartoonist identified as "editors." At the helm of the skiff stood *Puck*'s mascot, poised to plunge a harpoon (whose tip bore the talismanic word "antimonopoly") into the whale's side.[52]

Other cartoonists lacked Keppler's confidence in the power of the press. Antimonopolists were in a "Perplexing Position," brooded one *Puck* cartoonist in late 1881. Now that antimonopoly had gained the endorsement of New York City's corrupt Democratic political machine, Tammany Hall, it was hard for men of good faith—personified here by the magazine's mascot—to choose between the "Monopolyville" of Vanderbilt and Field, and the "Anti-Monopolyville" of Tammany boss John Kelly. Kelly, an opportunistic antimonopolist, held aloft the banner "Down with the Bloated Monopolists" to cynically garner votes while sidelining sincere antimonopolists like Thurber—who was, quite literally, in Kelly's back pocket.[53] Here the cartoonist raised a challenging question that later historians would long debate: Had merchant antimonopolists like Thurber successfully co-opted the Democratic Party—with its large working-class constituency—or was it the other way around?

The only antimonopoly cartoonist who could rival Bellew and Keppler in sheer inventiveness was G. Frederick Keller. Unlike Bellew and Keppler, Keller rose to prominence not in New York City, but in San Francisco, where, for a few years in the 1880s, he published an arresting portfolio of antimonopoly cartoons for the satirical magazine *Wasp*—the West Coast equivalent of Keppler's *Puck*.[54]

Antimonopolists differed on many issues of strategy and tactics, yet on one point consensus prevailed. The wellspring of the antimonopoly movement lay not in the hinterland, but in the nation's largest cities—and, in particular, in New York, Brooklyn, Chicago, and San Francisco—while its earliest and most influential champions were neither farmers nor workers, but proprietary capitalists and the journalists who covered their beat. Indeed, it would be hard to point to a single antimonopoly theme that would be championed in the 1890s and beyond by a farm or labor leader that had not appeared before 1880 in a big-city newspaper or magazine. If New York City was a "monied metropolis" in which merchants and manufacturers formed a durable alliance, as one historian has claimed, then it was also an antimonopoly metropolis in which proprietary capitalists collaborated with journalists to expose the abuses of the emerging corporate order.

The vocabulary of antimonopoly was urbane and sophisticated, as one might have anticipated, rooted as it was in the moral philosophy of the eighteenth-century Scottish Enlightenment and the political economy of mid-nineteenth-century British and Continental social science. So too was its visual iconography. Bellew had been born in British India, and drew much of his inspiration from the London comic magazine *Punch*, to which he occasionally contributed. Keppler, in turn, hailed from Vienna, and would deploy to good advantage in *Puck* compositional techniques that he had absorbed from the Baroque architecture, sculpture, and painting of the Hapsburg Empire that he remembered from his youth.

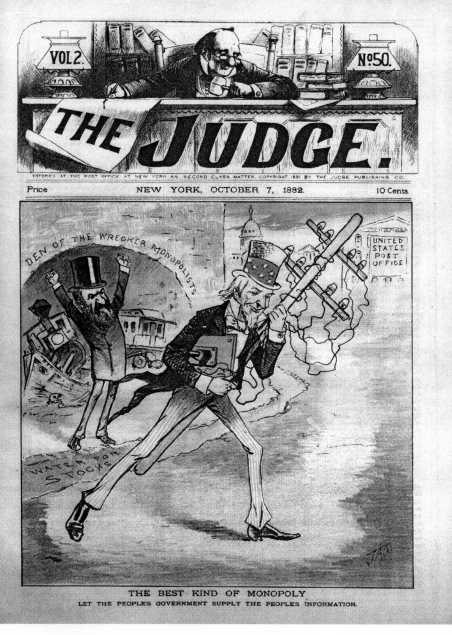

Figure 1.4. "The Best Kind of Monopoly," ran the caption for this hopeful 1882 James A. Wales antimonopoly cartoon endorsing the absorption of the telegraph by the Post Office Department. "Let the People's Government Supply the People's Information," the caption proclaimed, articulating a civic ideal that appealed to East Coast proprietary capitalists and that would soon be picked up by populists in the South and West. James A. Wales, "The Best Kind of Monopoly," *Judge* 2 (October 7, 1882): 1.

The urban pedigree of the antimonopoly movement was particularly conspicuous in its third, nationalist variant. Having accepted the inevitability of economic consolidation, nationalist antimonopolists took the further step of endorsing government ownership.

Government ownership today is often looked upon as a bizarre and foreign idea alien to the country's supposedly antistatist past. In fact, it has a distinguished American pedigree. For many late nineteenth-century antimonopolists, including Lloyd and Edward Bellamy, the much-touted success of the Post Office Department silenced any doubts regarding its practicality. For many Americans in the 1880s, 1890s, and 1900s—and not just for socialists, radicals, and Bellamyite nationalists—government ownership seemed far more compelling than corporate control. It was, after all, an age in which many Americans defended the public over the private, and not just for nationwide combines such as Western Union, but also for municipal franchise corporations with a mandate to provide the entire population—and not just that segment of the population who had the ability to pay—with gas, water, public transportation, and even telephone service.[55]

The relative equanimity with which Americans contemplated government ownership owed much to the antimonopoly appeal. For the antimonopoly cartoonist, the corporation was invariably a malign and often frightening monster. The republic's civic ideals, in contrast, were typically personified as a gracious and ingratiating, if often somewhat ineffectual, Uncle Sam. Government ownership was the "Best Kind of Monopoly," declared cartoonist James A. Wales in a forthright endorsement of the congressional buyout of the telegraph network that ran in the resolutely establishmentarian humor magazine *Judge* in October 1882. To illustrate this theme, Wales depicted an unusually resolute Uncle Sam wrestling a telegraph pole out of Jay Gould's hands and confidently striding out of the "den of the wrecker monopolists" and, to Gould's immense chagrin, across the river of watered stock that the "wrecker" could not ford and on to its future home in the Post Office Department. Like a latter-day Moses, Wales's Uncle Sam had led his people out of Egypt, across a river that their tormentor could not cross, and toward the promised land. The moral was unmistakable: government ownership was the solution to the problem that corporation-enabled speculative finance had spawned. Lest some dimwitted subscriber miss the point, Wales's caption spelled it out: "Let the People's Government Supply the People's Information" (Figure 1.4).[56]

The specter of corruption provided antimonopoly cartoonists with a wealth of material. The trick was to render this danger visually compelling. To help convince his audience that the republic was truly "In Danger," Keppler depicted the corrupt nexus of lawmakers and business interests as a slithering snake ("monopoly") that had wrapped itself around the congressional dome.[57] The specter of corruption would be rendered even more compellingly a few years later in Keppler's "Bosses of the Senate," in which a phalanx of overfed lobbyists for different monopolies (the "Standard Oil Trust," the "Sugar Trust," the "Copper Trust") had shut the public out of the legislative chamber.[58]

Equally artful was Grant E. Hamilton's "In the Clutch of a Grasping Monopoly," an 1888 slap at the nation's largest telephone company, in which the "Bell Telephone Monopoly" became a grasping spider angling to entrap the federal legislature in its web.[59] The corporation-monster hybrid reached something of an apotheosis in 1904, when Keppler's son, Joseph Jr.,—who, like his father, was a cartoonist for *Puck*—updated the by-then venerable rendering of the monopoly as an octopus to accuse the Standard Oil Company of trying to corrupt the presidency. In Joseph Jr.'s, rendering, the Standard Oil octopus had already wrapped its tentacles around the state legislatures and Congress, and had set its sights—"Next!"—on the ultimate prize: Theodore Roosevelt's White House.[60] As if to answer Keppler's implicit question, one of his colleagues reassuringly responded the following year with news that the "Standard Oil Serpents" of Rockefeller and Henry H. Rogers had not overmastered Roosevelt (the "Infant Hercules"), but, instead, that the youthful president was successfully wrestling them to the ground.[61]

* * *

This essay has traced the popularization in the 1880s of an antimonopoly critique of corporate capital that had been crafted by proprietary capitalists in conjunction with their journalistic admirers. The central role played in the antimonopoly movement by these groups, rather than by farmers and workers, has long been obscured by the mistaken assumption that late nineteenth-century politics revolved around a contest between the *people* and the *interests*, with the interests being more or less congruent with business. In fact, the antimonopolists regarded the interests of the people and the interests of proprietary capitalists to be fundamentally aligned. For them, the primary fault line was not the *people* versus *business*, as a later generation of progressives would contend. Rather, it was *business* versus *monopoly*, a very different configuration that aligned *business* with the *people* and *both* against *monopoly*. This distinction will remain obscure so long as historians continue to view the period through a Manichean people-versus-the-interests lens. "Monopoly is not business," explained an editorialist in a New York City periodical in 1884, in a particularly pithy distillation of the conventional wisdom. On the contrary, monopoly "kills business," an accusation that antimonopolists made repeatedly not only in stirring prose but also in the stunning visual iconography that remains one of the movement's most enduring legacies.[62]

The pivotal role of proprietary capitalists in the enactment of late nineteenth-century regulatory legislation is well known. New York City merchants drafted key provisions of the Interstate Commerce Act in 1887, and shippers rather than farmers led the fight for the establishment of state-level railroad commissions—a fact that has long been obscured by the uncritical adoption by historians of the once sneering dismissal by seaboard elites of this legislation as farmer-backed "granger laws."[63]

This revisionist characterization of the antimonopoly movement rests not only on an analysis of the divergent economic interests of proprietary and corporate capitalists, but also on the media politics of its critics and supporters. This analysis calls into question the propensity of historians to characterize the media politics of the period as tawdry and superficial, the rise of the corporate order as uncontested, and the progress of economic consolidation as unchallenged. Only in history books did antimonopoly bubble up more or less organically from the agricultural hinterland, with little or no input from proprietary capitalists in the nation's major cities. The ubiquity of such a flat, one-dimensional, and fundamentally mistaken people-versus-the-interests story line has its origins not only in the wishful thinking of historians and the gullibility of journalists, but also, and much more insidiously, in the publicity campaign mounted by big-business lobbyists such as Francis B. Thurber. Thurber's post-1893 anti-antimonopoly counteroffensive had been intentionally designed to sabotage the antimonopoly movement by blaming it on farmers and workers, two groups far less powerful—and for this reason markedly less threatening to the status quo—than proprietary merchants. It was, in short, the mirror image of the pro-antimonopoly campaign that Thurber himself had led in the 1880s, prior to his bankruptcy, to protect the interests of proprietary capital against a rising—though still morally vulnerable—corporate order.

The failure of all but a tiny handful of historians to fully grasp the character and significance of the late nineteenth-century antimonopoly movement is a testament not only to the extent to which historians have misunderstood the past, but also to the way the past has come to be remembered. By ignoring the interests of proprietary capitalists and the visions of the journalists who championed their cause, historians have provided yet one more reason to perpetuate the seductive, yet highly misleading, people-versus-the-interests mythology that had led so many to dismiss the 1880s as a reactionary "Gilded Age." The recovery of these neglected voices reminds us of the extent to which this decade deserves to be remembered—no less than the Progressive Era for which the antimonopoly movement of the 1880s would serve as a prelude, inspiration, and goad—as an age of reform.[64]

CHAPTER 2

Progressive Political Culture and the Widening Scope of Local Newspapers, 1880–1930

Julia Guarneri

In his 1925 article "The Natural History of the Newspaper," sociologist Robert Park defended what many people saw as the trivial parts of the newspaper. The society weddings, the divorce announcements, the petty crime stories: "local news," he said, "is the very stuff that democracy is made of."[1] Why did such seemingly mundane local stories matter for democracy? Because they defined for readers their "village"—the group of people they knew and cared about, even if that knowledge came only through reading the news. If democracy was to survive, wrote Park, "the newspaper must continue to tell us about ourselves. We must somehow learn to know our community and its affairs in the same intimate way in which we knew them in the country villages."[2]

What I am proposing in this essay is that we take Robert Park at his word, and consider the political consequences of *all* portions of daily newspapers. Coverage of local elections is obviously political news. But what about sports pages? Advice columns? Theater reviews? In my research on the metropolitan newspapers of the late nineteenth and early twentieth century, I have seen that these seemingly frivolous parts of the paper did hard political work, defining the scope of readers' sympathies and, therefore, their political commitments.

At the turn of the century, city newspapers expanded dramatically, with extensive news reporting, with the new genre of "feature" news, and with advertisements. Editors of this era assumed that readers had both personal and political stakes in their cities—that the city was, in Park's words, their "village." By reporting on it, papers gave readers the means to understand its problems and to rally for change. Newspapers thus gave rise to an active, civic, Progressive politics. By the 1910s and 1920s, this curious and committed local news coverage was on the wane. Many urban newspapers broadened their circulations into suburbs, small towns, and rural hamlets. Regional reporting began to crowd out urban news and features, and it pushed newspaper editorials toward a politics that benefited the metropolitan region rather than the city itself. Meanwhile, syndicates and chains gradually built a market for mass-produced news and features that spoke to national, rather than local, readerships.

The growing emphasis on regional and national news in the early twentieth century carried political consequences. Newspapers' material often urged readers to identify more closely with their metropolitan region, with their state, or even with a particular slice of the population (athletes, teenagers, home seamstresses . . .) than with their city. Few papers reminded readers of the unique textures, peoples, and rituals of their city, and those that did tended to package the city as entertainment rather than framing it as a community in which the reader played a role.

When we ask why all the energy and momentum of Progressive politics seemed to dissipate in the 1920s, the news may, in part, offer an answer. Newspapers did not heed Robert Park's call and "continue to tell us about ourselves." Americans no longer read in much detail or color about their neighbors. The scope of papers' political concern widened but also weakened. Newspapers asked readers to care about region and nation, yet encouraged them to identify only with people like themselves.

*   *   *

When turn-of-the-century readers opened a copy of the *San Francisco Call*, or the *New York World*, or the *Baltimore Sun*, they encountered the city itself rendered visible, audible, and intelligible on the page. Readers could grasp the scale and energy of the city by browsing the events listings: the fifty plays and ten music concerts running at once, the hundreds of preachers, rabbis, and priests speaking to their congregations at the same time. They could visit otherwise mysterious spaces in the city—the wings of a Broadway theater, the smoky floor of a German-language cabaret—by following intrepid reporters

there. Readers could imagine the sounds of Italian or Chinese neighborhoods, because reporters spelled out accents and explained immigrant
vocabulary. They might tour the dank depths of a city prison, or listen in on
the dealings of the city's political bosses. Newspapers treated the city as readers' environment, their entertainment, and their object of concern.

The late nineteenth-century blossoming of local news and features—
which created such rich urban experience on newspaper pages—owed more
to new news technologies than to editors' civic convictions or political commitments. In the last decades of the nineteenth century, cheap wood pulp
paper (as opposed to expensive rag paper) gave editors nearly endless space
to fill. The invention of the stereotype plate and the halftone let every publisher illustrate his paper. Merchants pushed their way out of the classifieds
and bought space to run elaborate ads. The ads themselves became incentives
to print more news; if a publisher had sold eight pages worth of advertisements, he needed to come up with a respectable amount of news to run
alongside. Hoe presses, gradually adopted by news publishers in the mid- to
late nineteenth century, could easily print, fold, and stack separate sections.
Over the course of the 1890s, newspapers became sprawling, multipart affairs, and the annual per capita consumption of newsprint rose from six to
sixteen pounds.[3]

Editors filled their expanding papers with local material in part because
it was the easiest to obtain. They could hire local reporters cheaply, and those
reporters could quickly pick up leads from police stations or city missions.
They could send illustrators or photographers along at no great expense. Yet
editors must also have sensed readers' appetites for information about their
ballooning cities. Newcomers and longtime residents, the rich and the poor,
natives and immigrants were unlikely to know one another. Their everyday
conversations and gossip could not catch them up on all the local news. Cities
seemed to be outpacing residents' experiences and their understanding. Just
at this moment, metropolitan newspapers began offering daily tours, intro-
ductions, and explanations, all for a price of just a few cents.

Articles carried readers through cities' different physical spaces and
explained their specialized worlds. Illustrations brought readers to gambling
dens, amusement parks, and museum galleries. Cross sections peeled back
surfaces to reveal the city's many levels, layers, and systems.[4] The 1885 *Boston Globe*'s "Scenes of the Subway" told readers about the transportation
marvel being built right under their feet.[5] Illustrated features took readers
up to the tops of the city's new skyscrapers and showed them the dazzling

views. These images helped readers to see how their urban territory fit into the rest of the city, and allowed them to imagine their lives playing out in relationship to the entire metropolis. Newspaper tours could also fortify readers' stake in their growing cities. If readers knew what went on in cities' offices, theaters, alleyways, and tunnels, it was easier to claim those cities as their own.

Turn-of-the-century newspapers offered readers an omniscient perspective on the city that rendered it quantifiable and comprehensible. Daily events listings gave readers exhilarating glimpses of the many city activities unfolding simultaneously. The *New York World*'s magazine feature called "The Busiest Hour on Earth" quantified a single New York hour. The feature listed the staggering numbers of things happening in that single hour: "150,000 cross Brooklyn Bridge," "12 people die," "500,000 people dine," "39,746 letters mailed."[6] Real estate sections printed maps of undeveloped lots; articles on city plans gave bird's-eye views of traffic flows. Newspapers took bewildering metropolises and organized them into statistics, charts, and maps. By supplying data and some critical distance, newspapers equipped readers to change their cities in systematic and organized ways.

Turn-of-the-century "travelogues" and human interest features introduced readers to city residents of varying ethnicities, professions, tastes, and habits. The *Chicago Daily News* reprinted lengthy conversations with the city's street peddlers.[7] The *Milwaukee Free Press* interviewed the city's corps of messenger boys and explained their many duties.[8] New York City papers interviewed wig makers, casting directors, rescue workers, and bridge engineers.[9] Many newspaper reporters visited immigrant institutions—Jewish street stalls, Hungarian dance halls—and reported back. These articles positioned the imagined reader as culturally neutral, and the subjects as culturally exotic; it could seem that the foreign-born were always written *about*, not *for*. And yet these articles did encourage curiosity about immigrant cultures, teaching readers Yiddish expressions and explaining the queue worn by Chinese men. They acknowledged immigrants as interesting members of the urban public. And newspaper profiles gave readers deeper and more multidimensional understandings of their neighbors than they were likely to get on the street.

Newspaper reporters, unlike most of their readers, also dared to enter the world of the very poor. They followed crime stories into destitute households, and gave readers vicarious tours. Theodore Dreiser investigated the impoverished St. Louis household where a man had murdered his family, and described everything from the family's pantry to their closets to their kitchen utensils.[10] A *New York Times* reporter talked to the unemployed men who spent their days on park benches, and told readers about the life paths that had brought the men there.[11] A *New York World* article on the Lower East Side's "Murderer's Alley" included a map to show readers exactly where the alley lay, and included sketches of the alley's fire escapes, its garbage, and its ragtag inhabitants.[12] These features traded in voyeurism and sensationalism. Yet in encouraging city dwellers to learn about each other, they forged a consciousness of "how the other half lives," and—because articles on poverty usually conveyed alarm—a sense that the situation needed to change.

Muckraking articles went even deeper into the city spaces unfamiliar to readers, and turned city dwellers' ignorance of their growing cities into part of the story. Information often failed to travel through cities' many strata of class and geography, so citizens might not learn of filth and corruption in meatpacking plants or political machines. Reporters dug into those worlds. Jacob Riis, who covered the New York City police headquarters for the *New York Tribune* and then the *New York Sun*, wrote about the misery he witnessed in the tenements, sweatshops, and flophouses of the city's poorest neighborhoods. Nell Nelson, of the 1880s *Chicago Times*, exposed dangerous conditions for women workers.[13] Papers in Louisville, Denver, and Philadelphia uncovered coal companies' price-fixing schemes and then distributed coal themselves to temporarily solve the problem.[14] In each case, reporters asserted that even in metropolises all problems could and should be made visible, and refused to resign themselves to the opaque processes and divided worlds of modern cities.

Muckraking reporters assumed and expected that readers would feel a sense of connection to their city as a whole—not just to their own class, party, neighborhood, ethnicity, or trade—and that the connection translated into a duty to solve city problems. Their articles consistently spoke of interconnected and interdependent cities. An 1897 *World* editorial called "Drag Up the Slums" drove home this idea:

> It is in such places that small-pox, measles, scarlet fever, diphtheria, consumption and all the most deadly diseases breed, to spread until the cleanest and wealthiest quarters are involved.
>
> Before New York can be a clean and healthy city the east side must be renovated with better homes, better drainage, more playgrounds, more parks and more baths.

The old proverb which says that it is our concern when the next wall is burning fits this situation exactly. If we do not drag up the slums, the slums will drag down New York.[15]

In this urban vision, a problem in one part of the city became everyone's problem. This stance blurred the line between altruistic reform and self-interest; the *World* editorial framed poverty as not just an evil but a threat to the middle and upper classes. Still, when papers expressed outrage about households that went without coal fires on cold nights or about neighborhoods with no green spaces, they did set the expectation that city people would notice and take responsibility for their neighbors, including the most vulnerable.

We have solid evidence that newspapers succeeded in engaging readers in the well-being of the whole urban community. Jacob Riis's articles inspired citizens and politicians to pass child labor laws, to construct city playgrounds, and to expand the Croton aqueduct, which supplied the city with uncontaminated drinking water.[16] The *New York Evening Globe* ran a muckraking series on tainted food production; its investigations led to arrests in the industry.[17] In Kansas City, the *Star* exposed an attempt to monopolize the streetcar system, and successfully campaigned for public parks and free baths.[18] Newspaper campaigns helped catapult cities into an age of energetic reform and established a norm of nonpartisan problem solving.

Papers in small and midsize cities tended to write in a tamer style. Working within the narrower social circles and economies of cities like Pittsburgh, Milwaukee, and Buffalo, editors had to be careful not to lose readers, advertisers, or friends with sensational reporting and populist rabble-rousing. A Charleston resident noticed the absence of such fiery news in the *Charleston News and Courier*: "It is never looking for sensations, never sticking its nose into the nether places to find out what is wrong. For this reason Charleston is poorly informed as to itself." Because neither of the city's two papers went digging for dirt, said this reader, "they do not educate their own people in political progressiveness."[19] Newspaper charity campaigns, however, provided a civic-minded and Progressive form of news that nearly all publishers could embrace.

In 1882, the *New York Tribune* sponsored the first long-running newspaper charity, the Fresh Air Fund, which sent New York City tenement children on two-week vacations in the countryside. The *Tribune* kept the fund's director on salary; he wrote articles that appeared in the paper nearly every day through the spring and summer, soliciting donations.[20] The *New York World*, *Journal*, and *Herald* followed in the *Tribune*'s footsteps. During the depressions of 1893 and 1897, each paper set up funds providing free ice, clothing, coal, and food. By the 1910s and 1920s, seemingly every city had a newspaper drive or charity. A 1921 *Philadelphia North American* article described fundraising "porch parties" held all over town and ran photographs of the disabled children who would be helped by the funds.[21] The *Cleveland News* enlisted readers and teachers to nominate needy children for its Christmas drive, and ran stories on exceptionally generous donors.[22] In smaller cities working to boost their own reputations, newspaper charity campaigns could rally for improvements without admitting that there was anything wrong to begin with, as when the *Tacoma Ledger* and *News* raised money for a high school stadium and a YMCA building.[23]

Charity articles' savvy strategies created an emotional connection between reader and subject, or between the reader and a larger community. Excerpted letters or quoted conversations put readers into print dialogue with those receiving aid.[24] The *New York Times*' "Neediest Cases" profiles devoted special attention to subjects' endearing qualities and their sympathetic situations. "No one can help liking 11-year-old Jimmy Sharp, and no one can help smiling into the joyous little face, with its brown eyes, wide mouth, and straight, narrow nose," explained one 1918 profile.[25] Nearly all charity drives printed lists of donations every day or week. By gathering names together on a page, around a shared cause, these lists created print representations of communities in which every member mattered. Finally, newspaper charities showcased readers' generosity and caring by reprinting the letters that came in with donations. "Please give this money to the Neediest Cases," wrote Elihu Robinson of Newark, in a letter reprinted by the *New York Times*. "My sister and I saved it for Christmas gifts for our family, but we decided that these cases need it more."[26]

The carefully crafted image of a benevolent and effective community was in many ways a fantasy that existed only in print. Yet charity articles successfully mobilized city readers. *New York Tribune* subscribers, for example, donated anywhere from $18,000 to $52,000 to the Fresh Air Fund in every year between 1882 and 1912, and sent between four and fifteen thousand tenement children annually on countryside vacations.[27] By implying that all city dwellers ought to care about the health and welfare of all others, newspapers' charity campaigns fashioned their reading audiences into more involved and reform-minded publics.

When in 1911 O. H. Chamberlain, a *Chicago Tribune* reader, wrote a short essay expressing his opinion of the newspaper, he revealed how the paper had in fact shaped his own relationship with and attitude toward his city. "I have felt that the 'Tribune,' with other Chicagoans, was too complacent with Chicago," he wrote. "I love Chicago, and yet I never can become used to some of the horrors here. The Harrison Street police station, the levee, the food adulterations, and the conditions which make little children suffer, are some of the municipal sores which, to me, deserve the front page forever."[28] Chamberlain complained that the *Tribune* did not devote enough space to the city's problems. Yet the source that most likely taught him about those problems was the *Tribune* itself. None of these issues (except for food adulteration) would have directly affected a middle-class Chicagoan, and yet they pained and urgently concerned this reader. Newspapers' city articles, by widening readers' circles of concern beyond their own jobs, families, and neighborhoods, encouraged readers to become civically invested. In the case of Mr. Chamberlain, at least, it worked.

*   *   *

The expanding cities, new technologies, and curious reading audiences of the late nineteenth century had rendered it both popular and profitable for papers to report in great detail on their own populations. Yet these cities, technologies, and audiences continued to evolve, and what had once been profitable did not remain so. Suburban growth began to outpace urban growth; distribution networks spread newspapers ever farther outside cities; and syndicate services turned daily news into a standardized, mass-manufactured product. By the 1910s and 1920s these changes had turned the focus of city newspapers from inward to outward, from urban to regional, from local to national. Newspapers that had once inspired Progressive reforms became agents of a blander, more passive participation in regional and national culture.

City newspapers had made efforts to attract suburban readers as early as the 1870s and 1880s, when they ran short "Suburban" columns. These sections seemed to expand each decade, until by 1927, the *New York Herald Tribune* was printing eight pages of society news from the boroughs, Westchester, Connecticut, and New Jersey.[29] Many publishers used their classifieds to hold onto suburban readers; the *Philadelphia Inquirer* and the *Chicago Tribune* both operated dozens of branch offices in peripheral neighborhoods and suburbs.[30] It made financial sense for newspapers to pursue suburban readers; turn-of-the-century suburbanites did much of their shopping in the city, so city advertisers were eager to reach them.

When it came to farther-flung populations, most nineteenth-century city dailies had not bothered to solicit their subscriptions. But in the 1880s, the Post Office contracted with regional railroads to run the first express mail trains, and in 1885, it dropped the postal rate for newspapers to one cent per pound.[31] After these changes, residents of Dubuque or Peoria could subscribe to Chicago papers for just slightly more than Chicago residents paid, and they would receive their papers on the morning that they were printed.[32] The passage of Parcel Post, in 1913, drastically lowered the shipping fees for small packages, which created a strong incentive for advertisers to reach rural readers and offer them goods by mail. City papers' Sunday editions became veritable mail-order catalogs, with detailed illustrations of goods that rural people could order from city shops. Cars again expanded urban papers' trade radius. Regional traffic through cities meant that nearly any kind of urban retailer could improve sales by advertising in newspapers to readers within a day's drive.

In pursuit of regional audiences (and the advertising business they would bring), city papers created regional editions and gathered more regional news. E. W. Scripps created a Kentucky edition of his *Cincinnati Post* in the 1880s, and Joseph Pulitzer printed a special New Jersey edition of the *New York World*.[33] By the 1920s, the *Des Moines Register* and *Tribune* (morning and evening papers with the same owner) were reprinting their front pages up to twenty times to appeal specially to the interests of readers in different regions of Iowa.[34] The 1920s *Chicago Tribune* printed a special Springfield edition, which focused on Illinois rather than Chicago politics. Printers shipped that edition off extra early so that readers in central and southern Illinois would have papers waiting on their doorsteps in the morning.[35]

Not every paper prioritized suburban or regional audiences. The *Chicago Daily News*, the *New York World*, and the *Cleveland Press*, for example, focused on pleasing city readers and therefore reported intensively on city issues.[36] But the many papers that catered to suburban and regional readers created notably regional political platforms. The *Boston Post*, which claimed the biggest Sunday circulation in New England at the turn of the century, advocated for "the advance of New England"—not just Boston—on its editorial page.[37] Regional papers in the 1920s stopped talking about the urban problems that turn-of-the-century papers had rallied around, such as crowded slums, dirty water, and sweatshops. They focused instead on suburban and regional infrastructure. The *Chicago Tribune* printed its platform "For Chicago" above each day's editorials beginning around 1920, advocating for a commuter trolley system, wide roads into the country, and regional rail stations.[38] The paper added a platform "For the Middle West" on Sundays, which included regional highway systems and flood prevention for the Mississippi.[39]

Articles on regional history and landscapes turned newspapers into stewards of metropolitan and regional identity over and above urban identity. The *Columbia State* explored South Carolina's history and its wildlife in its Sunday editions.[40] The 1920s *Baltimore Sun* ran a series of articles on Maryland's twenty-three counties and then published them as a book, *The Spirit of Maryland*.[41] *Chicago Tribune* reporter James O'Donnell Bennett set out on a motoring tour of the Midwest in 1926, and in the resulting series of articles he coined the term "Chicagoland."[42]

By the late 1920s, one could learn as much about suburban and rural life in the pages of the daily newspaper as about city life. Readers encountered stories on suburban high school sports, columns full of suburban weddings, and listings for suburban theaters. They saw images of freestanding single-family homes (rather than apartments) and read about players' golf scores at suburban country clubs. Department store ads no longer presumed that readers would be familiar with downtown; they spelled out streetcar routes, driving instructions, and parking locations. Catering to rural readers, city papers regularly ran poultry pages, advice columns on potato blight or sheep shearing, and advertisements for tractors.

These more regional papers of the 1910s and 1920s did not drop urban features entirely, but they often collected them in new "Metropolitan" sections that assumed less familiarity with city life than had urban features of previous decades. Artfully observed and illustrated vignettes could function as complete substitutes for, rather than supplements to, city life. The *Chicago Herald*'s Sunday "Humor and City Life" section printed a series of illustrations, "Our Neighbors Across the Way," that reproduced the mini-dramas urbanites glimpsed through their neighbors' windows.[43] Editors ran features that defined and publicized their cities' distinctive traits, effectively "branding" their city. The *Philadelphia Public Ledger* constructed local identity out of local history; its fictionalized columnists bore the names of city founders and prominent families.[44] Articles that slickly packaged urban life moved newspapers away from Progressivism's earnest engagement and quest to improve urban community.

As many papers shifted their focus from urban to metropolitan and regional, they also came to rely on syndicated news. By the early twentieth century, independent companies—the Central Press Association, McNaught Syndicate, Metropolitan Newspaper Service—offered features such as comic strips, advice columns, or even entire Sunday magazines for purchase. The nation's biggest newspapers, too, began to sell single articles, full-page features, and entire sections to papers in midsize and smaller cities. Syndication offered the editors of smaller papers material they could never have afforded to commission themselves, such as on-the-ground reporting on the Russo-Japanese war, expert instruction on sprinting technique, or beauty tips from film stars. Readers then came to expect the more lavish, global, and cosmopolitan news that syndicates made possible.

Syndication turned local papers into much leaner operations, since they outsourced so much of their labor. By the 1920s the typical newspaper's Sunday staff dwindled from a turn-of-the-century high of dozens to just a handful of editors who selected and laid out syndicated content.[45] Successful editors often spent more time assembling choice syndicated features than commissioning local reports. In a critique of the syndication system, journalist Will Irwin quoted a newspaper executive who compared a newspaper editor to "a moving-picture exhibitor. He doesn't have a thing to do with production of the film he runs. He just looks over the offerings of the production company, selects the one that he most believes in, dresses up the house a little, and runs them."[46] Not surprisingly, many local papers lost much of their distinctiveness. A reader in Albuquerque found his city's two papers "monotonously alike. Both print practically the same news matter, the same cuts, and sometimes even identical editorials. Like other papers of this size, they are dependent upon the great news-gathering associations and upon the so-called plate services for much of their material; hence their similarity to each other and to the thousand and one other papers of the country."[47]

Newspaper chains, like syndicates, capitalized on economies of scale in the news industry, and as a consequence they de-emphasized and defunded local reporting. Ira Copley bought out the midsize cities of California, while Gannett Newspapers seemed to control all of upstate New York. By 1923, thirty-one chains accounted for one-third of the nation's total daily circulation, and nearly one-half of its Sunday circulation. William Randolph

Hearst owned twenty-two major metropolitan newspapers by 1930; E. W. Scripps owned twenty-five.[48] By 1935 Hearst alone would control 11.1 percent of daily circulation in the U.S.[49]

The papers in the Hearst chain upended the standard newspaper formula that had emerged in U.S. cities over the preceding three decades. Instead of hiring a solid team of local reporters and supplementing their work with syndicated features, Hearst built his papers around shared material and merely decorated them with local news. He ran the column "Today, by Arthur Brisbane" as the front-page featured editorial of every paper he owned. Editors at each paper sprinkled just a few local features among the syndicated stories, such as the *Wisconsin News*'s "The Inquisitive Reporter," which polled random Milwaukee citizens on mundane questions such as "On what salary should a man marry?" or "Have you found stout persons better natured than thin ones?"[50] E. W. Scripps's chain of papers, too, skimped on local news; for every four local stories that appeared in his competitors' pages, Scripps's papers ran only one.[51]

Syndicated material could highlight commonalities and nurture affinities. But rather than speaking to populations that shared a city, syndicated articles spoke to groups that shared a circumstance or an interest. Feature writers targeted a range of demographics: new mothers, motorists, gardeners, bicyclists, outdoorsmen. All of these populations, not coincidentally, made prime targets for a corresponding set of advertisers. Syndicate writers drafted their articles to appeal to home cooks or radio enthusiasts across all U.S. regions, and made sure that their messages harmonized with the kinds of advertisements that local papers placed alongside them. So the political stakes that had been present in local news essentially evaporated in these syndicated features, which connected the reader only to an amorphous, anonymous population of other readers with similar interests.

Early syndicated material, appearing from the 1890s through the 1910s, did treat urban experiences, but those experiences were generic ones, applicable to nearly any city. Syndicates used the ethnic humor of only the most common immigrant groups, such as the Irish "Mr. Dooley" and the German "Katzenjammer Kids." "Among Us Mortals, by W. E. Hill"—distributed by the *Chicago Tribune*—observed city people in broadly recognizable scenarios: "The Amateur Vaudeville," "The Apartment House," and "At the Jeweller's."[52] By the 1920s, many syndicates' journalists stopped commenting upon the urban experience altogether. Because features that spoke only to big-city readers would not sell well in smaller cities, towns, or suburbs, most syndicate writers and illustrators instead played upon issues and situations familiar to nearly anyone, no matter where they lived. The syndicated feature "Home Town Folks" chatted with readers about all the conflicts and desires of various household members.[53] George Ade's series "In Our Town," which appeared in the mass-produced *Illustrated Sunday Magazine*, sketched characters familiar to any community, such as "The Actor" longing to see his name in lights.[54] When the city did appear in 1920s syndicated material, journalists presented it less as a familiar context than as a fantasy setting. The lavishly illustrated series "The Adventures of Prudence Prim," running in Hearst's *American Weekly*, chronicled the escapades of a young woman visiting New York. Rather than setting Prudence in scenarios familiar to city readers—the office, the streetcar, the luncheonette—cartoonist Nell Brinkley sent her off to late-night cabarets and luxurious beauty parlors.[55] In features like this, the city became a space of exotic intrigue rather than shared everyday experience.

A new crop of syndicated features addressed broad, universal needs and experiences rather than particular interests. Journalism professors and syndicate managers urged writers to stick to a few essential categories. Willard G. Bleyer listed "the fundamental sources of satisfaction" in a 1919 manual, including "(1) timely topics, (2) unique, novel, and extraordinary persons, things, and events, (3) mysteries, (4) romance, (5) adventure, (6) contests for supremacy, (7) children, (8) animals."[56] Syndicated authors earned royalties proportional to the number of papers that bought their pieces, so they worked hard to craft articles with the broadest possible appeal.

The rise of nationalized news carried several consequences for news readers, and I believe it carried broad ramifications for the politics of the early twentieth century. Syndicated news laid the foundations of a truly national culture; its features encouraged Americans to build the same houses, play the same games, and use the same words. Newspapers helped to construct a broadly understood American "way of life" that would become a touchstone of U.S. domestic politics and international relations through the entire twentieth century. When wartime propaganda marshaled residents' pride in the American way, or when radio or television pandered to audiences' commonalities, they did so using the shared vocabularies and shared values that newspapers had helped to spread.

But as syndication—as well as metropolitan and regional news—built up new kinds of affinities, commitments, and commonalities, it diminished or even devastated local feature reporting. It is worth asking whether the shrinking presence of local news and features damaged Progressive urban politics not only for concrete reasons (since readers learned less about their cities than they had in the past) but also for less tangible ones. Newspapers no longer covered urban populations as though the fate of every group mattered to every other. They no longer assumed that readers felt a strong loyalty and duty to their city. The widening scope of the local newspaper channeled readers' sympathies and directed their attention to their regions, to their nation, and to the world. Syndicated features helped them to recognize qualities and interests that they shared with readers all over the country. But readers no longer heard much about their neighbors. "We must somehow learn to know our community and its affairs in the same intimate way in which we knew them in the country villages." By the time Robert Park wrote this in 1925, newspapers may not have been of much help with his project.

CHAPTER 3

The Ominous Clang: Fears of Propaganda from World War I to World War II

David Greenberg

In 1914, with the outbreak of the European war, George Sylvester Viereck, a thirty-one-year-old German-born American poet, launched a weekly publication called *The Fatherland*. Passionately devoted to his native land, Viereck declared that he intended to combat what he called "misstatements and prejudices" toward Germany in the American press—"to place the German side of this unhappy quarrel fairly and squarely before the American people." That fall, when the German army rampaged through Belgium, slaughtering civilians and laying waste to public buildings, the tales of German atrocities horrified Americans: the kaiser's armies, it was said, chopped off babies' hands and women's breasts, or literally crucified enemy soldiers and shipped them home to be made into soap and grease. Germany's supporters insisted that these horrors were the inventions of British propagandists, and probably some were, though there was also enough barbarism to render such embellishment unnecessary.[1]

Though Viereck presented himself as a truth-teller, merely correcting a record shaped by the distorting propaganda of the Anglophile press, he was of course engaging in propaganda himself. In short order, his enthusiasm on behalf of the German cause piqued the suspicion of the U.S. Secret Service. Agents monitored his contacts, and on July 24, 1915, two officers were watching him as he visited the offices of the Hamburg-American Steamship Company on lower Broadway in New York. At three o'clock, Viereck emerged from the building with a companion, and the agents tailed the pair over to the Sixth Avenue El and onto a car.

At 23rd Street, Viereck got off. One agent followed him, while the other stayed on to watch the second man. A few stops later, the German man who had been riding with Viereck suddenly looked up from his newspaper and noticed that he had reached his stop. In his haste to rush off the car, he forgot his brown briefcase. The Secret Service agent grabbed it, and a chase ensued. Eventually the agent escaped with his unintended quarry, which he delivered to William Flynn, chief of the Secret Service.[2]

The bag's owner turned out to be Heinrich Albert, a German embassy attaché, and the sheaves of documents it contained detailed a sweeping campaign of espionage, sabotage, and propaganda designed to sway American opinion toward Germany in the war. The schemes were traceable to German Chancellor Theobald von Bethmann-Hollweg. The papers showed that Berlin was secretly subsidizing not only Viereck's *Fatherland* but other American publications as well. The Germans were planning, too, to buy a controlling interest in the *New York Evening Mail* and had plans to bankroll films, lecturers, and pseudo-indigenous movements to promote the German line. Worse still, these propaganda efforts were yoked to plans of sabotage and espionage: to foment strikes in American munitions factories; to acquire the Wright Brothers Aeroplane Company to use its patents; even to blow up the Welland Canal in Canada.

Flynn delivered the sensitive materials to Treasury Secretary William McAdoo, who in turn took the cache to Cornish, New Hampshire, the summer retreat of Woodrow Wilson. During the summer of 1915, the president was struggling mightily to maintain neutrality—to satisfy what he called "the double wish of our people," meaning to put an end to German offenses against America and yet also avoid war.[3] Wilson worried that the latest German mischief would thwart his diplomacy and inflame public opinion. He became convinced, as he told his adviser Edward House, that the country was "honeycombed with German intrigue and infested with German spies." McAdoo for his part "saw an opportunity," as he recalled, "to throw a reverberating scare into the whole swarm of propagandists—British and French as well as German—and I decided that this could be done most effectively through publicity."[4]

They decided to leak the documents to Frank Cobb, editor of the *New York World*. Cobb's paper proceeded to run a series of front-page stories in August about the German intrigues.[5] Day after day, revelations about the secrecy, funding, and scope of Germany's propaganda blitz outraged Americans—including antiwar journalists. Relations between Berlin and Washington deteriorated as the German ambassador to Washington was sent home. Viereck, for his part, continued to insist that neither he nor the German government had done anything wrong. Berlin was merely countering the Allies' lies, he said, and the *World*'s story was part of a British propaganda plot.[6]

The question of propaganda was a heavily fraught topic during World War I, and it would remain so for years—even to the point of shaping attitudes two decades later toward the next world conflict and beyond. The term *propaganda* had originated with the Catholic Church, and for centuries it carried no particular negative connotations: it meant ideas that were to be propagated. But after World War I, the use of propaganda by the Germans, as well as by the Allied forces and the U.S. government itself, left a bitter aftertaste. The word propaganda, as the political scientist Harold Lasswell wrote, came "to have an ominous clang in many minds."[7] (Lasswell, a realist when it came to such things, tried in vain to preserve the term's neutral meaning.) This shift in meaning was a function of what Steven Pinker has called the "euphemism treadmill"—when a word refers to something we dislike, even a sanitized euphemism we've invented eventually takes on the negative connotations of its referent, forcing the invention of still newer euphemisms.[8] *Propaganda* would eventually give way to a host of other words, from *public relations* to *psychological warfare* to today's favored term of art, *spin*.

But it wasn't just the word *propaganda* that fell into disfavor with World War I; it was the practice. Until the United States entered the war in 1917, Americans were bombarded with all manner of propaganda from both sides in the European conflict; and after the United States joined the fighting, Wilson set up his own propaganda agency, the Committee for Public Information, under the leadership of the muckraker George Creel, which bombarded them some more. The American experience with propaganda in these years would thus nurture a deep and lasting skepticism among the public about the government provision of information.

Distrust of political rhetoric, to be sure, wasn't new in the World War I era. As far back as Plato's dialogue *Gorgias*, philosophers have argued that rhetoric, the coin of democratic politics, is inherently untrustworthy. For Plato, the problem is that rhetoric, unlike philosophy, aims to instill not truth but merely conviction. Just as cosmetics, which seeks to impart only the semblance of good health, is a corrupted form of medicine, so rhetoric, in Plato's account, is a degraded form of philosophy. But Plato's view was not uncontested. Aristotle, notably, took a more benign view of rhetoric, arguing that it could be used for good or for ill. "If it be objected that one who uses such power of speech unjustly might do great harm," he wrote, "that is a charge which may be made in common against all good things except virtue, and above all against the things that are most useful, as strength, health, wealth, generalship."[9] Nonetheless, the Platonic attitude toward rhetoric has persisted.

In the American political context, the distrust of political rhetoric was wedded early on to the new nation's distrust of centralized political power. The result was a strong streak of suspicion about not just White House power but also White House communication. Any president who was at all bold in his exercise of authority, especially if he was popular, came under attack for using manipulative rhetoric. Whig critics, for example, called the *Washington Globe*, the newspaper run by Andrew Jackson's cronies, "the President's thinking machine, his writing machine—aye, and his lying machine."[10]

Suspicion of political communication assumed a special place in American consciousness during the Progressive Era. More than any of his predecessors, Theodore Roosevelt made the White House into the seat of policymaking and a platform for mobilizing public opinion to achieve his agenda. Toward this end, he devised countless new methods for making his case to the public: holding press conferences, staging publicity stunts, hiring press agents for his pet projects, cultivating journalists, undertaking "swings around the circle" to promote his policies, and making extensive use of the bully pulpit, which, by naming, he fairly invented. For Roosevelt, the expansion of the White House's policymaking capacities and the proliferation of its channels of public communication went hand in hand.[11]

Roosevelt has been celebrated for these innovations in creating what the political scientist George Edwards has called "the public presidency."[12] But Roosevelt also had his critics. One of them was the one-eyed South Carolina Democratic senator "Pitchfork Ben" Tillman, who had earned his nickname by threatening to spear President Grover Cleveland with a farm implement. In January 1906—the same year Roosevelt mobilized public opinion on behalf of regulating the railroads, the meat packers, and the food and drug industries—Tillman caused one of the political kerfuffles of the year when he assailed Roosevelt from the Senate floor for his appetite for publicity and his manipulation of the press. The president, Tillman bellowed to the galleries during a two-and-a-half-hour tirade, was a sham, a self-promoter who had exaggerated his achievements ever since the Spanish-American War. "He had press agents with the Rough Riders down at Guantanamo," Tillman sneered. "Theodore Roosevelt owes more to newspapers than any man of his time, or possibly of any other time," reciting the president's practices for shaping his news coverage—stiffing unfriendly reporters, muzzling cabinet officials, using the White House secretary to drug the press with his talking points on Panama, railroad rates, and "everything pertaining to public affairs. . . . The newspapers are the men who have made him what he is."[13]

Tillman and Roosevelt had a history between them, but this eruption was more than the fallout from a grudge. In the Jeffersonian tradition, Tillman considered limited executive authority to be sacrosanct, and he watched with alarm a growing shift in power from Congress to the presidency, which had begun under McKinley, if not earlier. TR's manipulation of the press, Tillman charged, enabled his arrogation of power. It made him no different from "Andrew Jackson or Napoleon Bonaparte."[14]

If the long-term shift of power from Congress to the White House was the underlying reason for Tillman's outburst, the more proximate cause was Roosevelt's hiring of Joseph Bucklin Bishop as secretary for TR's Panama Canal project. Not long before, Roosevelt had appointed his friend, a journalist at the New York Globe, to manage the day-to-day affairs of building the canal, including the public relations—making Bishop, according to most accounts, the first dedicated government public relations officer. Tillman and others on Capitol Hill went ballistic, decrying the very idea that the president needed hired "press agents" to advance his agenda. Roosevelt and Bishop, for their part, insisted they were simply countering misleading propaganda from big business—the railroads in particular stood to suffer from a canal—and providing neutral factual information. "I give out the situation as it is," Bishop said flatly.[15]

The fight over Bishop would last for months, and it reflected a deep congressional reluctance to authorize any executive public relations officers, even passing prohibitions on their hiring.[16] Even after the controversy passed, the distrust of executive publicity continued. In 1913, Congress passed an amendment to an appropriations bill barring federal funds from compensating publicity experts.[17] Asked at a press conference if he would veto the bill, Woodrow Wilson, the new president, said no, agreeing that the departments shouldn't employ publicity agents. But then he added, with a smile, "It won't affect [this] office. We'll have publicity, I can promise you that."[18]

Wilson was true to his word. He built on Roosevelt's work in fashioning a public presidency, regularizing his press conferences (at least until he found them unbearable), making speeches to Congress and swings around the circle, and acquiescing uncomfortably in newsreels and other photo opportunities. Wilson also sought early in his presidency to establish an information ministry—an office that at the time wasn't seen as an Orwellian bogeyman but was considered a practical vehicle for coordinating the growing journalistic demand for official news and information.

Prodded by a number of progressive journalists, Wilson finally set up such an office when America entered the world war. He appointed the progressive muckraker George Creel to run the Committee on Public Information, tasked with providing the news media with official data from the White House, the cabinet departments (except State and War, which jealously guarded their own turf), and wartime agencies like the National War Labor Board, the War Industries Board, and other bodies. Creel, true to his muckraking roots, resolved to hew to the facts, hoping that the truth would of its own persuasive power summon the needed morale from the American public. He insisted he had no wish to see the government cooking up falsehoods, as the European governments were doing: no phony claims of battlefield routs, no cover-ups of embarrassing setbacks, no hyperbolic atrocity tales. Instead of suppression, the goal would be expression; instead of secrecy, publicity.[19] "We did not call it 'propaganda,'" Creel said, "for that word, in German hands, had come to be associated with lies and corruptions."[20]

Despite its goal of responsibly conveying information, the Creel Committee over time developed a reputation for fomenting hate and prejudice. Historians have handed down a grossly distorted, even cartoonish picture of Creel as a hyperpatriotic, intolerant zealot. The charge that the Creel Committee went overboard wasn't altogether without merit. The body's most visible and memorable efforts included some inflammatory material, including a handful of infamous posters demonizing the Germans. The activities of the Four-Minute Men, local volunteers who recited committee-issued pro-war themes in movie houses and public squares, also struck many Americans as excessively jingoistic. Creel himself admitted that his bureau became "a vast enterprise in salesmanship," with "energy exerted to arouse ardor and enthusiasm." Along with the German and British propaganda that battered

Americans before the United States entered the war, the Creel Committee's work did its part to give propaganda a bad name—despite his efforts to avoid the term.[21]

It is frequently forgotten, however, that during the war Creel was attacked less often for drumming up war fever than for being too restrained and insufficiently chauvinistic. The American Defense Society, a right-wing outfit, complained that Creel's "pacifistic" committee was "giving comfort to the enemy." The National Security League, another pro-war group, denounced one of the committee's more innocent pamphlets as "a masterpiece of Hun propaganda." Within the administration, Assistant Secretary of War Benedict Crowell berated Creel for not doing enough to boost the soldiers' morale. "May I suggest," he asked Creel in his gentlemanly way, "that a little savagery be added to the carefully prepared and exceedingly moderate statements of the official news?" When Creel refused to spread uncorroborated atrocity tales, Republicans attacked him for downplaying German ruthlessness. "Conservatives call me a radical," Creel sighed, "and the radicals all call me a conservative."[22] The idea that Creel fed the infamous wartime excesses of Attorney General Thomas Gregory and Postmaster General Albert Burleson—with whom he often tangled—became gospel only after the war, in the wake of Wilson's failure to win a just and lasting peace. Only after 1919 did Americans, experiencing buyer's remorse, adopt in full measure the revisionist view of the Creel Committee.[23]

The revised assessment of Creel stemmed from the disappointment that set in with Wilson's failure to implement his postwar international vision. But it also owed something to the hyperkinetic culture of the 1920s, which witnessed the rapid growth of private and government publicity operations. The cultural critic Silas Bent called the 1920s the "Age of Ballyhoo"—a decade of flashy display and cheerful salesmanship. In Times Square, neon signs and blinking streams of bulbs hawked toothpaste, Coca-Cola, and cigarettes amid the blinding dazzle of theater marquees. Ad men and public relations agents tapped out self-consciously snappy prose that moved to the syncopated rhythms of the Jazz Age. Newspapers not only teemed with advertising; they also reflected the values of promotion, as gossip-filled tabloids served up arresting photographs while glossy magazines featured beguiling illustrations. Technological invention, a humming economy, and a revolution in manners and morals chased one another in a dizzying whirl.[24]

In the new, booming economy, advertising and public relations enjoyed unprecedented chic. Writers flocked to the lucrative warrens of Madison

Avenue. "It is a great responsibility to mold the daily lives of millions of our fellow men," declared copywriter James Wallen, "and I am persuaded that we are second only to statesmen and editors in power for good."[25] The agencies were changing the culture; what had been luxuries, they sought to make necessities, using the latest insights. The J. Walter Thompson Agency, seizing on a vogue for psychology, hired John Watson, a founder of behaviorist psychology—a move that symbolized the profession's intention to use "science" to plumb the unconscious. The senior men in the field fancied themselves statesmanlike interpreters of public opinion, giving voice to popular yearnings. "The product of advertising is . . . public opinion," declared a pamphlet from Barton, Durstine and Osborn (BDO), an up-and-coming firm, "and in democracy public opinion is the uncrowned king." This democratic language aimed to dispel impressions that their business was deceptive and mercenary. Yoking its aims to the spirit of Progressivism, it sought to legitimize advertising's place in the political sphere.[26]

Among the leading evangelists for advertising was Bruce Barton, a partner in BDO.[27] A magazine journalist, best-selling author, advertising executive, public relations adviser to presidents, and, later, a congressman, Barton was a hard-charging, almost manic, insomniac, who despite periodic visits to clinics and spas juggled his multiple roles deftly. During the war, he had worked for the United War Work Campaign, an ad hoc group assembled by the War Department to promote the YMCA, the Jewish Welfare Board, and the Salvation Army. Afterward he pivoted to commerce. "And they shall beat their swords into—Electroypes," he prophesied in a December 1918 article that proposed harnessing advertising's know-how to the peacetime goals of security and prosperity. With Roy Durstine and Alex Osborn, colleagues from the United War Work Campaign, he founded BDO (renamed, when it merged with the George Batten Agency in 1928, BBDO), headquartered a block and a half west of Madison Avenue in midtown Manhattan. With a staff of fourteen, their company built an august client list, including General Electric, General Motors, and General Mills—the top brass of the business world—emerging by 1923 as the fourth largest advertising firm in the country. Barton also emerged as a best-selling author with the publication in 1925 of *The Man Nobody Knows*, a portrait of Jesus Christ as a "magnetic personality" and charismatic entrepreneur. By marrying a vibrant religious faith to an appreciation of hustle and acquisition, the book signaled that a life of goodness wasn't incompatible with the good life—and helped ratify the view of advertising men as the apostles of the age.[28]

Public relations, too, boomed after the war. Journalists fretted that the end of the European conflict had uncorked a geyser of what Frank Cobb, in a 1919 speech to the Women's City Club of New York, called "private propaganda"—a flood of one-sided news, worked up by corporate shills, who were now laboring on behalf of every conceivable cause. Before the war, a New York newspaper survey had found some 1,200 press agents employed at different companies; now they were uncountable, serving corporations, banks, railroads, "all the organizations of business and of social and political activity," Cobb noted, "even statesmen." While conceding that "in some respects they perform a highly valuable service," he argued that the hired guns existed "not to proclaim the truth, the whole truth, and nothing but the truth," but merely to convey "the particular state of facts that will be of the greatest benefit to their client—in short, to manipulate the news."[29]

Here the key figure was Edward Bernays.[30] Born in Vienna in 1891, the nephew twice over of Sigmund Freud, Bernays began a career in what was derisively called "press agentry" before going to work for the Creel Committee. Opening his own private practice as a "public relations counselor" after the war, he tried to invest his trade with the weight of science and professionalism. He boasted that he taught the first university course in public relations, at New York University in 1923, and he defended public relations practitioners against attacks in the newspapers and advertising trade journals. He also shamelessly played up his connection with his legendary uncle, though Bernays's own knowledge of psychoanalysis was actually fairly skimpy, having come, as he once admitted, mainly from "osmosis."[31] Where Barton put his ideas forward in *The Man Nobody Knows*, Bernays did so in a pair of books, *Crystallizing Public Opinion* and *Propaganda*, briefs for the importance of public relations work. In the latter volume, he tried to salvage the once-neutral term, explaining, "The conscious and intelligent manipulation of the organized habits and opinions of the masses is an important element in democratic society," he wrote. "Those who manipulate this unseen mechanism of society constitute an invisible government which is the true ruling power of our country."[32]

Both Bernays and Barton, notably, became advisers to the Republican presidents of the 1920s, who steadily augmented the White House communication machine. Warren Harding, who relied on the advertising executive Albert Lasker, also hired the first presidential speechwriter in Judson

Welliver. Calvin Coolidge emerged as the first chief executive to master radio while also becoming, the *New York Times* wrote, "the most photographed person . . . on earth outside of movieland."[33] Coolidge, too, relied on Barton to help fashion his image as "Silent Cal," the rock-solid embodiment of Yankee virtue, and, when that persona seemed too aloof, he turned to Bernays to show the public that he could enjoy a good laugh. Herbert Hoover, for his part, was deemed by Drew Pearson to be "one of the great super-promoters of the age, a man who had been able by a consummate sense of publicity to create the illusion of heroism and greatness and to attain world acclaim."[34] Or so it seemed until the Depression struck. The Democrats, too, embraced professional publicity in these years, hiring the newspaperman Charlie Michelson to launch daily attacks in the press against Hoover.[35]

This flood of propaganda, from the White House as well as the business world, did not go unremarked upon. On the contrary, it fed an intense backlash against the practice and the practitioners of persuasion. Despite the efforts of men like Bernays and Lasswell, Americans looked upon propaganda with growing cynicism. It became a convenient scapegoat for explaining away their former enthusiasm for the World War. Embracing Harding's "normalcy" and the "Coolidge Prosperity" of the 1920s, shunning the high ideals of Progressivism, regretting their European adventure, Americans now told themselves that they had gone to war only because propaganda had insidiously played upon their emotions. Propaganda became a way for critics to make sense of the brew of groupthink, nationalism, and repression that they suddenly wished to disavow.

In the 1920s, this new culture of suspicion produced a cottage industry of antipropaganda tracts that cemented a lasting distrust of publicity. In many of these works, Creel came in for particular criticism. One author said that his committee had engineered "the greatest fraud ever sold." Another declared that "truth was crucified during the war."[36] Perhaps the cruelest attack came from a series of articles in the *Saturday Evening Post*, later collected in a 1931 volume called *Spreading Germs of Hate*, which was graced by an introduction from a penitent Edward House. The author of this pious manifesto mocked Creel as a "messianic spirit" and "chief evangelist of American propaganda." (Wilson was its "High Priest.") The book pinned blame on Wilson and Creel for whipping up American anger toward Germany and making the country so "war mad" that the president, during the peace negotiations, had to jettison his Fourteen Points. The author of this tract, a formerly discredited writer who had lately been rehabilitated, was George Sylvester Viereck.[37]

*   *   *

One year after the publication of *Spreading Germs of Hate*, Adolf Hitler came to power in Germany. Viereck, remarkably, resumed propagandizing on behalf of his native country. He traveled to Germany to interview Hitler, Josef Goebbels, and Hermann Goering. He also edited a volume of self-justifying essays by the Nazi leaders and probably ghostwrote, or at least translated, Hitler's contribution.[38] Back in New York, in May 1934, he headlined a rally of some 20,000 Nazi sympathizers in Madison Square Garden, for which the arena was converted, Nuremberg-style, into an ideological hothouse, with swastika-laden bunting, the German eagle, and other Nazi iconography hanging from the rafters. Eight hundred men, dressed in high boots, military trousers, and Nazi armbands, stood erect in the aisles, policing the crowd. On stage, Viereck sang the praises of the Reich and attacked Jews and Communists. This behavior got him hauled before the new House Committee on Un-American Activities, designed to monitor pro-Nazi activities. Viereck confessed to working with Carl Byoir, a leading American public relations man (and onetime deputy to Creel), to secretly promote German interests in the United States. Viereck's self-defense was the same as it had been in 1915. The Nazis, he insisted, had no nefarious intent. Their propaganda was merely "a proper defensive measure against a flood of billingsgate."[39]

These revelations were shocking, but the public remained resistant to intervention against Nazi Germany, owing to the lingering regret over World War I. Many well-intentioned liberals, seared by the experience of World War I, had grown irrationally fearful of their own government's messages. It fell to a handful of far-sighted intellectuals to question why so many of fascism's natural enemies on the left had become complacent isolationists. In many analyses, fear of propaganda—not the Nazis', but the American government's—was a major reason for the failure of nerve. The pioneering communications scholars Paul Lazarsfeld and Robert Merton called this overweening fear of being misled "propaganditis."[40]

Among the most vocal critics of the isolationist left was the poet and playwright Archibald MacLeish, whom Franklin Roosevelt had named librarian of Congress in 1939. In the spring of 1940, MacLeish assailed antiwar novelists, including his friends Ernest Hemingway and John Dos Passos, for having unintentionally fostered a debilitating distrust "of all slogans and . . . all words, . . . of all statements of principle and conviction, all declarations of moral purpose." Nothing did more than this postwar cynicism, said MacLeish, to "disarm democracy in the face of fascism" a generation later.[41] For these remarks, the poet faced a hail of denunciations, but he wasn't alone in his diagnosis of the problem. The journalist Max Lerner also decried the undue fear of propaganda he saw about him, which arose, he argued, "because we have felt cheated and disenchanted by our role in the last war, and are determined never again to be tricked." This self-imposed vigilance, he concluded, was clouding judgments, blurring distinctions, and diverting attention from the danger Hitler posed.[42] Likewise, the historian Allan Nevins dismissed "these warnings to guileless Americans to look under the bed every night for propagandists"; after decades of "propagandistic" appeals to the public by "the Abolitionists, the Prohibitionists, the Suffragists, the Populists, the Protectionists, and the innumerable other 'ists' who strew our history," he observed, the public had developed "the most constant practice in detecting and resisting it."[43]

Perhaps the most eloquent of these voices was that of the critic Lewis Mumford. In a postwar revision of an essay first penned in 1940, Mumford deplored what he termed a "pathological resistance to rational persuasion [that] characterized a great part of the civilized world" in the late 1930s and early 1940s. "Analysts of propaganda," he explained in a lengthy footnote to the essay, "exposing the rhetorical devices of persuasion, themselves put over one of the biggest propaganda frauds of our time: namely, the conviction that the important part about a statement is not its truth or falsity, but the question whether someone wishes you to believe it." Pointedly, Mumford belittled those "who still believe that the horrors of the German extermination factories are but the figments of propaganda," tracing that incredulity to the dismissals of Germany's World War I atrocities, which Charles Beard, for example, called a "tale for babes." This was no smear or baseless attack on Mumford's part. After all, Beard's fellow World War I revisionist and isolationist Harry Elmer Barnes would follow his belief system to an extreme conclusion, going on to become a key figure in launching the Holocaust denial movement. There was a clear and disturbing progression from Barnes's fashionable post–World War I isolationism, with its casual dismissal of "propaganda stories," to his subsequent opposition to fighting Nazism, and then to his embrace of one of deepest crimes against history and morality.[44]

Few propaganda skeptics went to such malign extremes as Barnes. Yet by World War II the rise of publicity had instilled in Americans a robust suspicion of official pronouncements. For a few years, the war itself seemed to mute these concerns, as the national mobilization to fight against fascism encouraged a trust in the president and the government. But the abiding American anxiety about propaganda did not disappear. In the postwar era, it returned with a vengeance—as seen in such phenomena as the panic about brainwashing, popular films about political manipulation like *A Face in the Crowd*, and the runaway success of Vance Packard's book on the deceptive nature of advertising, *The Hidden Persuaders*. That anxiety would only grow stronger in the ensuing decades with the rise of television and the advent of professional political consultants.[45]

Just as rhetoric was an inherent part of ancient politics, propaganda—or spin, as we call its modern-day variant—is a permanent part of ours. It's understandable that we should fall into a Platonic mood and want to wish it away, but we can hardly imagine politics without spin. There is a "No-Spin Zone" on television, but the fact that it's hosted by the highly opinionated, provocative, and staunchly conservative pundit Bill O'Reilly should tell us something about those who claim to be offering information uncolored by ideology or personal viewpoint. Indeed, the long history of rhetoric, propaganda, and spin suggests that propagandists or spinners have invariably claimed to be truth-tellers who were simply dispelling falsehoods, while those aiming to dispel falsehood have seldom resisted the temptation to propagandize or spin.

Of course, citizens should—and do—call out those politicians who distort, exaggerate, or lie. In an aphorism attributed to Daniel Patrick Moynihan (but first coined, with a slightly different wording, by Bernard Baruch), everyone is entitled to his own opinion but not to his own facts.[46] Usually, though, determining which facts are relevant or important is part of the challenge—and the disagreement. Instead of trying to somehow banish propaganda from the kingdom of politics, we'd be better off, like the critics who battled against the debilitating propaganditis of the pre–World War II years, trying to inculcate a critical sense that helps us question and evaluate it, and maybe, just once in a while, to know when to believe it.

CHAPTER 4

When the "Mainstream Media" Was Conservative: Media Criticism in the Age of Reform

Sam Lebovic

Apart from their law degrees and their success in politics, Spiro Agnew and Archibald MacLeish had almost nothing in common. As Richard Nixon's vice president in the late 1960s, Agnew built a reputation as a champion of the "silent majority" and a caustic critic of leftists and liberals. MacLeish was an upper-class liberal whose moment of political influence had come three decades earlier, when he served in various roles in Franklin Delano Roosevelt's administration. Educated at Harvard and Yale, MacLeish was a poet, a New Dealer, and an internationalist, and he counted Dean Acheson and Ernest Hemingway among his close personal friends. He was, in short, exactly the sort of East Coast liberal that Agnew liked to pillory in the late 1960s.[1]

So it is interesting that MacLeish and Agnew shared a surprisingly similar antipathy to what each thought of as the mainstream media. In November 1969, Agnew gave two famous speeches in which he criticized the news media for its irresponsible and biased coverage of the government's policy in Vietnam. He began by criticizing the power of the television news: "the news that forty million Americans receive each night is determined by a handful of men responsible only to their corporate employers and filtered through a handful of commentators who admit to their own set of biases." The following week, he extended this criticism to the press, arguing that "the American people should be made aware of the trend toward the monopolization of the great public information vehicles and the concentration of more and more power in fewer and fewer hands." "Many, many strong independent voices have been stilled in this country in recent years," Agnew observed. "And lacking the vigor of competition, some of those that have survived have—let's face it—grown fat and irresponsible." Agnew therefore challenged the media to "relate their great freedom with their great responsibility."[2]

In 1941, as a spokesperson for another administration facing media criticism of its war policies, Archibald MacLeish similarly asked whether the press was going to "accept, as a consequence of its traditional right to influence American opinion, a responsibility for the opinion which results?" He complained that there were "minority elements of the American press which are actively engaged in influencing American opinion in directions which lead not to victory but to defeat" and regretted that the rest of the press was not criticizing these "cowardly, half-hearted publishers, and the venal editors of their staffs."[3] Only a few years later, MacLeish expanded on his views of the irresponsibility of the media when he drafted a report on the state of the media as part of an intellectual commission exploring the meaning of modern press freedom. Like Agnew, MacLeish observed in the media a "tendency toward concentration of ownership, and therefore of control, in fewer and fewer hands." And like Agnew, MacLeish worried that monopolization of the press by an unelected and unrepresentative minority threatened the American public's ability to receive accurate news: "the greatest danger a self-governing nation faces is the danger that ideas and information will be kept from the people by dominant political or economic or religious or social groups."[4]

Of course, the two disagreed about something quite fundamental— Agnew was incensed that the media was monopolized by a coterie of irresponsible liberals; MacLeish that it was monopolized by a clique of selfish conservatives. But beneath the difference in partisan flavor, the logic and rhetoric of their critiques was almost identical. Agnew and MacLeish even buttressed their criticisms of media monopoly by citing judicial opinions from the same Supreme Court case—the Justice Department's antitrust suit against the Associated Press in 1943. That case had been controversial in MacLeish's time, for it was seen by conservative newspaper publishers as a New Deal effort to regulate the free economics of the newspaper industry and thus to bring the free press under the dictatorial heel of FDR. New Deal liberals like MacLeish, though, had argued that some state action was needed to break apart media monopolies—they were pleased that the antitrust suit was judged constitutional by Judge Learned Hand, and that the Supreme Court had upheld Hand's decision in its 1945 ruling on the matter. So it was un-surprising that MacLeish would favorably cite Hugo Black's pronouncement that "the widest possible dissemination of information from diverse and antagonistic sources is essential to the welfare of the public." But it was strange that Agnew, in 1969, would buttress his assault on the liberal media by quoting similar sentiments from the opinion of Learned Hand, who was a liberal, in the AP matter, which had been understood as a liberal victory.[5]

And therein lies an interesting historical puzzle. Conservative criticism of the mainstream (or "lamestream") media became a fixture of American political culture in the years after Agnew's speeches, and historians have done important work in unearthing the origins of right-wing media criti-cism in conservative movement culture after World War II.[6] But criticism of media monopolization and bias began in an earlier era, and it was not origi-nally a discourse of the right. Beginning in the late nineteenth century, pro-gressives and liberals had first criticized media consolidation, arguing that the media was becoming a homogeneous block, hostile to diverse voices. And they had thought that the capitalist nature of the mass media had made it overwhelmingly conservative, hostile to liberal and leftist and working-class voices in particular. By the time of the New Deal, it was almost an article of faith that the mass news media was a conservative force in society. New Deal-ers and Popular Fronters regularly decried the probusiness, biased conser-vatism of the press. Conservatives and media figures responded that liberals were simply seeking to shackle the free press—they argued that the news me-dia industries needed to be protected from government and political med-dling. Those partisan dynamics changed rapidly after World War II. Agnew's assault on the media in 1969 was criticized by one Democratic congressman as a "creeping socialistic scheme against the free enterprise broadcast in-dustry."[7] It was easy for Agnew to brush off the charge. "That is the first time in my memory anybody ever accused Ted Agnew of entertaining socialist ideas," he quipped.[8] But the barb captured, however unintentionally, a deeper truth. In criticizing the political bias of the mainstream media, Agnew had inherited a left-wing discourse.

This essay reconstructs antimedia populism from the era before World War II, when it was a populism of the left, not the right. It begins in the late nineteenth century, when muckrakers and press commentators first noticed that commercial transformations in the press were creating a more homogenous news media and when they first worried about the implications of those developments for American politics. Such media criticism moved into the mainstream of American politics during the Depression, when the Popular Front and the New Deal regularly clashed with what they understood to be the "conservative press." The progressive, liberal, and left-wing critique of the mainstream media is an interesting moment in its own right—it captures a fascinating intersection between media and politics, and provides a window into the political culture and intellectual currents of the long age of reform. And consideration of the curious echo of this critique in right-wing populism after World War II also raises broader questions about the historical transformations of American political culture, and about the relationship of the mass media to political life in the modern United States.

*   *   *

Criticism of the news media was, of course, as old as American politics. Thomas Jefferson had famously decried the press's "abandoned prostitution to falsehood," and suggested that the "malignity, the vulgarity and mendacious spirit" of the press was "rapidly depraving the public taste."[9] And throughout the nineteenth century, political partisans and moralists alike had found content in the press to which they could object. The very point of a partisan press, after all, was that it appealed to one political faction—by definition, that was going to be objectionable to others. And as the penny press and then the yellow press sought to reach ever-larger markets of readers through sensationalist journalism, their sensationalism raised questions about their respectability; the rise of urban crime reporting, in particular, caused much hand-wringing about the prurient appeal of the news.[10]

But in the late nineteenth century, a new form of press criticism began to emerge. More than simply criticism of the moral turpitude of the press, more than partisan swiping at the biases of individual editors or stories, the new criticism began to suggest, first, that the press was becoming ominously homogeneous and, second, that it was becoming homogeneously conservative. The criticism was a response to very real changes in the political economy of the newspaper industry—the rise of newspaper chains, the growth of monopoly papers, the dependency on advertising revenue, and the declining numbers of daily newspapers (which began in 1909, and was noticed shortly thereafter).[11] By 1909, Hamilton Holt documented the ways that the "preponderating weight of commercialism" was transforming the press.[12] The next year, the *Atlantic Monthly* observed that "more and more the owner of the big daily is a business man who finds it hard to see why he should run his property on different lines from the hotel proprietor. . . . The paper is likelier to be run as a money-maker pure and simple."[13]

Populists and Progressives quickly argued that such commercialism was producing a conservative press, dominated and distorted by capitalist self-interest. Following his 1896 electoral defeat, William Jennings Bryan argued that the press had been aligned against him, and worried about the "predatory interests which own newspapers and employ brilliant editors to chloroform their readers while the owners pick their pockets."[14] In 1906, Henry George argued that the press had become a "pleader and champion for Privilege" because of its financial "bondage."[15] Muckrakers trained their eye on the manipulation of the press by business interests—Ray Stannard Baker revealed "How Railroads Make Public Opinion," and William Kittle documented the corrupting role of the Associated Press in "The Making of Public Opinion."[16] "The charge of conspiracy to suppress the truth is rife on every hand," journalist Oswald Garrison Villard observed in 1915: "I hear constantly that we have all agreed to perpetuate this outrage or that wrong. . . . I was myself asked the other day in a mass meeting: 'is it not true that you are owned by Wall Street?' "[17]

Two particularly important works of the new press criticism emerged from the muckraking impulse. In 1911, after a year of research and writing, Will Irwin published in *Collier's* a landmark series of fifteen articles on the history and operation of the press. Surveying the commercialism of the press, and documenting cases of graft both major and minor, Irwin discovered what he thought to be an "unhealthy alliance" between advertising and the press. He worried about the fact that the press was paid for by big business: "about one per cent of the population, and often the very one percent united, in the present condition of American society, with the powers most dangerous to the common weal." "Publicly," he concluded, the modern newspaper "assumes to exercise its ancient office of tribune of the people. Privately, it serves wealth. . . . The system is dishonest to the marrow."[18]

Almost a decade later, Upton Sinclair came to similar conclusions in his book of press criticism. In *The Brass Check*, named for the tokens used as payments in brothels, Sinclair set out to do for the newspaper industry what he had earlier done for meatpacking. Sinclair considered *The Brass Check* his "most important and dangerous book"—he was apparently worried that it would produce more than fifty libel cases—but it was in truth a far less successful book than *The Jungle*. Partially written in the mode of autobiography, the self-published book was self-indulgent and self-righteous and often seemed to be an opportunity for Sinclair to settle scores. But the book helped to synthesize the nascent critique of the conservative, probusiness press, and it sold 150,000 copies. "It is the thesis of this book," Sinclair stated plainly, "that American newspapers as a whole represent private interests and not public interests." And Sinclair pulled no punches in making the case that the press was a functionalist tool of capitalist hegemony: "journalism is one of the devices whereby industrial autocracy keeps its control over political democracy."[19]

With the "return to normalcy" in the 1920s, press criticism became more muted, focusing largely on professionalization and self-improvement.[20] But the worries of the muckrakers continued to reverberate. In 1921, for instance, sociologist Alfred H. Lloyd suggested that Sinclair's book was "not to be taken whole," but he nevertheless criticized the "peculiar conservatism of the press," its "venal sensationalism," and its tendency to "duplicity" and a "certain habit of fabrication."[21] Oswald Garrison Villard published portraits of the press that emphasized the rise of chains, the consolidation of the press, and its political conservatism—what he called the "prevailing tendencies in the rake's progress of our press, due to the commercialization of what should be the noblest of professions."[22] In their classic sociological portrait of Middletown, the Lynds remarked that "it is usually safe to predict that in any given controversy the two leading papers may be expected to support the United States in any cause, the business class rather than the working class, the Republican party against any other."[23] In 1927, in the most extensive criticism of Jazz-Age journalism, Silas Bent intermingled complaints about business consolidation with worries about the immorality of the press.[24] That seemed to sum up the press criticism of the decade: the concerns about press conservatism had receded, and been diluted, but they had not gone away.

*　*　*

In the 1930s, in response to the Depression and the polarization of the New Deal polity, criticism of the conservative press reached a crescendo. At first, the rosy press coverage of the early Depression raised concerns that the papers were deceiving the public. At the 1933 meeting of the American Society of Newspaper Editors, one editor introduced a motion criticizing the newspapers for creating a sense of "false economic security." John Dos Passos was blunter, confessing to Edmund Wilson in 1931 that "I'm beginning to think that every printed publication ought to be required by law to print at the bottom of each page: NB: THIS IS ALL BULLSHIT."[25] New Deal investigations into market failures also produced new evidence that business interests corrupted the press. Fiorello La Guardia's investigations into financial reporting revealed press manipulation and press incompetence. ("If newspapers spent one-third as much for an intelligent analysis of financial news as they do for sports," he concluded, "the loss of billions of dollars by American people in worthless stocks would have been averted.")[26] Extensive Federal Trade Commission investigations into the power trust also revealed that power companies had bought up newspapers and planted stories to resist public regulation. Press critic George Seldes called it "the greatest scandal in the history of the American press."[27]

At the same time, the rise of organized labor and the Popular Front heightened dissatisfaction with the range of opinions presented in the media. "It is a well known fact," Harold Ickes declared in 1939, "that, by and large, the press is unfriendly to organized labor." Representatives of labor agreed, decrying the biased and slanted coverage of strikes, negotiations, and industrial disputes in the New Deal polity.[28] Ferdinand Lundberg, author of a muckraking attack on the concentration of American wealth, decried what he called the "press of the plutocracy" and the "centralized class control over the American press by the very rich."[29] Journalist Max Lerner asserted that the American press was the "most class conscious segment of big-business, since its stock in trade consists of the legends and folklore of capitalism."[30]

Despite the rise of the radio, public debate about media monopoly and political bias remained fixated on the newspaper industry. This was because the radio was only just emerging as a discrete news medium. Through the mid-1930s, the radio networks both relied on newspapers for information and, following the Biltmore Agreement with the newspaper industry, limited themselves to two five-minute bulletins a day. The agreement was often violated, and it soon unraveled, but as late as 1938 67 percent of Americans still said they got most of their news from the newspapers.[31] Liberal critics of radio therefore focused primarily on the banal commercialism of radio—its very lack of political discussion constituting the problem—or on worrying signs that the newspaper publishers were about to extend their monopolistic influence over the new medium. By the end of the decade, in fact, almost one out of every three radio stations was owned by a newspaper, and the critique of media monopoly began to focus on what were soon dubbed mixed-media empires. And it was the publishers, not the broadcasters, who were in charge of those empires.[32]

Public debate about conservative media bias therefore fixated on the power of the newspaper baron—larger-than-life political figures such as William Randolph Hearst, Robert McCormick, and Frank Gannett. These men did, in fact, mobilize their media holdings as a platform from which to attack the New Deal as a threat to American liberty. McCormick compared the National Recovery Act to fascism, and complained that "business cannot prosper when the President of the United States embarks upon a campaign to destroy the constitution." In a front-page interview with the *New York Times*, Hearst argued that the New Deal was "wasting the people's money in futile and fantastic experiments" and called for the end of the "NRA and its Nonsense, Ridiculous, Asinine interference with national and legitimate industrial development." Later in the decade, Gannett funded a Committee to Uphold Constitutional Government to attack FDR's plans to pack the Supreme Court and reorganize the executive.[33]

And come election time, the press threw its weight behind Republican challengers to FDR. In 1936, Hearst helped to fund and organize Alf Landon's campaign, McCormick paid a large network of Landon volunteers to turn out the vote, and FDR received editorial endorsement from only 37 percent of daily newspapers.[34] "The electorate went to the election booths," observed Oswald Garrison Villard, "under the strongest impression not only that the press was mainly Republican, but that it was fighting not for the country as a whole but for its own personal interests." As the election results came in— FDR would win 60 percent of the vote—pro-Roosevelt crowds in Chicago celebrated by assaulting the *Chicago Tribune*, setting fire to a delivery truck and egging its building.[35] In 1940, even fewer papers endorsed FDR—only one in four preferred him to Wendell Willkie.[36] After that election, journalist Irving Brant decried the existence of the "Press for Willkie" club, noting that the "alliance between the press and Big Business throws into the political scales, all on one side, a crushing weight of propaganda and money."[37] In reality, FDR's comfortable reelection in both 1936 and 1940 suggested that the media were not as powerful as these critics feared.[38]

But in the polarized political climate of the 1930s, the conservatism of publishers like Hearst and McCormick produced concerns about the disruption of democracy, as well as a vitriolic reaction. In the summer of 1936 a group of Chicagoans canceled their subscriptions to the *Tribune* because of McCormick's "genius for distorting political news."[39] In 1936, Harold Ickes observed in his diary that there was "more widespread anti-Hearst feeling among the people than there has been for a great many years, if ever. I am told that when his name appears on the screen in some movie theaters, he is hissed."[40] Boycotts and mass meetings were held to protest the Hearst press's "attempts to glorify Fascism." In 1936, a Communist Party of California meeting featured a parade of papier-mâché–headed villains of American democracy: Hitler, Landon, and Hearst.[41]

In the late 1930s, an administration frustrated with press hostility took up the critique of conservative media bias. Harold Ickes, the secretary of the interior, was the figure most responsible for bringing the assault on the mainstream media to the center of politics. In 1939, he published a book criticizing the newspapers for their "misrepresentation of individuals and propaganda directed against the public welfare in the interest of the further enrichment and enhancement of the power of our economic royalists, among whom our Lords of the Press occupy a preferred status."[42] Ickes' debt to the leftist critique of the press was clear—the phrase "Lords of the Press" was the title of radical journalist George Seldes's 1938 critique of the conservative press; Ickes' book was entitled *America's House of Lords*. But coming from a prominent member of the administration, accusations of conservative media bias gained a wider hearing and a stamp of official imprimatur. In 1939, Ickes conducted a public debate with Frank Gannett on the state of American press freedom in which he continued his attack on the press. In front of a sold-out New York Town Hall and a national radio audience, Ickes bemoaned the "lack of a free press" in the United States and argued that the newspapers' "vast financial investment, running high into the millions, binds them closely to the business world from which they draw their sustenance. Freedom is impossible . . . when the counting office holds the whip hand."[43] Ickes and Gannett continued the argument in public letters in the press over the following weeks; in 1940 and 1941, Ickes publicly complained again of the "bias and narrow partisanship" of the press.[44]

Other members of the administration, too, took up criticism of the press. In 1938, Sherman Minton added that the press was so opposed to the New Deal that "the administration can't get a headline in the newspapers" and criticized the "propaganda that appears in the sheets of this country."[45] In 1940, Edward Flynn, chair of the Democratic National Convention, said that the newspapers "are under a real dictatorship, a financial dictatorship of their advertisers and stockholders."[46] Even FDR, who regularly noted that "85%" of the press was against him, insinuated that the press was dominated by probusiness interests and edited "from the counting room."[47] Behind the scenes, it seems that there was even more administration animus toward the press. "Almost every week," observed a June 1937 *Kiplinger Washington Letter*, "there's some White House 'crack' against newspaper publishers as a class—off the record and unpublished."[48]

How much of the public believed in that critique is impossible to quantify precisely. Perhaps very few did. According to one Gallup poll, approximately 75 percent of respondents believed the papers were fair to the administration between elections, and 50 percent of FDR voters thought the press had been fair to the president in the 1940 campaign.[49] But by the end of the 1930s, there was little doubt that *if* the press had a political bias, it was a conservative, probusiness bias. A 1938 Roper poll, for instance, found 61 percent of the public thought that the newspapers soft-pedaled news that was unfavorable to big advertisers in at least some cases, and one in two thought it soft-pedaled news that was unfavorable to business in general. While the majority of the public couldn't decide whether the press was too antagonistic or friendly to the wealthy or to labor, 27 percent thought the papers too friendly to people of wealth, and only 8 percent thought the papers were too antagonistic. Only 9 percent thought the papers were too friendly to labor.[50]

And in some places, it seemed that the critique of the conservative press was becoming almost a form of political common sense. Walter M. Harris, managing editor of two papers in Oklahoma, calmly observed that "a big newspaper is first of all a factory . . . no doubt publishers shade policy to what they think is the protection of their property. The country club influence is a definite class influence. Few editors become publishers without becoming conservatives."[51] In 1939, a study of administrative publicity announced that "there is no denying that newspapers are preponderantly the reflectors of the views of business which has a first interest in making profits and a second concern for the public welfare."[52] In 1946, the introduction to a study of the press by working journalists declared that the volume wasn't "warming up the trite accusations that advertisers control the press, or that owners are in a conspiracy to suppress the news." Nevertheless, the journalists observed that "there is a widespread belief that most of the press favors property interests," argued that the "overwhelming majority" of papers "show unmistakable hostility to labor," and reported that "careful study of many newspapers across the country produces a strong impression that labor is consistently a victim of slanted news stories and prejudiced editorials."[53]

*   *   *

This critique of the conservative media would never disappear entirely from American political life, but it had hit its peak in the late New Deal. In the second half of the 1940s, some of the interwar critics of media monopoly continued to decry the ongoing consolidation and conservatism of the press. In 1946, Morris Ernst decried the "vanishing marketplace of ideas" created by media monopolies; in the same year journalist George Marion argued that the press was "a tool in the hands of a few finance capitalists."[54] Between 1940 and 1950, George Seldes continued his press criticism in a newsletter called *In Fact*, which documented the political deceptions of the corporate press as part of a leftist challenge to "American as well as foreign fascism, the corrupt newspapers, labor-baiters, anti-semites, and the great and powerful forces of money and greed." The newsletter was short-lived, but it helped to pass the torch of radical press criticism to future generations: both Howard Zinn and Ralph Nader read *In Fact* in their youth, and Seldes strategized with I. F. Stone when Stone began his weekly newsletter in 1953.[55] In the last decades of the twentieth century and the first decades of the twenty-first, a renewed critique of corporate media monopoly would be taken up by Noam Chomsky and Edward Herman, Ben Bagdikian, Robert McChesney, and others.[56]

But the critique had lost its purchase on the mainstream of politics—it is hard to imagine a member of the Carter or Clinton administrations drawing on Bagdikian or Chomsky in the same fashion that Ickes had drawn on Seldes in the late 1930s. And in the 1950s, as a number of historians have shown, a populist critique of media monopoly would emerge from the right. Grown in the hothouse of conservative movement culture and nourished by the ferment of the 1960s, accusations of liberal media bias became a fixture of mainstream politics. It is Agnew's attacks on the liberal media that resonate in contemporary politics, not Ickes' assault on the "financial ties" or conservatism of the press. By the 1990s, according to one study of press coverage, there would be seventeen mentions of liberal press bias to every one reference to conservative bias.[57]

The displacement of the left-wing critique of the mainstream media by a conservative critique was a significant moment in American political culture. It was a remarkably quick reversal, raising questions about broader transformations in American politics. It is, of course, possible that media content itself underwent a radical transformation from conservatism to liberalism in these years. But while we lack content analyses of this issue, such a change doesn't seem particularly probable. Postwar newspapers, for instance, overwhelmingly continued to endorse Republican candidates for the presidency—Nixon received between 54 and 71 percent of the endorsements in his three presidential campaigns; his opponents, including JFK, received between 5 and 15 percent.[58] Such editorial policy tells us nothing about the bias of the news content, which was the main concern for conservative media critics, but it does upset any idea of a homogeneously liberal media. Rather than a wholesale change in ideological bias in the press, it is more likely that coverage of certain issues triggered a conservative reaction. We know, for instance, that conservatives were troubled by the mainstream media's belated attention to the civil rights struggles in the South, seeing it as a sanctimonious form of meddling.[59]

In any case, the rapidity and ideological extremity of the shift in media criticism suggests that the content of the media was less important than the lens through which the media was being viewed. Midcentury media critics were not always careful social scientists, parsing close studies of content coverage. They were themselves political actors, making political arguments according to their own normative frameworks about the sort of issues and opinions that deserved coverage in the "mainstream" of American media culture. That makes the transformation of media criticism an interesting moment in the history of American political culture and intellectual life. It suggests that a precondition for the conservative critique of the press was the displacement of an earlier left-wing critique. That displacement can be explained by the broader dynamics of midcentury politics—the impact of World War II and the Cold War, postwar prosperity, the marginalization of leftist critics and critiques during the Second Red Scare. But remembering the decline of the leftist critique of the mainstream media reminds us that the establishment press that was criticized as part of the "liberal consensus" was not considered to be particularly liberal as it was coming into view in the 1930s. And it therefore casts into relief the novelty of conservative accusations of liberal bias.

Comparing left-wing and right-wing criticisms of the press also reveals the marginalization of structural critiques of capitalism after World War II. The long history of press criticism had fixated on the problems of commercialism, industrialization, and capitalist self-interest to explain the inadequacies of the press. But postwar conservatives who criticized the liberal press avoided such issues, which were hard to square with their broader commitments to free market economics.[60] And they found it tricky to explain why advertisers and corporate owners of the press would encourage and support inimically liberal journalistic enterprises. In 1962, in the pages of the conservative newsletter *Human Events*, the business and financial editor of the *New York Herald Tribune* engaged in rare reflection on this issue and was left wondering why businesses were continuing to advertise in the liberal media: "I am tired of defending a system that is headed by such muddled thinking as to ignore its own warriors and pay tribute, glory, and riches to its enemies."[61]

Most conservative critics therefore avoided this can of worms and fixated instead on the political biases of journalists, which were best explained not by economic factors but by the cliquish culture of liberal elites. Agnew, for instance, focused on the fact that journalists were a small group who "live and work in the geographical and intellectual confines of Washington DC or New York City" and who "read the same newspapers and draw their political and social views from the same sources. Worse, they talk constantly to one another."[62] And while Edith Efron insisted that she did not believe in conspiracy theories of liberal media bias, she nevertheless attributed the twisting of the news simply to "tacit determination by a ruling intellectual elite to hold onto a position of influence which is now entrenched."[63] Such conspiratorial and pop-sociological explanations for media bias were not absent from the liberal critique of the conservative media, which regularly worried about the "country-club" influence on the journalistic elite.[64] But the earlier critique usually, if not always, married that sociological explanation to a structural explanation—as Will Irwin put it in 1911, "the financial brake on free journalism is intertwined with the social brake."[65] In the conservative critique of the liberal media, the question of finances dropped away as social factors and cultural politics became all important.

Important as these differences in form are, a comparison of left-wing and right-wing critiques of media bias also reveals an important continuity: populist critiques of the media were a recurring feature of the twentieth century. Perhaps this is just what modern politics looks like: when liberals are in the ascendancy, and run up against media criticism, they decry its irrational conservatism; when conservatives are ascendant, they decry the biased liberalism of their critics. (If one were to look at this situation through particularly rosy glasses, one could even conclude that this is exactly the sort of criticism that a watchdog press should inspire among government partisans.) But in a long enough historical perspective, the similarity between antimedia populism before and after World War II captures something distinctive about the modern media. By the middle decades of the twentieth century, the media were more consolidated than at any earlier point: the major networks dominated the new broadcast media, the overall number of newspapers was declining, and the remaining papers were increasingly monopolistic. And the consolidated media were, by definition, increasingly remote from the mass of the public that depended on them for their news. As the illustrious Hutchins Commission put it in 1947, "the press has been transformed into an enormous and complicated piece of machinery. As a necessary accompaniment it has become a big business. There is a marked reduction in the number of units of the press to the total population. . . . The owners and managers of the press determine which person, which facts, which versions of the facts and which ideas shall reach the public."[66] Assaults on the bias of the "mainstream media," however paranoid, inaccurate, or hyperbolic, seem to have been an important mechanism through which the public sought to make sense of the unprecedented role of the mass media in American politics.

Since the 1980s, the rise of cable and the Internet have begun to break apart this mass, creating the potential for a more diversified media, as well as niche programming and new worries about the atomization of the public sphere. If those trends continue, it might make sense to inter the critique of mainstream media bias as a relic of an earlier era—it is already unclear whether there still really is a "mainstream media" of the sort that emerged in the twentieth century. Whether it will persist into the twenty-first century, however, the critique of the mainstream media was a constant in the twentieth. Its surprising history provides a lens through which we can spy some of the broad trends of modern politics: the partisan clashes that defined and then ended the New Deal order; the marginalization of structural critiques of capitalism; the displacement of leftist populism with a postwar populism of the right; the confusing emergence of newly powerful media entities. At the end of the day, perhaps MacLeish and Agnew did share something else in common—as twentieth-century politicians, they provided a channel for a persistent populist feeling that the mass media were distant, different, and dangerously unaccountable.

CHAPTER 5

"We're All in This Thing Together": Cold War Consensus in the Exclusive Social World of Washington Reporters

Kathryn McGarr

At seven o'clock in the evening on Saturday, April 11, 1953, the dinner bell rang in Washington's Hotel Statler. Wearing white ties and tails, five hundred of the most influential men in American politics, business, and publishing—or, as one leftist political columnist referred to them in his diary, "the assembled throng of fat-cat publishers, millionaires, hucksters and what-have-you"—had fifteen minutes to find their seats.[1] Then President Dwight Eisenhower would take his place at the head banquet table, the lights would be turned off, the United States Marine Corps Band would begin playing the traditional "Music in the Air," and the president of the Gridiron Club would deliver the customary "Speech in the Dark."[2] The Gridiron Club, founded in 1885, was an elite group of fifty Washington reporters, representing newspapers from across the country, that hosted biannual "stag" dinners at which they performed skits and song parodies. The Gridironers excluded women reporters from both the club and the dinner on the pretext of being a purely social group. In reality, the Gridiron's professional importance was so well understood that most of the men's employers covered their dues as business expenses. While the club's sole mandate was to host its formal dinners, members saw each other frequently at meetings, rehearsals, and social events like the annual golf tournament hosted by the well-connected president and chairman of the board of Washington's Riggs National Bank.

The fellowship among Gridiron men fostered a shared perspective on politics and journalism. Ideological differences remained, of course, but essential commonalities prevailed among Washington's top reporters, especially their maleness (demonstrable in the drag performances among their skits), their whiteness (even more pronounced for these gentlemen, sometimes performing in blackface and always surrounded by black waiters), and their heterosexuality (or, at least, a tolerance of off-the-record homosexuality, which made an allowance for the blue-blooded, Harvard-educated, and barely closeted Joe Alsop, who was a columnist and not himself a Gridironer).[3] One characteristic skit from that evening in April 1953—poking fun at Eisenhower's cronies—included a scene in a golf club locker room with four white businessmen golfers interrogating Ike's dialect-speaking black caddy, "Cemetery Poteet," about the president's policies: "1st Golfer: Did he say anything about our anti-trust suit? Poteet: (scornfully) Anti-Trust. Anti-trust? Why dey ain't no anti in dat man. He trusts everybody."[4]

Invitations to these evenings of expensive sherry and champagne, as well as private cocktail receptions throughout the hotel before and after the dinners, were as coveted as invitations to the White House, but more rare. Among the guests that night in April were the secretaries of the treasury (George M. Humphrey), defense (Charles E. Wilson), agriculture (Ezra Taft Benson), and interior (Douglas McKay); the attorney general (Herbert Brownell Jr.) and the postmaster general (Arthur E. Summerfield); the ambassadors of Norway, France, Brazil, Egypt, and Australia; all of the joint chiefs of staff (including the chairman, General Omar Bradley); Allen Dulles, director of the CIA; the chairmen of the boards of U.S. Steel and RCA and the presidents of both Gimbel's and Macy's; Governors Thomas Dewey, James F. Byrnes, Christian Herter, and Theodore McKeldin; at least eighteen senators; Speaker of the House Joe Martin and assorted congressmen; and almost every major American publisher.[5] These powerful men from around the country and the capital gossiped freely, with the Gridiron president's annually repeated promise that the dinner had "but two rules—ladies are always present—reporters are never present." Both maxims were rhetorical: women were not allowed to attend, but the jokes would be appropriate even for "mixed" company; the fifty most powerful reporters in Washington were hosts, but everything said at the dinner, except information from the club's prewritten press release, was "off the record" and could not be published. The exclusivity of the proceedings emphasized the presumption that what political elites said for public consumption and what they said over Maryland terrapin stew, the club's signature dish, could be different.

"Guests of the Gridiron," began Duke Shoop of the *Kansas City Star*, the club's president in April 1953. He paused before delivering his first punch line, "—and fellow applicants for membership in Burning Tree." The exclusive Burning Tree Club was a men's golf club in nearby Bethesda, Maryland, already an essential social space for some of the wealthier local guests, and, since Eisenhower's arrival at the White House three months earlier, a necessity for men seeking presidential access. Washington had long been a city of clubs for journalists—who enjoyed a higher social status there than anywhere in the nation—as much as for politicians and officials. In the capital, political administrations changed, but reporters remained. With the population boom that accompanied the rise of the New Deal administrative state, Washington lost its small-town intimacy, and social ties and friendship networks became even more important to gaining access to sources. And as the government grew, so too did the press corps that covered it. In this period, Washington supplanted New York City as the "nation's news center," which meant the press corps grew from a few hundred in the early 1930s to over a thousand by the 1960s.[6] "What is relevant for our purposes is that the intensification of federal power has heightened the meaning of what takes place in Washington," wrote political scientist Leo Rosten in his 1937 book *The Washington Correspondents*. "The capital has entered into the consciousness of the American people to a degree unparalleled in times of peace. This assigns an unprecedented importance to news from Washington."[7] Washington's status in waging World War II further solidified it as the news capital of the nation, and, by the early 1950s, according to those living there, of the world. The interactions between men in places like Burning Tree and at the Gridiron dinners reinforced a sense of common purpose conducting the nation's affairs during the "troubled times," as they saw them, after the war—a war most men at the Statler that night had participated in, the significance of which will be discussed further below.

Duke Shoop set up his next joke: "We meet tonight on the hearthstone of good cheer and fellowship. Or to put it another way, why worry—we're all in this thing together."[8] He got a laugh because the line was true: they *were* all in "this thing" together. Whether reporter, industrialist, or public servant, they were the elite American political class, responsible—or so most thought in this era of U.S. nuclear and military dominance—for the well-being of the world.

Historians have well established that there was no national liberal consensus in the early Cold War years, as conservatism continued to flourish at the grassroots level as well as among intellectuals. Similarly, both foreign and domestic policy remained subject to partisan ideology. But, as Wendy Wall has demonstrated, the *idea* of consensus held sway because of conscious efforts by certain groups to promote a single American way of life.[9] Among an elite group of men in Washington and New York who set the nation's news agenda, those efforts were often conscious, but just as often innate—a product of their everyday social and professional routines. The lived reality of their daily lives created consensus about the role America would play in the world, that Washington would play in America, and that "responsible" reporters, as most Washington journalists considered themselves to be, would play in maintaining national security during a time of global political uncertainty. Only by excavating the social world of Washington does the contested concept of Cold War consensus make sense.[10]

In this instance, the controversial word "consensus" characterizes the more widely accepted theory of "pack journalism," which Timothy Crouse infamously described in his book about the reporters covering the 1972 presidential campaign, *The Boys on the Bus*. "Trapped on the same bus or plane, they ate, drank, gambled, and compared notes with the same bunch of colleagues week after week," he wrote.[11] As a result, they filed similar stories, even when they knew they were not giving accurate accounts of the campaigns. Unlike a campaign, which might last several months, the insularity of Washington meant *year after year* of men attending Gridiron dinners, playing golf at the Chevy Chase Club, lunching at the Metropolitan Club, drinking at the National Press Club bar, dining at the 1925 F Street Club, and holding off-the-record stag dinners with government sources at the Mayflower Hotel.[12] The daily working lives of Washington reporters included a widespread, institutionalized blurring of the social and the professional that made dissent on major issues of national security all but unthinkable. The elaborate network of favors and counter-favors was routine and unremarkable for those participating in it, and therefore has been little studied. But the sense of fellowship it created among men—men who naturally had differences of opinion—tempered potential disagreements by the time they made it to print, creating what communications scholar Daniel C. Hallin has identified as three spheres: a Sphere of Consensus, a Sphere of Legitimate Controversy, and a Sphere of Deviance.[13] This chapter seeks to explain how reporters built those spheres in real life and operated within them, creating a sphere of consensus surrounding American Cold War strategy.

Men claimed that lunches at the National Press Club and the Metropolitan Club, and annual stag banquets, like those given by the Gridiron, the Alfalfa Club, and the White House Correspondents' Association (WHCA), to name just three of the most famous on a long list of stag dinners, were purely social occasions, disingenuously demarcating a line between their professional lives and their social lives that did not exist. Women reporters actually did belong to the WHCA, but still could not attend the annual dinner until 1962. "The dinner may be 'off-the-record' for immediate news, but it is of considerable professional value for a newswoman to attend," one woman reporter wrote to another in 1954. "She observes news figures in action. Her prestige—to her employer and in her working associations—is increased. If the woman reporter can bring a guest, or guests, so much the better. It never hurts a reporter to treat a news source, or boss, to a glamorous event—as the men well know."[14] The men, most of whom would not acknowledge the professional injustice publicly, did know this. Just ten days after the above letter between women reporters was written, James B. "Scotty" Reston (nicknamed for his Scottish roots) of the *New York Times* wrote to Secretary of State John Foster Dulles, with whom he was not especially close—although close enough to address him as "Foster" and to sign off as "Scotty"—to invite him as his guest to the WHCA dinner the next month. *Times* reporter Bess Furman was one member of the Women's National Press Club (WNPC) who worked toward their inclusion at the correspondents' dinner. As Furman wrote to a fellow WNPC member in 1954, "I didn't even take up the Gridiron Club—too fantastic."[15]

The sense of exclusivity and being "in the know" was heightened for the men of the press who were privy to certain people and spaces in Washington to which others did not have access. Even the enormous National Press Club (NPC)—a professional necessity for all reporters in Washington, not just the fifty most prominent, like the Gridiron Club—was technically a private club, and did not accept black journalists until 1955 (and then only one, the conservative Louis Lautier) or women journalists until 1971.[16] In the early 1950s, the club had approximately one thousand active members and over 4,500 total members of all classifications. The NPC's enormous building on Fourteenth and F Streets, in which some newspapers had bureaus and some syndicated columnists had offices, included as part of its private space a restaurant and bar, where reporters gathered daily to gossip and drink. The

NPC Bar Committee's report for 1953 estimated an average of 1,700 drinks per day. ("Your committee knows the Club Members have manfully done their duty because one member at least was present at the Bar at all times," one joked in the report.)[17] In an introduction to a 1958 book commemorating their fiftieth anniversary, one member wrote of the club, "It's a hang-out, a drop-in, with overstuffed chairs for lazy bones. It's a restaurant, a bar. It's an auditorium where big shots make their speeches and lesser fry make their contacts. But, more than anything else, it is a place where men meet and talk, talk, talk. They talk mainly about the news of the day or the week. They roll it around, punch it and pat it, and sometimes twist it for a bit of shape."[18]

Men also gossiped, swapped stories, and ate—though with more decorum and at higher prices—at the Metropolitan Club, so central in the life of many elite Washington men that, among themselves, they referred to it simply as "the Club." The Metropolitan Club, the type of men's club commonly established in large cities in the nineteenth century, seemed to be on the verge of closing in the 1930s, with a total membership (resident and nonresident) of less than one thousand in 1939. However, the war—and with it, the deep pockets of a new group of men arriving in the capital with defense industries, as well as a housing shortage—increased demand for the club's facilities. The restaurant, which operated with an $8,059 deficit in 1941, enjoyed a $6,419 profit in 1943.[19] By 1946, there were almost 1,500 total members, and a slight postwar dip was "soon offset by the march of international politics," as the club's 1963 centennial history proudly put it. The Cold War kept the club solvent; in the words of the club's historian: "The global military and economic commitments of the United States made Washington even more the hub of world-wide leadership, attracting to it a representative segment of the nation's talent."[20] In the 1950s, the dining room became so congested at lunchtime that they added an entire additional dining room where previously there had been billiard tables. In this period, it was de rigueur for publishers, top editors, columnists, and a few elite reporters to belong to the Metropolitan Club. Arthur Krock of the *Times* ate there almost daily for lunch, and in 1961 the *Times* bureau moved from a ten-minute walk to the club to a five-minute walk; Eugene Meyer, the publisher of the *Washington Post*, went straight from the office to the club nearly every afternoon after work, even if he had also had lunch there earlier the same day.[21]

Literal boys' clubs played an important role in establishing norms and consensuses, deciding what should be reported and what should be withheld. Understanding the pervasiveness of this clubby world is essential to recognizing how constant fellowship and togetherness could have inhibited radical thinking. "It was no coincidence that some of the toughest pieces on the 1972 Nixon campaign came from Sarah McLendon, Helen Thomas of UPI, Cassie Mackin of NBC, Marilyn Berger of the Washington *Post*, and Mary McGrory," wrote Timothy Crouse in *The Boys on the Bus*. "They had always been the outsiders. Having never been allowed to join the cozy, clubby world of the men, they had developed an uncompromising detachment and a bold independence of thought which often put the men to shame."[22] Among foreign affairs correspondents in the 1950s, there were few women who could have put the men to shame, even if they had wanted to. Entrée to male spaces was so essential for this kind of reporting that newspapers would not have risked assigning a woman to the diplomatic beat. The two women who did cover international affairs regularly during this period did not do so from Washington: Marguerite Higgins of the *New York Herald Tribune* was a foreign correspondent based overseas, usually at the battlefront, and Anne O'Hare McCormick, a columnist for the *New York Times* until her death in 1954, lived in New York City.

Although press institutions like the Gridiron Club and the National Press Club existed prior to World War II, the war considerably strengthened a shared sense of community. Wartime experiences also reinforced the legitimacy of all-male spaces. The "shadow of war" from the Second World War, which historian Michael Sherry argues created the country's militarization in the 1950s, hung over reporters especially darkly. Sherry acknowledges that postwar memories of "universal experience of unity and common purpose" were later shown to be false, since "just beneath the surface of public culture, with its omnipresent talk of victory and freedom, lay sharply varied experiences shaped by gender, race, ethnicity, religion, region, age, and other factors."[23] However, as we have seen, members of the Washington press corps were a remarkably homogenous group; the variety of experiences was minimal, shaped foremost by their maleness and their whiteness. And, almost to a man, reporters in the capital after the war had, in some way, participated in World War II, making it the all-consuming "total war" of American mythology.

Wartime experiences knit these men closer together, whether they shared foxholes or simply the memory—especially salient for the generation of reporters practicing their trade in the 1950s through the 1970s—of being a part of history. As CBS correspondent Larry LeSueur put it in an interview forty years later: "Murrow, Collingwood, Sevareid, Bill Downs, myself, we shared tremendously indelible experiences. We shared in the making of *history* in World War Two; we knew what it was like to be scared together."[24] Whether they felt that at the time, they certainly cherished the feeling of brotherhood for decades. The experience was not limited to the broadcasting "Murrow boys" that LeSueur listed, but to almost *all* the boys in national news. The men mentioned below are merely a representative fragment of the large majority of reporters who "shared tremendously indelible experiences." Elmer Davis, a *New York Times* reporter, then a famous radio correspondent before and after the war, served (unhappily) as the head of the Office of War Information (OWI). The *New York Times* "loaned" Scotty Reston to the government to reorganize the OWI's London branch, before he returned to reporting for them on the war. Ferdinand Kuhn had been at the *New York Times* before the war and served for four years in the OWI before taking up his position as diplomatic correspondent for the *Washington Post*. Herbert Block ("Herblock"), who joined the *Washington Post* after the war as a syndicated cartoonist, was a sergeant in the Information and Education division of the Army. Russell Baker, who covered the White House when he joined the *Times* in 1954, had served in the Naval Air Force. John Oakes, then at the *Washington Post* (later the *Times*' influential editorial page editor), as well as Wallace Deuel, who before and after the war was diplomatic correspondent for the *Chicago Daily News*, served in the Office of Strategic Services (the OSS, predecessor to the CIA).[25] Even the men who remained reporters during the war—they performed an "essential service" and could therefore be exempt from the draft—still wore army uniforms overseas, a significant and proud marker of identity for the men who wore it. Reporter Drew Middleton, who joined the *New York Times*' London staff in September 1942, received a Navy Certificate of Merit in 1945 for his coverage of World War II, and in 1947 both the Order of the British Empire (Military Division) and the U.S. Medal of Freedom (the latter prize going to eighteen "news men" in total).[26] For years, World War II remained fresh in the minds of those who had lived through it. One *New York Times* national desk editor in 1951, in a memo about requesting the Pentagon's permission to cover exercises at Stewart Air Base, wrote, "I personally feel that, with the growing consciousness of the need for closer security in what's given out to the press (my old days as a Navy censor, no doubt, conditioned me somewhat), we may have difficulty getting clearance. If they don't want us poking around, it's perfectly okay with us."[27]

Whether they had worked for the government devising censorship policies or covered the war and adhered to them, these men shared in the sense of having fought for peace together, and now of having a stake in the world's collective security. Most of the press establishment in Washington, therefore, bought into the idea of a "Cold War" that necessitated certain wartime-like concessions. Bob Lovett, the under secretary of state (and future secretary of defense), told reporters in an off-the-record press conference one Saturday in October 1947 that all nations are "conditioned by history" to transition to peace. "Instead, we witnessed a transition from war to invisible aggression, a new kind of international situation in the handling of which we seem to be curiously inept."[28] The ineptness was off the record, and fear that their leaders were, indeed, inept kept reporters eager to help the cause for peace. For instance, in the fall of 1948, *Times*man (as they referred to themselves) Scotty Reston went on a short trip to Germany, London, and Paris and reported his main conclusions to Arthur Krock, who was chief of the *Times*' Washington bureau from 1932 to 1953. The first conclusion was that U.S., British, and French officials "are not nearly so confident about their Berlin policy as they say they are in public." But revealing the discrepancy could be bad for morale at home and peace abroad. "All this, I think raises a newspaper problem," Reston acknowledged. "Probably we should not report at this time that our officials are saying one thing in public and another in private."[29] Men like Reston, who considered themselves "responsible reporters," were not going to cause World War III.

Individual dissent remained about American policy overseas. But individuals did not have voices in the mass media. Instead, layers of editors, publishers, producers, and executives, who had the final word on what information became public, filtered out disagreement. While working for CBS, Edward R. Murrow lived in New York City, where the news division was headquartered, but his circle of friends extended to Washington and was circumscribed in ways similar to his colleagues in the capital; he belonged to the Century Association in Manhattan ("a real oasis in this miserable city," as he wrote to fellow newsman Charles Collingwood in 1959, telling him that he "must by all means become a member") and went duck hunting with General Omar Bradley.[30] When Murrow went to Korea in August 1950, he recorded a radio dispatch from Tokyo that began, "This is a most difficult broadcast to do." He explained that he had never believed correspondents should criticize commanders while a battle was in progress. "However, it is now time to cast up an account of the past ten days. For the question now arises whether serious mistakes have been made."[31] The transcript came over the New York newsroom teletype to CBS producer Wells Church, who took it to Ed Chester, who took it to Joe Ream of the legal team (and who, a few years later, would be in Washington as the first civilian deputy director of the National Security Agency). Ream took the typescript to the twentieth floor, where chief executives William Paley and Frank Stanton were in a conference room together and where the dispatch was killed entirely.[32]

The CBS executives justified their action by saying the broadcast would give comfort to the enemy and could be used as Soviet propaganda. Murrow had been shockingly critical in his report, writing, "I met no officer in South Korea who believes we can mount an effective offensive with our present strength. . . . And yet, correspondents here have received cables from their home offices indicating that air-conditioned sources in Washington think the thing can be wound up this fall. To paraphrase the GI's in Korea—that ain't the way it looks from here."[33] To the men in the air-conditioned offices of the CBS "black rock" building in New York, this seemed like, as they put it, "unfair criticism of those quoted as being in air-conditioned offices."[34] They suggested that the men that Murrow talked to might not know what was *really* happening, and when Murrow himself returned to the air-conditioning, he would regret the broadcast: "Murrow is probably tired, probably wouldn't have written same piece if back home to reflect." If he were back home, these executives were thinking, he would be able to reflect as part of the "pack," and after some time at CBS and at the Century, the independent thinking would subside. Murrow struggled with his independent thinking for the next several years, and the more controversial he became, the less airtime and sponsors he enjoyed. Finally, in 1961, he gave up entirely, moving to Washington to run the United States Information Agency for John F. Kennedy. (His friends saw a tragic irony, but at least he would be on the government's payroll.)

Pressure was not always, or even often, exerted from the top down as in the Murrow case, but simply manifested itself as groupthink or peer pressure. The daily work practices of Washington reporters contributed to the appearance of consensus, or the "echo chamber" of Washington. For one thing, almost every foreign affairs reporter read the same few newspapers— the *New York Times* and maybe the *Herald Tribune* and *Baltimore Sun*, the *Washington Post*, and the *Evening Star*. Stories carried in the *Times* were ipso facto newsworthy, causing other papers then to pursue the same item or follow-up stories.[35] Furthermore, because there were no national newspapers (the *New York Times* did not have a national edition until 1980; *USA Today* launched in 1981), reporters were not typically in competition with each other. They frequently collaborated, sometimes by sharing with each other black carbon copies of stories they had filed with their home offices, a practice colloquially known as "blacksheeting."[36] According to an interview that Scotty Reston gave to political scientist Bernard C. Cohen in 1958, as Cohen was researching what would become his 1963 *The Press and Foreign Policy*, blacksheeting was "passé" by then. "Of course there is an exchange of ideas," Reston conceded at the time. "I'll see Walter Lippmann once every couple of weeks, maybe oftener, and we talk shop about what's going on the world."[37] But this practice, Reston emphasized, was "quite different" from the blacksheet. That Reston saw Lippmann "maybe oftener" was more accurate. Besides living down the street from each other, both men belonged to the Metropolitan Club "Table," where they often had lunch. And when the Lippmanns vacationed in Maine and the Restons vacationed in Virginia, the two men kept in touch by post. As Cohen wrote in his book, "The ever-present need to validate one's news sense forces the foreign affairs correspondent to keep in close contact with his colleagues—not really a novel pattern of social behavior, to be sure, but a substantively significant one nonetheless."[38] At the same time, their use of passive phrases, such as "It can be stated on reliable authority," "it is now learned," "it is generally agreed," "his view apparently was as follows," "is understood to have taken this opportunity in Washington to make these points"—all of which appeared in a single front-page *Times* article by Reston about the French premier, Pierre Mendès-France, in November 1954—allowed reporters to obscure the scenes and sources of their reporting. The provenance of this particular Reston story, which a *Times* editor in New York gave the flashy headline, "New Red Divisions in Indochina Stir U.S.-French Alarm," developed after Scotty went to the home of *Washington Post* owner Eugene Meyer at six o'clock the prior evening for "a private meeting," as Reston called it in his diary, with Mendès-France. Reston wrote privately, for his own files, "He told us, not for quotation, that the situation in Indo-China was getting much worse and that the Communists had added three new divisions, two of them armored, since the Armistice in that country last Summer. Accordingly, I rushed down from Meyer's to the office and wrote a long story, which led the paper."[39] Earlier in the day, Reston had also attended a men-only lunch at the NPC at which Mendès-France spoke.

As a city, "official" Washington (as distinct from the economically diverse, racially segregated actual metropolitan area) was unlike any other city in the expectation that personal and public lives were the same. The five-thousand-dollar business expense account that the *New York Times* provided Arthur Krock in 1953 was double the amount they gave to their managing editor in New York City—the highest-ranking editor of the newspaper, at the paper's headquarters.[40] Judging by reporters' justification of their behavior when their own words were "on the record," reporters were entirely aware that conflicts could arise when constantly breaking bread with each other and their sources. Columnists and brothers Joseph and Stewart Alsop, in their 1958 book *The Reporter's Trade*, disingenuously downplayed their active social lives, denigrating in particular cocktail parties and the "hat-bearing females" (likely a dig at columnist May Craig, famous in Washington and on *Meet the Press* for her haberdashery) who attended them. "We have never heard of any case of a leak at a cocktail party, possibly because we almost never go to cocktail parties ourselves," the brothers wrote.[41] Perhaps their loophole was that they did not *go* to cocktail parties; all manner of parties came to them. And they counted every party they hosted as a business expense, keeping a careful record for reimbursement purposes of who attended and exactly how much money was spent on food and liquor. Tellingly, during some months, they listed "deductions for parties which were partly personal," even further implicating themselves in the social-professional system they obscured for the public and, presumably, obscured for their guests, few of whom would have appreciated being written off as business expenses. For example, for a large, forty-six person luncheon on May 3, 1953, Joe Alsop contributed $85 to the total bill of $243.84, because that was the amount he felt was "personal." He did the same twice more that month, contributing $15 of a $71.61 bill on May 24 and $10 out of $57.65 on May 31. It is unclear if he calculated personal expenses based on the percentage of guests who did not provide news or the percentage of minutes spent discussing private matters. Either way, he rounded. In that single month, May 1953, Joe Alsop hosted eight luncheons and two dinner parties, while his brother and sister-in-law held one additional dinner.[42]

Conversations at these ostensibly social affairs, which were paid for out of business accounts, were off the record. Even so, and even if no one leaked specific information, common understandings emerged from shared knowledge, and leads were given—to be followed up back at the men's offices later in the week. Only readers already within Washington would have known this, though. "The Alsops entertain their guests in the grand manner, with the proper wines and all the trimmings," a palpably annoyed Peter Brandt, the chief Washington correspondent for the *St. Louis Post-Dispatch*, wrote his editor back in Missouri in 1951, explaining how sensitive military information kept appearing in the Alsops' columns. "Both are clever and, with their background, can piece together the bits of information gathered during conversations."[43]

To be sure, Joe Alsop was an extreme on the entertainment scale, not just by virtue of his family background and position, but because he was unmarried and without children; he simply had more free evenings than most of those in his profession. But Scotty Reston, with three boys (whose school, St. Albans, provided one more point of interaction among Washington's elite), participated in the social-professional "merry-go-round" of Washington, as they liked to call it, as well. The eminently responsible Reston was sensitive to charges that he was leveraging friendships for his work on the *Times*. In a 1984 oral history interview for an internal New York Times Company collection, Reston commented derogatorily about his predecessor as the *Times*' Washington bureau chief, Arthur Krock, that, "He believed, as I do not believe, in social journalism. That is to say, that you gather news at dinner parties at night. He was very social."[44] Certainly compared to someone like Joe Alsop with his cocktail-soaked dinners, Reston was not a partier. But Reston was the top Washington correspondent for the newspaper that was most widely read by Washington's officials.

Reston's social and professional lives were inextricable, and he knew it. To the outside world, he pretended otherwise, and not just in that 1984 interview, after Watergate and Vietnam supposedly changed the way the press viewed officials. In an *Esquire* magazine profile of Reston published in 1958, entitled "Washington's Most Powerful Reporter," Joe Kraft recounted Reston's activities throughout one day. "At lunch, at his home, Reston talked trade with the Canadian and Dutch ambassadors. 'Ordinarily,' he said later, 'I don't believe in white-tie reporting. Booze cuts three hours off the working day. But these were old friends.'"[45] He felt the need to disparage what he called white-tie reporting. Again, within the city, out of the public eye, his colleagues knew better. One correspondent at another newspaper warned his editor back home of the learning curve for their new foreign affairs man: "Reporters like Reston and Deuel have their subject in mind during all their waking hours. Their social acquaintances are carefully chosen from persons who can help them professionally. Their reading is primarily in their chosen field. They have built up their own libraries with publications relating to foreign affairs. Their conversation is on foreign affairs."[46]

Reston's New Year's Eve of 1949 is instructive. On January 1, 1950, Reston wrote one of his occasional diary entries, noting that, "We are living in what is in many respects the most interesting community in America, at a time when decisions taken here are of fundamental and even decisive importance for nations all over the world."[47] At the time, he and his wife, Sally, were recovering from ringing in the new year at the home of Walter and Helen Lippmann on Woodley Road, near the National Cathedral—down the street from where Sally and Scotty would move the following year. Reston, who had just turned forty, considered the sixty-year-old Lippmann to be a mentor. Reston's 1942 book *Prelude to Victory*, about the necessity of America's involvement in the war, had gained wide acclaim and brought him to the attention of important internationalists, among them Lippmann, as well as the publisher of the *Times*, Arthur Hays Sulzberger, who soon brought Reston into the inner circle of the Ochs-Sulzberger-Dryfoos family. By 1950, the *Times* was paving the way for Scotty to become Arthur Krock's successor as their Washington bureau chief, which he officially became in 1953. Reston and Lippmann kept in close touch. The younger man often forwarded off-the-record memos that Lippmann could use in composing his columns. When, in the 1960s, Reston was no longer doing "leg-work" himself, he had his reporters brief Lippmann; years later, David Halberstam remembered returning from Africa to have Reston immediately trundle him off to lunch with the elderly columnist, who had no formal affiliation with the *Times* and, in fact, published with their competitors.[48]

Also at the Lippmanns' on that December 31, 1949, were six other couples, whom Reston named in his diary entry: "Bonnets, Fulbrights, Ellistons, Grahams, Tarchianis, Bruggmanns."[49] The men were Henri Bonnet, French ambassador to the United States; Senator William Fulbright; Herbert Elliston, the editorial page editor of the *Washington Post*; Philip Graham, the publisher of the *Washington Post*; Italian ambassador to the United States Alberto Tarchiani; and Swiss ambassador (and brother-in-law to former Vice President Henry Wallace) Charles Bruggmann. Phil and Kay Graham and Scotty and Sally Reston, of the same generation, grew so close in Washington that the Grahams designated the Restons their children's legal guardians in the event of their deaths. Phil, and later Kay, also made overtures to Scotty to join the *Post*, but Reston was a loyal *Times*man who enjoyed his unparalleled platform. Reston continued in his account of that New Year's Eve, writing,

"Talked mainly about whether the United States should occupy Formosa, with most everybody being against. Last year everybody was relaxed enough to sing Auld Lang Syne with some zing, but this year everybody looked vaguely embarrassed in trying to be merry at midnight."[50] After the Lippmanns, they went to Ferdie and Delia Kuhn's house for what Reston called "first-footing," a Scottish tradition of visiting friends after midnight of the new year and being the "first foot" in the door. Kuhn had been at the *New York Times* before the war and served for four years in the OWI, before taking up his then-current position as diplomatic correspondent for the *Washington Post*. Also at the Kuhns' were Elizabeth and Ned Kenworthy. Ned, too, had been at OWI and was at that point, in 1949–50, serving as executive secretary of Truman's Committee for Equality of Treatment and Opportunity in the Armed Services, which would successfully recommend desegregating the Army. (Kenworthy would soon become a Washington reporter himself.)

In private memos, Reston found it less necessary to obscure the social dimension of his Washington reporting. His purchase in 1951 of his family's house in Cleveland Park was explicitly a business expense, which he bought with a $12,000 loan from the Sulzbergers, since he needed space to entertain for work. "My professional obligations are increasing as my contacts in the embassies and the government increase, and I must either plunge even deeper into the rental market here to find adequate quarters or buy," Reston wrote in a letter to Arthur Sulzberger in March 1951.[51] A year and a half later, he was still struggling to entertain his guests in the manner to which they had become accustomed, prompting the *Times* to set up a slush fund for this purpose, for which Reston wrote a sheepish thank-you to Sulzberger, or "Mr. Gus," as Reston affectionately called the older man in personal correspondence. (The men had used nicknames for each other in letters of this nature since taking a seven-week trip to the Soviet Union together in 1943; "Gus" was short for "Guspadine," a play on "mister" in Russian, *gospodin*; Sulzberger, in turn, called Reston "Pectoh," the Cyrillic rendering of his last name.) In that note, Reston joked that he had always been against "secret funds, regardless of origin or destination," but that he would now have to qualify that statement. "This entertainment business, though, I must confess, was perplexing. I could not do my job here without going to the embassies, and particularly, seeing the men at the counselor and first secretary level, who really know what's going on." He felt obligated to repay the invitations, and "this was a drain, even though my reverse lend lease wasn't precisely what it ought to have been," he joked.[52] Having the deep pockets of the *Times* was, as always, useful; the poor *Post-Dispatch* bureau chief had been unable to reciprocate for the off-the-record dinners he attended "because we have no cook."[53]

Arthur Hays Sulzberger was very much part of the elite press establishment of Washington, though he resided in New York, and the *Times*' managing editor, Turner Catledge, had himself been a Washington reporter in the 1930s and 1940s; they never questioned Reston's social life. But editors and publishers who were outsiders to the Washington community could clearly see how problematic the atmosphere might be. Ben Reese, managing editor of the *Post-Dispatch*, wrote to their newly minted diplomatic correspondent, Richard Stokes, in May 1947, on behalf of himself and Joseph Pulitzer: "We don't want you to swallow whole all American foreign policy. We want you to look into the other side at all times. Sometimes, when one begins to attend social functions and dinners with State Department dignitaries, one is liable to see only one side—the American side—of the picture."[54] That was easy for Reese to say, since he only made occasional trips to Washington. The D.C. bureau correspondents had to live in a bubble where all dinners were, by definition, working dinners. By the time many of these men returned to their typewriters to write an "objective" story that broke no confidences and revealed no sources, there was little dissent across the spectrum, no matter how far to the left leaned the Pulitzers of the *St. Louis Post-Dispatch* or, for that matter, how far to the right were the McCormicks of the *Chicago Tribune*.[55] Reporters had to get in line with the American side or be excluded from private conferences. "It should go without saying, of course, that there are deviations from this norm," Bernard Cohen concedes in his 1963 study, "and that individual reporters violate the rules of the game from time to time; but the very fact that 'violations' can be observed, and described, and even accounted for reinforces the normative code of behavior for reporters who cover foreign affairs."[56]

The normative code withstood intense pressure less than a week before the 1953 spring Gridiron Dinner, on Monday, April 6, when several of the attendees were in the basement level of the Carlton Hotel for dinner. About twenty foreign affairs reporters had invited the new secretary of state, John Foster Dulles, to a private dining room for a "background session." After preliminary cocktails, they had a dinner of steak and strawberry ice cream sundaes at one enormous table. Then the gentlemen of the press began their questioning and remained until about 10:15, when the room had grown unbearably hot. Dulles's information fell under the Lindley Rule, named after Ernest K. Lindley, *Newsweek*'s Washington correspondent since 1937 and a frequent background dinner participant. Members of the Washington press corps understood the Lindley Rule to be the "rule of compulsory plagiarism," meaning reporters could use an idea from a background dinner only if they presented it as their own, without quotation of or attribution to a source. Specific information could also be put "off the record," meaning not for use of any kind. Dulles, who had worked as a special advisor to the State Department during the Truman administration—as well as having partly grown up in Washington under the eye of his secretary-of-state grandfather—well understood these ground rules. That night, among other revelations not for attribution, Dulles said the new administration's policy on Korea was to consider settling for a division at the "narrow waist," and that they would entertain a United Nations "trusteeship" for Formosa. In writing about the dinner in his diary, Wallace Deuel, by that time the diplomatic correspondent for the *St. Louis Post-Dispatch*, revealed the sphere of consensus at work: "But it is agreed informally afterwards among the newspaper men present that it would be a mistake from our own selfish point of view and quite possibly from the point of view of the national interest for us to rush into print with much of this stuff and it is left rather vaguely that we will confer tomorrow before anybody writes anything about it," noting that some of the men had left by the time this was decided.[57] (Deuel had been a foreign correspondent before the war, served in the OSS for the duration, and then spent nine years as a diplomatic correspondent in Washington. In 1954, he returned to intelligence work, to the OSS's successor agency—working for "my favorite Dulles," as he liked to put it, Foster's brother Allen, director of the CIA from 1953 to 1961.)

Walter Waggoner, the *New York Times'* State Department correspondent, attended dinner and then gave his notes to a fellow reporter in the Washington bureau, Anthony Leviero.[58] On April 9, the *Times* ran Leviero's story on its front page, emphasizing its significance with a large map of Korea, and similar stories appeared in other newspapers. Senator William Knowland, furious that a new foreign policy had apparently been devised and announced without his knowledge, called Dulles, who supposedly denied the story and assured him that no one at State was the source, which Knowland then stated in a release. White House Press Secretary James Hagerty—after having frantically tried to reach the *Times* reporter by phone all morning—then had to issue a denial, as well. (This was after Hagerty first accidentally confirmed the story to Reuters, because he knew perfectly well Dulles had leaked the information a couple of days earlier.) The *Times* position with the Eisenhower administration on this story was weak because Leviero had not actually been at the dinner, which Dulles realized and mentioned in a telephone call to the *Times*' Arthur Krock on April 9, during which he said if he were revealed as the source, "the New York Times would never get another interview."[59] The *Times* printed a correction the following day, April 10, also on the front page. In that story, their most trusted correspondent, Reston, wrote mischievously, "In fact, so many responsible reporters here have written similar articles in the last forty-eight hours that it was generally assumed that they had been inspired by a high official of the Government," knowing full well that Dulles had inspired the story and that, by now, everyone in Washington knew it too.[60]

In summarizing the incident for Krock, Tony Leviero wrote, "In the circumstances I believe we were circumspect. You will recall that I expressed amazement over some of the things that Mr. Dulles had said and I recommended that the New York Times should not publish without attribution his statement that Russia could take all of Western Europe and that we could not stop her. You agreed out of a sense of responsibility for national security we should not publish that when so much peace talk was in the air."[61] What the *Times* chose *not* to print and what Deuel wrote in his journal reveal the ordinariness of their assumptions that national security and world peace were as much reporters' responsibility as the secretary of state's. That assumption was new to the early Cold War period, conditioned by World War II. As Reston wrote his editor just a few weeks later, on April 30, 1953, "We are obviously in a period when it is not always easy to be a good newspaper man and a good citizen; therefore, some information will have to be withheld."[62] The "period" to which he refers is one in which everyone in Reston's social-professional set believed the world could be on the brink of war. For Reston and his fellow reporters, that conclusion was "obvious"—so obvious it merited little scrutiny and became a routine assumption, reinforced through the institutions and practices in which they participated.

A few months later, the Gridiron Club elected Scotty Reston to membership. The club's secretary, Lyle Wilson of United Press, wrote to him sarcastically, "It is my pleasant chore to advise you that on October 10, 1953, you were elected to active membership in the Gridiron Club of Washington, D.C. From that moment, you became possessed of all rights and privileges accruing to an active member, including the headaches of rehearsal, wistful dreams of additional seats for guests who must be THERE and one (1) full vote in the most democratically run outfit which I know. You will even come to know, in time, the Democrats who run it, and to understand why you must vote as they suggest that you vote. . . . Your sponsors took solemn oath that you sing, dance, compose, act and prefer black-face to all other parts."[63] At the next Gridiron dinner, December 12, 1953, Reston performed onstage in the banquet hall of the Statler, in front of an audience of five hundred of the most influential men in America, wearing white tie and tails.

CHAPTER 6

Objectivity and Its Discontents:
The Struggle for the Soul of American
Journalism in the 1960s and 1970s

Matthew Pressman

From a twenty-first-century perspective, the 1960s and 1970s seem like a golden age for the American press—especially for leading newspapers such as the *New York Times* and the *Los Angeles Times*. The "just-the-facts" approach to reporting that had prevailed in the 1940s and '50s crumbled, and journalists began to focus instead on the more exciting work of explanation, interpretation, and investigation. They found themselves at the center of great national crises such as the civil rights struggle, the Vietnam War, and Watergate, which gave many journalists the opportunity to launch brilliant careers and influence the course of history. Perhaps most importantly, it was a time of healthy profits and steady expansion. Layoffs were almost inconceivable, and editorial departments spent freely, even extravagantly. The *Los Angeles Times* insisted that its staffers always fly first class—never business class.[1] The situation did not look so rosy to the people running these newspapers at the time, however. They were proud of their successes, but they had deep, almost existential concerns about the future.

In 1971, *L.A. Times* editor in chief Nick Williams wrote to a colleague, "I have a terribly uneasy feeling that journalism has reached both a pinnacle and a crossroads. I suspect it has gained enormously in power and has lost credibility . . . with an alarming percentage of the people." If that trend were to continue, Williams said, "we [will] have destroyed or weakened a keystone of our Constitution."[2] Williams's boss, *L.A. Times* publisher Otis Chandler, also believed newspapers such as his faced a crisis. In a 1969 speech about the hippie generation's disdain for the mainstream press, Chandler noted that the problem went even deeper. He said, "The far right does not like us; they see us as too soft on communism [and] as too sympathetic with rioting minorities. . . . The far left does not like us; they see us as a tool of the rich and feel that we filter the news to suit them. . . . Middle-class establishment adults do not like us. We are not tough enough on student uprisings. We are not supporting the police enough in their efforts to enforce law and order."[3]

Like many other established institutions in the late 1960s, the press had become a political battleground. As historians have shown, nearly all sources of traditional authority were being challenged during this era.[4] Newspaper managers recognized this at the time, but it provided them little solace. "To say that there has been an overall decline in public confidence in established institutions is a cop out," a *New York Times* executive wrote in a 1973 memo addressing the paper's declining credibility. "When this feeling attacks the fundamental base of this newspaper, we cannot afford to accept this answer."[5] The ballast supporting that "fundamental base" was American journalism's most cherished principle: objectivity. The news industry's professional associations adopted objectivity—meaning some amalgam of fairness, accuracy, impartiality, detachment, and independence—as an ethical standard in the 1920s, and it became even more entrenched in the next few decades.[6] Earning a reputation for objectivity enabled news organizations to enhance their credibility, and therefore their potential appeal, among the broadest possible audience. By the late 1960s, however, that strategy was no longer working. Polls, surveys, and letters to the editor showed the public's distrust and dislike of the press rising sharply.[7] People began to speak of a "credibility gap" between the news media and the public, adopting a term that the press itself had coined to describe misleading U.S. government pronouncements about the Vietnam War.

Editors and publishers fixated on the credibility gap as a major long-term threat. In a 1966 memo about the challenges facing journalism, Nick Williams emphasized "the feeling on the part of a large segment of the public that newspapers slant their news, or select their news, to accomplish a specific and not always honorable purpose." He noted, "We sell credibility. . . . It is probably our most important asset."[8] Williams's successor as *L.A. Times* editor in chief, Bill Thomas, told the paper's business managers in 1972, "We must above all else remain credible, or we are of no value to anyone."[9]

At the *New York Times*, editor in chief A. M. (Abe) Rosenthal was obsessed with maintaining the paper's reputation for objectivity and credibility. His goal, he wrote in 1969, was to provide a newspaper "that a reader can turn to confident that he is getting the utmost possible in fairness and objectivity."[10] Upon hearing that many people considered the *New York Times* "a political journal" rather than "an information medium," Rosenthal confided to his journal in 1971, he took it as a serious blow.[11] When he rebuked reporters and editors for passages that he considered biased—something he did frequently—he often reminded them that these violations of objectivity could do irreparable harm to the paper's credibility.[12]

As editors and publishers wrestled with how to handle the knotty issues of credibility and objectivity, they received much unsolicited advice. The problem, said many people on the right, was that journalists had taken up the antiestablishment cause of the late 1960s—instead of being objective, they were slanting news coverage to suit their left-wing biases. Vice President Spiro Agnew famously leveled this accusation in a series of speeches in 1969 and 1970. At the same time, many on the left insisted that the problem was objectivity itself; in trying to be objective, they said, journalists inevitably became biased *in favor* of the establishment.

These competing critiques bore directly on the most pressing concerns of news organizations: preserving their credibility, maintaining the goodwill of advertisers, attracting and retaining talented staff, and appealing to a broad cross section of readers, especially the younger generation. Furthermore, the sources of these critiques made them impossible to ignore. Agnew was the vice president, and he seemingly spoke for much of the Silent Majority, judging by the way his popularity shot up after his inflammatory speeches.[13] And the fiercest left-wing critics of objectivity were journalists themselves, often well-respected ones working for high-profile publications. News organizations therefore needed to reassess their fundamental values and practices. This essay examines how that process unfolded at two of the county's most influential newspapers, the *New York Times* and the *Los Angeles Times*.

*   *   *

The importance of objectivity was an article of faith at most American news organizations in the early 1960s, but it was especially central to the identity of the *New York Times*. In a famous 1896 editorial, publisher Adolph Ochs promised to "give the news impartially, without fear or favor." This championing of objectivity earned his newspaper great financial success and even greater prestige, and many others emulated it.[14] Ownership of the paper has remained in Ochs's family ever since, and its editors have venerated him and his commitment to objectivity—none more so than Abe Rosenthal, who led the newsroom from 1969 to 1986.

In October 1969, two months after becoming managing editor, Rosenthal sent a memo to the entire staff in which he listed seven core beliefs on which "the character of the paper" rested. Five of the seven concerned objectivity:

> The belief that although total objectivity may be impossible because every story is written by a human being, the duty of every reporter and editor is to strive for as much objectivity as humanly possible.
> The belief that no matter how engaged the reporter is emotionally he tries as best he can to disengage himself when he sits down at the typewriter.
> The belief that expression of personal opinion should be excluded from the news columns.
> The belief that our own pejorative phrases should be excluded, and so should anonymous charges against people or institutions.
> The belief that presenting both sides of the issue is not hedging but the essence of responsible journalism.[15]

Rosenthal did not accuse anyone of failing to honor those beliefs. "I am bringing all this up," he wrote, "not as a warning nor as a cry of alarm, because neither is needed, but simply as a reaffirmation of the determination to maintain the character of The Times as we grow and develop."[16] That was disingenuous—privately, he felt there was indeed cause for alarm. He had adapted the memo from a letter he wrote the year before to James Reston, then the paper's executive editor. That letter included the same core beliefs and the same emphasis on the *New York Times* maintaining its character, but Rosenthal also warned of a serious internal threat to that character. "There are more reporters on the paper who seem to question or challenge the duty of the reporter, once taken for granted, to be above the battle," he wrote. "Inevitably, more young reporters reflect the philosophy of their age group and times—personal engagement, militancy and radicalism."[17]

This generational conflict was roiling newsrooms throughout the country. Writing in the fall of 1969, the longtime *Hartford Courant* editor in chief Herbert Brucker noted that, a decade earlier, "everyone agreed . . . that an accurate, unbiased account of the event reported was journalism's purest gem. . . . Today objective news has become anathema to young activists in journalism."[18] In a May 1970 speech, the editor in chief of the *Wichita Eagle* observed that many journalism students "regard . . . objectivity as obscene."[19] A June 1970 headline in the newspaper trade journal *Editor & Publisher* described the situation succinctly: "Attack on Objectivity Increases from Within."[20] After an article in the *Wall Street Journal* mentioned Rosenthal's staff memo and quoted excerpts from it, editors and journalism professors from around the country requested copies of the complete memo, saying they felt objectivity needed to be defended from its detractors in the younger generation.[21]

Not all of those who dismissed objectivity were brash youngsters, however. The *New York Times* was being "attacked from within" on objectivity, as Rosenthal complained to the publisher, by a member of its top brass: associate editor and columnist Tom Wicker.[22] A standout Washington correspondent in the early 1960s, Wicker became Washington bureau chief in 1964. But he was an ineffective manager, and he left Washington after four years to devote himself full-time to the opinion column he had begun writing in 1966.[23] As a consolation for losing the prestigious bureau-chief job, Wicker received the title of associate editor. Although he had no editing or managerial responsibilities, his name appeared on the editorial-page masthead alongside the paper's publisher and top editors.

As a columnist, Wicker had free rein to express his opinion, in the *New York Times* and elsewhere. Writing in the *Columbia Journalism Review* in 1971, he declared objectivity to be the American press's "biggest weakness." By objectivity, Wicker said, he meant the press's "reliance on and its acceptance of official sources"—that is, privileging the perspective of the powerful. "The tradition of objectivity," Wicker explained, "is bound to give a special kind of weight to the official source, the one who speaks from a powerful institutional position."[24] Rosenthal objected strongly to Wicker's article. In a letter to *Times* publisher Arthur Ochs "Punch" Sulzberger, he lamented: "Here we have a man whose name appears on the masthead telling his readers that what The Times promotes and what is at the base of its existence are not worth having. . . . It seems to me fairly obvious that these people inside the paper who wish us to drop objectivity and comprehensiveness will receive comfort and inspiration from Wicker's article, thus making our job even more difficult than it is or need be."[25]

Rosenthal was right to be concerned about "people inside the paper" who shared Wicker's view. Wicker hit on what many journalists found to be the most convincing critique of objectivity: that it privileged establishment perspectives while excluding others. The 1968 student uprising at Columbia University made young *New York Times* staffers acutely aware of this issue. Steve Roberts, at the time a twenty-five-year old reporter, recalled decades later, "We felt that the coverage of Columbia was heavily influenced and tilted toward the police version and the administration version, and that the *Times* would not allow us to give voice to the protesters' side of things."[26] This frustration increased when Rosenthal wrote a front-page article that sided openly with Columbia's embattled president and demonized the student protesters.[27] Such episodes led some *Times* journalists to equate Rosenthal's brand of objectivity with his relatively conservative political views, and thus to reject it. Those who clashed with Rosenthal most fiercely tended to be passionate left wingers.[28] But the dispute went beyond politics. On controversial issues, there are certain viewpoints that journalists feel merit inclusion in their coverage—these viewpoints fall into what the political scientist Daniel Hallin calls the "sphere of legitimate controversy." Other viewpoints journalists consider unfounded or too extreme—these fall into the "sphere of deviance" and rarely get discussed. Noncontroversial views are contained in the "sphere of consensus."[29] In the case of Columbia, some *Times* journalists (most notably Rosenthal) felt the views of radical leftist students fell into the sphere of deviance, whereas others (such as Roberts) felt they belonged in the sphere of legitimate controversy.

Even if they did not think of it in precisely these terms, most journalists understood that, in practice, objectivity entailed deciding which viewpoints deserved serious consideration and which did not. Therefore, those who sympathized with viewpoints outside the mainstream—in particular the New Left—often rejected objectivity. Similar disagreements about which viewpoints merited serious consideration made many African-American journalists skeptical of objectivity. Gerald Fraser, who became a *New York Times* reporter in 1967, recalled the paper spiking a story he had written about black college students in the late 1960s. "I just went out and asked the black students what they thought, and that's not what the *Times* wanted," Fraser said. "Had I interviewed the deans and college presidents and said, 'How are you dealing with the black students now?,' [my editor] would have liked that."[30]

Fraser said he and his fellow black reporters at the *Times* recognized "that our viewpoint was different than the general viewpoint on the news." Along with African-American journalists working for other publications in New York, they formed a group called Black Perspective, which met regularly in the offices of Kenneth Clark, the renowned African-American psychologist at City College.[31] In that forum as well as in others, they discussed objectivity frequently. Earl Caldwell, whom the *New York Times* hired as a reporter in 1967, said that he and his black colleagues in the late 1960s thought the paper was failing utterly to be objective in its coverage of issues affecting people of color; therefore they found it hard to take their (white) editors seriously when they insisted on some murky standard of objectivity. As Caldwell recalled, "The objectivity thing—I never got caught up on that. I always just said, 'I'm going to try to be honest, and I'm going to try to be fair.'"[32]

The press's detractors on the right also took issue with whose perspectives received prominent coverage. As Spiro Agnew said mockingly in one of his speeches skewering the news media, "If a theology student in Iowa should get up at a PTA luncheon in Sioux City and attack the president's Vietnam policy, you would probably find it reported somewhere in the next morning's issue of *The New York Times*."[33] And yet, Agnew claimed, when a majority of congressmen signed a letter in support of Nixon's Vietnam policy, the *New York Times* did not report it.[34] This critique did not originate with Agnew. William F. Buckley Jr. founded the conservative journal *National Review* in 1955 partly because he felt most newspapers and magazines excluded right-wing views like his. Many white Southerners in the late 1950s and early '60s believed (correctly) that the country's leading news organizations sympathized openly with the civil rights movement and denigrated the perspective of segregationists, a posture that they attributed to the press's "liberal bias."[35] Agnew, however, helped bring the fixation on liberal bias from the fringes to the mainstream, and it has remained a central component of Republican orthodoxy ever since. This was a remarkable turnaround from earlier decades when, as Sam Lebovic writes elsewhere in this volume, liberal politicians criticized the press as a propaganda vehicle for conservative corporate interests.[36]

Antipress sentiment among conservatives had been building for several years prior to Agnew's offensive, deriving partly from a sense that the press was giving less attention to their perspective and more attention to left-wing or radical viewpoints. The *Los Angeles Times* was especially vulnerable to this criticism, because prior to Otis Chandler becoming publisher in 1960, it had featured right-wing perspectives prominently in its news coverage and had ignored most others. In 1969, the paper published a lighthearted profile of the unassuming, middle-aged woman in charge of the Communist Party in Southern California—this infuriated television commentator George Putnam, among others. Putnam declared that Americans should be "shocked into a rage" and told his viewers to protest "this insult to American patriotism."[37] Naturally, many people felt that the perspective of an avowed communist did not belong in a major U.S. newspaper, but more frequent complaints from the right accused the *L.A. Times* of devoting inordinate attention to the views of student radicals or the black community. A front-page article about dissatisfaction among African Americans with Richard Nixon's selection of an all-white cabinet in 1968 prompted an acquaintance of editor in chief Nick Williams to protest, "Don't you think all this propaganda about negro representation is overdrawn and for the grandstand? . . . I fail to understand why [one] minority group is so important."[38]

Seven years later, in 1975, the managers of the *L.A. Times* were still fielding complaints that they—and the press more broadly—overemphasized the perspectives of the discontented. This perception concerned Bill Thomas so much that he felt compelled to write a front-page article about it—the only article he wrote for the paper during his seventeen-year tenure as editor in chief. Under the headline, "The Press: Is It Biased Against the Establishment?" Thomas offered an explanation for why many people perceived the *L.A. Times* and other newspapers as antibusiness or anti-cop. "Until about 10 years ago, the press tended to rely almost solely on sources within so-called establishment institutions," Thomas wrote. "A crime story quoted police spokesmen; an economics story rested on business and industry and chamber of commerce sources; stories about racial problems came from the mouths of government spokesmen and sociology professors. One heard little from black people, the poor, the dissident, the accused criminal, and others who spoke without institutional blessing." Thomas implied that people who complained about antiestablishment bias simply were not accustomed to seeing nonestablishment perspectives in the news. But having identified the cause of the complaint, he had no intention of placating the critics. He argued, "Really, all that has happened is this: where establishment voices alone were heard, others have gained access. To some, this is anti-establishment; to us, it is not only fair but the only way to bring about sensible, informed decisions."[39]

Indeed, the *L.A. Times* would remain committed to conveying the perspectives of "black people, the poor, the dissident." In the late 1970s, some of

the paper's editors felt they were not devoting enough attention to the problem of poverty in Southern California. So they appointed a new city-county
bureau chief, Bill Boyarsky, whom they knew to be sympathetic to the plight
of the poor. He was allowed to recruit his own staff and was given a mandate
to remedy this shortcoming in the paper's local coverage.[40]

Like other major metropolitan newspapers, the *New York Times* began
increasing its coverage of antiestablishment perspectives in the 1960s. Abe
Rosenthal had reservations about this trend. A few months after becoming
managing editor in 1969, he sent a memo to the national and metropolitan
editors in which he remarked on how many articles in that day's paper
concerned protesters, poverty, or discrimination. He wrote: "I get the impression, reading The Times, that the image we give of America is largely of
demonstrations, discrimination, antiwar movements, rallies, protests, etc.
Obviously all these things are an important part of the American scene. But
I think that because of our own liberal interest and because of our reporters'
inclination, we overdo this. I am not suggesting eliminating any one of these
stories. I am suggesting that reporters and editors look a bit more around
them to see what is going on in other fields."[41]

This mildness of this memo, and the fact that Rosenthal rarely mentioned
the issue subsequently, suggests that it was not a priority for him. As his
reference to "our own liberal interest" indicates, he likely recognized that he
would not have enough support within the paper to reduce the number of
antiestablishment stories even if he wanted to. The section editors chose the
story topics, and the reporters chose whose views to include and emphasize.
Rosenthal had to pick his battles, so he concentrated on his primary concern:
keeping reporters' political opinions out of news articles.

*   *   *

On the question of perspectives, the critics of objectivity won. They may not
have seen it that way—many on the left continued to claim that the press ignored or dismissed views outside the mainstream—but from a philosophical perspective, most newspapers by the 1980s recognized the pitfalls of
overreliance on establishment sources and the importance of presenting
a range of viewpoints. However, many journalists in the 1960s and '70s
challenged objectivity on other grounds as well. For one thing, they said, true
objectivity was not humanly possible. This was something of a straw-man
argument, because even the staunchest proponents of objectivity, like Rosen-

thal, conceded that it was not wholly achievable. A more salient critique charged that in trying to be objective, journalists censored themselves and obscured the truth. They presented opposing views in an effort to achieve balance, but if they believed certain views were false or misleading, they withheld that belief from the public in the name of objectivity.

This critique, equating objectivity with meek neutrality, remains common today, and it was not entirely new in the late 1960s.[42] Seeking to explain how they had enabled the rise of Senator Joseph McCarthy during the Red Scare, many journalists faulted their colleagues for publicizing his accusations without telling readers how dubious they were. Partly as a result, newspapers began to include more context and analysis in news articles, permitting their reporters to express judgments, but not opinions. This was controversial initially—in a 1961 speech to California newspaper publishers, Nick Williams had to make a plea for "interpretive" reporting to his skeptical audience—but by the mid-1960s, most mainstream commentators accepted it.[43] In 1967 Irving Kristol, a founding father of neoconservatism, argued that objective journalism without analysis was "a rationalization for 'safe' and mindless reporting." He declared, "To keep a reporter's prejudices out of a story is commendable; to keep his judgment out of a story is to guarantee that truth will be emasculated."[44]

In the late 1960s, however, some journalists took this critique a step further, arguing that reporters should be permitted to express not only judgments but also personal opinions. Writing in *The Nation* in 1968, a former member of the *New York Times* foreign staff, Leslie Collitt, argued for the superiority of European newspapers, in which stories were "presented as the opinion of the reporter." In the American press, by contrast, "Various views on an issue are presented, point-counterpoint, and the only opinion omitted is the one that would matter most to the reader—the reporter's own."[45] In the same magazine a year later, *Boston Globe* reporter David Deitch said newspapers "must admit that the editorial function is inherently biased and that reporters have opinions." The solution, he said, was to imitate the respected Parisian daily *Le Monde*, which "makes itself credible by rejecting the myth of objectivity. It exposes all its biases to the reader."[46]

This push from some reporters for more freedom to write what they wished was part of a larger power struggle between reporters and editors. The editors—generally older, more cautious, and more wedded to the concept of objectivity—had the power to dole out assignments, change the text of articles, write headlines, and determine how prominently stories were displayed. Reporters had resented this ever since reporting became a profession, but they rarely challenged the editors' power until the late 1960s. In 1970, a group of prominent *New York Times* journalists began holding informal meetings during which they shared their grievances about heavy-handed editing and the paper's top-down decision-making process. They jokingly called themselves "the cabal."[47] Some, like star reporter J. Anthony Lukas, felt that the line between judgment and opinion was arbitrary. Covering the trial of the Chicago Seven, Lukas resented that the editors would not permit him to share his unvarnished impressions of the proceedings—he later wrote a book about the trial, compelled by his desire to explain "what really happened."[48] At many other news organizations, disgruntled journalists were challenging their bosses in similar ways, demanding a greater voice in determining news policies and some relief from the strictures of objectivity. Observing this phenomenon, the *Columbia Journalism Review* said a movement for "reporter power" was afoot.[49] Many journalists seeking greater freedom of expression left the daily newspaper business to work for magazines and journalism reviews, where the so-called New Journalism was flourishing: writers were free to include their own opinions and to use novelistic techniques in the interest of vivid storytelling and pointed commentary.[50]

But while some newspaper reporters felt they were being stifled or censored, the mirror image of that complaint came from the right. Conservatives believed that reporters were expressing themselves *too* freely; the press had crossed the line between reporting and commentary, they argued, and thereby sullied its objectivity. In Spiro Agnew's first speech about the media, in 1969, he decried the way TV news anchors slyly injected their personal views into supposedly objective reports. "A raised eyebrow, an inflection of the voice, a caustic remark dropped in the middle of a broadcast can raise doubts in a million minds about the veracity of a public official or the wisdom of a government policy."[51] Agnew thus implied that journalists reporting the news should not "raise doubts"; if they have doubts, they must keep them to themselves. Many journalists would consider that self-censorship or dishonesty, but Agnew considered it responsible journalism. In 1972, Tom Wicker wrote in the journalism quarterly *Nieman Reports* that objectivity should be abandoned "so that reporters can stop being mere transmitters" of information.[52] The conservative media-watchdog group Accuracy in Media (AIM), which had been founded in 1969, seized on this remark as indicative of the problematic direction in which the press was headed. In a letter to the editor of *Nieman Reports*, AIM's executive secretary wrote that unlike Wicker, "We would like to strengthen the tradition of objectivity. We want to see reporters become transmitters of accurate information, and we would not use the adjective 'mere.'" The journalist's appropriate task, according to AIM, was "to dig out and report facts accurately, even when the facts clash with deep-seated beliefs."[53]

The right-wing critics would have liked to see the press revert to 1950s consensus-style reporting, in which official sources were rarely questioned and interpretation was confined to the opinion columns.[54] But that would never happen. In addition to interpretive reporting having become firmly entrenched, the press was adopting a more adversarial posture toward those in power.[55] Conservatives may have recognized the hopelessness of their mission to turn back the clock, but as Nicole Hemmer suggests elsewhere in this volume, they could use objectivity as "a vital conceptual tool for undermining mainstream media"—a major long-term goal of the conservative movement.[56] The press might not change its behavior in response to charges that analysis and objectivity were incompatible, but it could at least be made to look hypocritical and untrustworthy.

*   *   *

Despite their influence, neither angry conservatives nor frustrated reporters could cause news organizations to change their fundamental values. Those decisions rested with the top editors and publishers. Thanks to the outspoken Abe Rosenthal, it was clear where the *New York Times* stood on objectivity: it remained the paper's guiding principle. Rosenthal did not, however, subscribe to the same definition of objectivity as Spiro Agnew or Accuracy in Media. In Rosenthal's view, objectivity allowed for analysis, interpretation, and colorful writing.[57] The *Los Angeles Times* had a more ambiguous position on objectivity, and it changed over the course of the 1960s. In 1964, Nick Williams composed a form-letter response to readers who complained about a left-wing slant in the formerly Republican paper. The letter stressed, "The Times does make every effort to be objective, complete and factual in reporting the news."[58] By the late 1960s, however, Williams no longer promised objectivity to disgruntled conservatives. To one such reader, he wrote in 1969, "We do try, if not always for objectivity, at least for fairness."[59] In a speech the following year, he said, "I want to quarrel a little with . . . the basic theory of so-called objective journalism." His quarrel, he explained, derived from his belief that objectivity was incompatible with interpretive reporting.[60]

Clearly, Williams defined objectivity differently than Abe Rosenthal. It was mainly the term, not the concept, that he disliked. Williams's successor, Bill Thomas, felt the same way. In a 1972 television interview, Thomas was asked, "Is there such a thing as objectivity, in your judgment, and can an editor expect it of his reporters?" He replied, "No. It's a word that's been tossed around so much that nobody knows what it means anymore. I don't think one can expect pure objectivity of anybody in any field at any time . . . it's probably not humanly possible." However, Thomas quickly added, "I think one can expect fairness, and that implies professional standards. In that regard, looking at objectivity through that definition, then I think you do have a right to expect that."[61] L.A. Times publisher Otis Chandler addressed the issue bluntly in a 1971 speech, saying, "I detest the word objective. Pursuing the word objective only leads you into a semantic jungle." He preferred to speak of "honest" journalism rather than objective journalism.[62] As Chandler sensed, if he embraced the term objectivity, he would open himself up to criticism from people, mostly on the right, who defined the term in ways that he and his editors found unacceptable. The critics might insist that interpreting the news or calling into question official statements violated objectivity. At the New York Times, Rosenthal was surely aware of this danger, but he clung to the term nevertheless—although he acknowledged on multiple occasions that many people "get hung up on" the definition of objectivity.[63]

The New York Times and the L.A. Times dismissed right-wing critics who asked for curbs on interpretive reporting, but they also disagreed with left-wing critics who wanted the freedom to insert their personal views into news articles. The L.A. Times was less strict on this question than the New York Times. In a 1970 memo to his most senior editors, Nick Williams took a cavalier attitude toward opinionated news coverage, saying he was "not persuaded" that the reporter's opinion should be included in news articles. He added, "Some of the finest writing in The Times in recent years has come very close to this border line of personal opinion."[64] The L.A. Times was considered "a reporter's paper," meaning reporters—especially the most talented writers among them—were given great freedom in choosing the topic, angle, style, and length of their articles. Rather than ask writers to strive for an ideal of objectivity that was difficult to define, impossible to achieve fully, and discredited in the eyes of many journalists, Williams, and later Bill Thomas, allowed them significant latitude, trusting their editors to guard the line between interpretation and opinion. The *New York Times*, on the other hand, had a reputation as "an editor's paper." Articles had to adhere to the paper's standards and house style—including the editors' standards of objectivity—and they were often rigorously edited to guarantee that they did so. A conservative who read the *New York Times* and the *L.A. Times* each day likely would have perceived more bias in the Los Angeles paper, but because of the *New York Times*'s greater national stature, it was a more frequent target of Agnew and other right-wing critics.

Yet despite their different approaches to enforcing editorial standards, the managers of the *New York Times* and the *L.A. Times* had the same basic philosophy. They believed that their coverage should emanate from the political center, so being attacked simultaneously from the right and the left made it easier for them to reject both critiques. In speeches defending the fairness and credibility of the *L.A. Times* or newspapers in general, Chandler and Williams mentioned, seemingly with pride, that both sides of the political spectrum found fault with them. As Williams said in 1966, "The American press, so vigorously attacked from both the left and the right—described as both the lackeys of capitalism and the dupes of communism— . . . is, I earnestly believe, the *most* responsible of *all* our American institutions."[65] When a reader complained to Chandler in 1968 that the paper was devoting more coverage to Richard Nixon's presidential campaign than to the Democratic candidates, Chandler responded that he found the letter "quite refreshing," explaining, "Much of my recent mail has criticized The Times for not giving Mr. Nixon enough space. One of the best tests of objectivity a publisher has is to check and see if he receives criticisms from both sides at the same time on the same issue. This usually means his newspaper is pretty close to down the middle reporting, which is my constant aim for The Times."[66]

This was a common view at the *New York Times* as well. Harrison Salisbury, an influential senior editor and roving correspondent, told a friend in 1971 that he was unmoved by criticism of the news media from "the extreme right and the extreme left. . . . It seems to me that this is just the conventional yapping by people who always complain if others do not reflect their opinions. As you know, we get plenty of it here at the Times, and in almost equal measure from radicals who think we are the establishment and reactionaries who think we are the revolution."[67] Seymour Topping, deputy managing editor in the 1970s, recalled, "When I was getting [criticism] from both sides of an issue, there was an indication to me that we were doing our job."[68]

Of course, to achieve "down the middle" coverage, it is necessary to determine where the middle is. The target audiences for the *L.A. Times* and the *New York Times* were not microcosms of the country as a whole—they were better educated and more left-leaning, among other characteristics. Nevertheless, the men running these papers misjudged the direction in which the United States was moving politically. Instead of seeking out a middle ground between the New Right and liberalism, they sought a middle ground between the old right and the New Left. This resulted partly from the concerns these men had about the future of their business. Both papers were financially healthy (indeed, the *L.A. Times* was a cash cow), but they worried about declining readership, especially among the younger generation. Pollster George Gallup investigated this issue in a confidential 1976 survey, and in his report to newspaper publishers Gallup underlined his main finding: "The greatest cause for concern is the loss of readers among the young adult group."[69]

This had been a major worry at the *L.A. Times* and the *New York Times* for at least a decade. Sizing up the challenges facing his newspaper in 1966, Otis Chandler wrote to Nick Williams, "Knowing now the audience to which we need to appeal in the next five years, obviously it is the young, swinging group—not just young chronologically but in spirit and interests."[70] As his use of the word "swinging" implies, Chandler equated young people with antiestablishment, countercultural attitudes. An influential survey a few years later by the pollster Daniel Yankelovich reinforced this perception. In a speech to newspaper publishers in 1969, Chandler cited Yankelovich's finding that 42 percent of eighteen- to twenty-four-year-olds were "radical," and that these were "the ones who are gaining power; the ones who will lead the group; and the ones who will influence and shape the opinions of the under-18 group."[71]

Decision makers at the *New York Times* also fretted over young readers and assumed that most were radical. In 1970, several executives debated adding a "youth section" to the paper but scrapped the idea after deciding that it would be condescending. As one executive wrote, "The kids of today are no longer swallowing goldfish and playing with hula hoops. They are now into stopping wars, de-polluting rivers, and marching on General Motors."[72] Nevertheless, the idea of a youth column was resurrected in 1976, with managing editor Seymour Topping telling several top news editors, "The paper needs to become more attractive to young people."[73] A few months later, Topping solicited memos from about a dozen editors and reporters with ideas about how the *New York Times* could attract more readers in their late teens and early twenties. One reporter in her thirties jokingly suggested, "Turn itself into a tabloid and change the name to Rolling Stone," the bible of radical youth culture.[74]

Management seemed less concerned about attracting or retaining older, conservative readers. These readers wanted a comprehensive, high-brow newspaper, and they had no other good options: the *New York Times'* main competitor, the *New York Herald Tribune*, had folded in 1966; in Los Angeles, the Hearst Corporation had shuttered its morning *Examiner* in 1962, leaving only its declining afternoon paper, the renamed *Los Angeles Herald Examiner*, as a competing broadsheet. The *L.A. Times* realized that for a certain type of reader, they were the only game in town. When people canceled their subscriptions because they disagreed with the political views expressed on the editorial page, Nick Williams often reminded them about the paper's unmatched news coverage. As he told one in 1970, "If at any time you feel that the overall coverage of The Times from its 18 foreign bureaus, its 7 national bureaus, and its staff in California reporting exclusively to Times readers, outweigh the work of two controversial cartoonists whose work occupies less than a column each day, the Editorial Department of The Times will be happy to welcome you back among our subscribers."[75]

By the 1970s, the *L.A. Times* seemed to have written off the staunch conservatives who had formed the core of its readership two decades earlier. Analyzing the results of a survey about canceled subscriptions, Bill Thomas acknowledged that there were many "random comments from unhappy conservatives," but he warned, "If we pleased these people, it's possible— even likely—that we would lose the others." Besides, he noted, only 2 percent of those who canceled cited as their primary reason "too opinionated: inconsistent reporting."[76] Given those numbers, the *L.A. Times* was not inclined to reconsider its approach to reporting based on right-wing critiques.

*   *   *

By the late 1970s, the peak period of concern regarding newspapers' credibility and objectivity seemed to have passed. The tumult of the previous

decade and a half had died down. Spiro Agnew, having resigned over corruption charges in 1973, was a fading memory. The left-wing journalism
reviews that reveled in the mainstream press's failings had begun to
fold.[77] The malaise of the Carter era dampened enthusiasm for attempts
to fundamentally transform institutions that, like the press, seemed to be
functioning relatively well (unlike, for instance, manufacturing, energy
policy, or the monetary system). Addressing an audience of journalists in
1978, Bill Thomas said, "We are closer than ever before to a position of real
and, importantly, *perceived* independence. . . . We're getting close to a goal
that looked unattainable, not so long ago: that of acceptance as a truly independent source of dependable information."[78] This was a far cry from Nick
Williams's pessimistic assessment of press credibility in the late 1960s and
early '70s.

Even Abe Rosenthal felt less of a sense of urgency to protect his paper's
credibility. The number of memos he sent about advocacy or editorializing
in the news columns declined sharply after 1975. In 1978, he collected several minor examples of instances "where we may have strayed" and sent them
to Punch Sulzberger. Five or ten years earlier, he had laced such memos with
warnings about the dire threat to the paper's principles and to American democracy. This time, he wrote, "My own belief is that in recent years we have
gone a hell of a long way to improving [fairness and the level of discourse]
and that whatever excesses that were in the past in American journalism
have largely been eliminated as far as The Times is concerned. . . . So I am
calling these to your attention not because they indicate a problem but just
as a matter of interest."[79]

Debates about objectivity, advocacy, bias, and credibility would continue into the 1980s and beyond—it is hard to imagine that they will ever be
resolved, as long as there is a free press. But beginning in the late 1970s,
those debates reached a kind of stasis. For decades thereafter, critics on the
right would level the same kinds of charges that Spiro Agnew had made: of
liberal bias, elitism, arrogance, insularity, and unwarranted power. Those on
the left would accuse the press of kowtowing to powerful interests and failing to report truthfully on the country's real problems. Neither side believed
for a moment that the press was actually objective. Yet most news executives
and journalists in positions of power continued to insist that they were guided
by something like objectivity, even if some preferred not to use that word.
This confidence in their core values, along with the immense profitability of
their businesses, enabled them to embrace other substantial changes to the

news product, from interpretive articles to soft-news sections. But they would not need to fundamentally reassess their values and business model again until the twenty-first century. This time the challenge would be technological rather than ideological—the Internet—and how it will reshape journalism remains to be seen.

CHAPTER 7

"No on 14": Hollywood Celebrities, the Civil Rights Movement, and the California Open Housing Debate

Emilie Raymond

In the summer of 1964, more than 150 Hollywood celebrities and industry insiders formed what they called "the most important group of performing artists, executives, directors, writers, and craftsmen from the broadcast and movie industries ever assembled for a single, political purpose": an Arts Division to defeat Proposition 14.[1] California governor Edmund "Pat" Brown had signed the Rumford Fair Housing Act in April 1963, but opponents in the real estate industry successfully initiated Prop 14 to repeal it. Brown made defeating Prop 14 the priority of his administration; he formed Californians Against Prop 14 (CAP) and worked with entertainers Sammy Davis Jr., Frank Sinatra, and Dean Martin to create an Arts Division within CAP hoping that the celebrities could provide "a unique gift—the gift of time, talent and the creative message to educate voters."[2] Davis and a handful of others had already laid the groundwork for celebrity civil rights activism, and in the coming months, more Hollywood stars became involved in fair housing than on any other racial issue up to that point. They took on myriad responsibilities and participated in politics in a personal manner, organizing an all-out fund-raising and media effort and stumping on the campaign trail. Although Prop 14's passage evokes the paradoxes of celebrity activism, as stars would later be characterized as part of a liberal elite "out of touch" with everyday people, this critique pales in comparison to the benefits celebrities can bring to political movements, particularly their adeptness in capitalizing on media interest to raise visibility and funds for various causes.

This essay, like Julia Guarneri's piece earlier in this volume, calls for an expansion of the traditional conception of media politics. There is a growing body of scholarship on the civil rights movement and the media. Scholars such as Donald Bogle, Thomas Cripps, and Richard Iton have explored the intersection between the civil rights movement and the popular media, particularly regarding the representation of African Americans in film and television.[3] Aniko Bodroghkozy, Christine Acham, and Steven D. Classen discuss how both the national and local news portrayed the movement.[4] However, these works do not explore how celebrities used the film and television media or their star status to advance the civil rights cause. This essay builds on the work of Donald T. Critchlow, Kathryn Cramer Brownell, and Steven J. Ross, who have brought more attention to the intersection between Hollywood and politics, and contribute to the literature on Proposition 14.[5] In determining the lessons of Prop 14's passage, scholars have emphasized its relation to the splintering of liberalism, the conservative ascendancy, and urban unrest, but they have not examined the significance of celebrity involvement in the fair housing debate.[6]

Prior to the 1960s, Hollywood did not have a particularly impressive record on civil rights matters. During the "studio era," black actors were relegated to menial roles, such as maids, porters, butlers, and the like, and often served as comic relief by using improper dialects and exaggerated mannerisms. Their pay was substantially less than that of their white costars, and the studios employed no black crew members, producers, or directors.[7] Residential patterns in Los Angeles were similarly discriminatory. Although public spaces such as theaters and beaches had been integrated since the 1920s, restrictive covenants in the real estate industry had resulted in "white" and "colored" sections of town. The well-known character actors Louise Beavers and Hattie McDaniel and a handful of other wealthy blacks moved into the West Adams enclave and successfully challenged racial covenants there in 1945, but most African Americans lived along Central Avenue.[8] When Sammy Davis Jr., moved to Los Angeles after World War II, no one in the Hollywood Hills would rent to him. He rented a hotel room on the very edge of the star-studded neighborhood until he could afford to buy a home, and even then only after a white business associate surreptitiously purchased it in his name. Davis became the first black resident of the neighborhood and experienced the indignities that came with this role. During his first December there, a vandal painted "Merry Christmas, Nigger!" across the garage door.[9]

Furthermore, the film industry had proven resistant to civil rights efforts even before the House Un-American Activities Committee (HUAC) drove many film workers out of liberal causes. In 1942, NAACP Executive Secretary Walter White began pressuring Hollywood studios to improve their portrayal of African Americans; although White won pledges from several sympathetic filmmakers, no enforcement mechanisms existed. Furthermore, the controversies associated with his visit led the studios to become wary of hiring African American actors at all.[10] With the exception of the Screen Actors Guild, the craft unions repeatedly proved hostile to expanding their memberships to include African Americans well into the 1960s.[11] After the HUAC investigations and adoption of the studio blacklist in 1947, any number of liberal causes became suspect and, given the Communist Party's professed commitment to racial equality, any organization or individual addressing racial injustice was deemed subversive. As the actress Dorothy Dandridge put it, "It was considered dangerous for the people in show business to endorse anything more controversial than toothpaste."[12]

However, changes in the industry allowed for a new generation of black stars who increasingly proved their willingness to speak out on racial politics. The breakdown of the studio system (instigated by the U.S. Supreme Court's so-called *Paramount* decision in 1948) gave rise to the independent directors behind postwar "message movies": films that featured liberal racial themes and better parts for black actors. The success of the 1949 films *Home of the Brave, Pinky, Lost Boundaries*, and *Intruder in the Dust* proved the financial viability of "the social problem" film. *Variety* reported, "Film's leading b[ox] o[ffice] star for 1949 wasn't a personality, but a subject matter."[13] Message movies presented welcome opportunities for black actors like Sidney Poitier, Ossie Davis, Ruby Dee, and Harry Belafonte, all of whom were involved in the Harlem-based American Negro Theatre.

They became fast friends, and all looked to the performer and activist Paul Robeson for inspiration, leading them to participate in various cultural initiatives in Harlem sponsored by the Communist Party. Due to Robeson's influence, Belafonte embraced his own folk music career, and the friends all performed in Community for the Negro in the Arts (CAN) productions, later identified by HUAC as a communist-front organization.[14] However, Robeson came under intense scrutiny as a Soviet sympathizer, and saw his career systematically destroyed. Soon thereafter, the black performers Canada Lee and Hazel Scott came under investigation by HUAC and were effectively blacklisted. Poitier says that Robeson cautioned them against appearing "too radical," and that they increasingly distanced themselves from such groups. Although Davis, Dee, and Poitier all managed to avoid signing loyalty oaths, and even spoke out against the blacklist, Belafonte denounced his past associations in the anticommunist publication *Counterattack*.[15] Nevertheless, as the modern civil rights movement—under the aegis of such groups as the NAACP, Martin Luther King Jr.'s Southern Christian Leadership Conference (SCLC), and the Urban League—took hold in the mid-1950s, Belafonte, Poitier, Davis, and Dee, along with Sammy Davis Jr., all became active participants in the struggle. Soon joined by Dick Gregory in the early 1960s, these Leading Six stars paved the way for celebrity involvement in the movement by setting examples and recruiting other entertainers into a northern liberal network of support.

They first became involved with the movement as participants, headliners, and even organizers of mass rallies and demonstrations. The 1956 Madison Square Garden rally in support of southern activists marked the first such event, and the 1957 Prayer Pilgrimage for Freedom to Washington, D.C., followed soon thereafter. Belafonte cochaired the Youth March for Integrated Schools in Washington, D.C., in 1958, and Sammy Davis Jr., helped organize a rally at the Los Angeles Sports Arena in support of the Freedom Ride movement in 1961. A combined 77,500 people attended these events, and the two rallies, where collections were taken, raised $37,000.[16] Moreover, the stars generated favorable media attention, entertained the crowds, articulated the civil rights message, and provided a psychological boost to the everyday marchers.

The Leading Six also performed in numerous benefit shows and concerts for civil rights organizations. Some of the most successful during the late 1950s and early 1960s included an Apollo Theater benefit that raised $4,000 for the NAACP in 1958, a Chicago Urban League jazz festival that netted $250,000 in 1960, a "Tribute to Martin Luther King, Jr." that generated $22,000 for the SCLC in 1961, and a Fight for Freedom dinner three months later that raised $60,000 for the NAACP.[17] All of these shows starred Sammy Davis Jr., and Belafonte helped organize the King tribute, as well as another benefit show with Sidney Poitier that raised $10,000 for the Committee to Defend Martin Luther King Jr., after King was erroneously charged with tax evasion in 1960.[18] Not only did the benefits raise hundreds of thousands of dollars for the cause; they served as an important source of news in which northern audiences could hear directly from southern activists and feel a sense of ownership and participation in the movement.[19] The increasingly swanky benefits also brought an air of glamour that had been absent from the movement and made it easier for the Leading Six to recruit more stars, including white stars like Davis's Rat Pack pals Dean Martin and Frank Sinatra, to perform for free.

Indeed, the Leading Six utilized their show-business connections to appeal to financial sponsors and shore up organizational support. Sammy Davis Jr., undertook a letter-writing campaign for the NAACP's Life Membership program, while Belafonte and Poitier made direct appeals to such Hollywood figures as television host Steve Allen and director George Stevens when raising money for King's defense. Ossie Davis and Ruby Dee hosted a Student Nonviolent Coordinating Committee (SNCC) "house party" in 1962—the first of many such intimate affairs where celebrities and student activists mingled with potential donors.[20] These activities generated considerable income and helped the organizations develop mailing and sponsorship lists for further actions and programs.

Only a few celebrities engaged in direct action or risked arrest during this period. Influenced by a longtime friend, the white actor Charlton Heston joined an NAACP-sponsored desegregation campaign in Oklahoma City for two days in 1961, and the Jewish actor and singer Theodore Bikel began working on SNCC's voter registration programs in Mississippi in 1962.[21] The celebrity who proved most open to the tactic of civil disobedience, and willing to endure the subsequent jail time, was the comedian Dick Gregory, whose frequent television and nightclub appearances had made him a household name. After being jailed along with Bikel (in segregated facilities) in Birmingham, Alabama, in May 1963, he would go on to be arrested at least eight times, bringing attention to isolated and dangerous SNCC projects in such locales as Pine Bluff, Arkansas, and Greenwood, Mississippi, which had received little media coverage until Gregory's involvement.[22] However, most stars were unwilling to risk jail, especially in the South. Singer Nat "King" Cole even called such activity "idiotic" for celebrities.[23] Despite this limitation, the advantages of celebrity involvement were apparent, and civil rights organizations heavily recruited them to raise money and awareness. African-American stars could speak to the racism they had themselves experienced, and the white allies who were their friends, having seen the indignities of racism up close, could also provide valuable commentary.

The summer of 1963 saw an upsurge of Hollywood engagement in the movement, as more A-list stars, such as Paul Newman and Marlon Brando, proved their willingness to organize on their own and risk controversy while doing so. The examples set by the Leading Six, as well as King's first visit to Los Angeles in June 1963, motivated them. Newman agreed to speak at a Rally for Freedom celebrating King's leadership at Birmingham, and a reception at Burt Lancaster's home with about 250 guests followed. Newman and Brando proved the top donors and soon went to Gadsden, Alabama, in an unsuccessful attempt to negotiate between city officials and civil rights activists.[24] King returned only a few weeks later in an attempt to promote the use of nondiscrimination clauses in union contracts; though largely unsuccessful, King did win Brando's and Heston's agreement to form an Arts Group for the March on Washington held in August 1963. They mobilized seventy-five Hollywood celebrities for the event, generating positive publicity in such publications as the *New York Times, Los Angeles Times, Variety,* and *Jet* magazine in the weeks preceding the march and serving as an inspirational and dramatic presence during the event itself. Moreover, in its immediate aftermath, more stars, such as Elizabeth Taylor and Ed Sullivan, volunteered for benefit shows, including a huge NAACP "Freedom TV Spectacular," a trend that led Sammy Davis Jr., Sinatra, Martin, and Count Basie to form a "Stars for Freedom" committee to help streamline civil rights fundraising and the distribution of funds.[25] Stars for Freedom provided the organizational basis for the Arts Division formed by Governor Brown during the Prop 14 campaign; meanwhile, the growing interest in grassroots organizing and even direct action resulted in an outpouring of celebrity activity for open housing.

Paving the way was Brando, whose involvement in the movement continued to deepen as he strove to "have racial equality represented in [his] daily li[fe]" on a more widespread basis.[26] King's visit to Hollywood had made Brando more aware of employment discrimination in the film industry, and, believing he should improve his own hiring practices, Brando added an African-American secretary to his payroll. He also met with studio chiefs about hiring more black actors and crew members, which led him to CORE and its fair housing campaign. In addition to actions in such locales as Philadelphia and Chicago, the organization had been orchestrating a series of pickets at segregated housing tracts in the Los Angeles suburb of Torrance.[27] Hoping to garner media attention for the issue, Brando joined that effort in July 1963. According to one activist, "There had been demonstrations, and arrests before our march. However, the presence of Marlon Brando sharply dramatized the situation and drew newspaper and TV reporters to the scene by the dozens." Arrested on at least one occasion, Brando was also targeted by hecklers as a "nigger-loving creep" and a "stooge for communist race-mixers." The first major Hollywood star to join demonstrations in Los Angeles, Brando received media praise for his decorous behavior, and the publicity from the campaign led the developer to permit integration of the neighborhood.[28]

Hostility over residential integration was characteristic of many northern states, but the issue of fair housing had become a pressing concern for California's liberal establishment.[29] Even though the U.S. Supreme Court had outlawed the enforcement of racially restricted covenants in the 1948 *Shelley v. Kramer* decision, realtors (as represented by the powerful California Real Estate Association, aka CREA), developers, and neighborhood associations continued to practice "informal" segregation by refusing to show, sell, or rent property to African Americans and other minorities, just as Sammy Davis Jr., had experienced.[30] The Rumford Act empowered the state's Fair Employment Practices Commission to handle claims of racial discrimination by realtors and owners of apartment houses and homes built with public assistance.[31] Significant exemptions (for investment property, for example) weakened the Rumford Act's coverage, but it nevertheless signaled a significant policy shift that elicited an immediate response from the real estate industry. Through an organization called the Committee for Home Protection, CREA wrote and gathered signatures for Prop 14, an initiative designed to repeal the Rumford Act, as well as earlier laws dealing with housing discrimination.

Brando's demonstrating foreshadowed greater celebrity involvement with the issue. With 150 celebrities and industry insiders, the Arts Division doubled the number who had participated in the Arts Group for the March on Washington. Several participants from the march served in leadership roles. Burt Lancaster, who had delivered a rousing speech at the Lincoln Memorial, served as the chairman, along with Gordon Stulberg and M. J. Frankovich, both vice presidents of Columbia Pictures Corporation. March veterans Polly Bergen, Judy Franciosa, and James Garner served on the executive committee, while other past supporters, such as Poitier, Heston, Richard Burton, and Elizabeth Taylor volunteered general support. Nat "King" Cole and George Stevens, both of whom had been ambivalent about "group action" in the past, joined. Between the governor's personal appeals and the Arts Division's recruitment efforts, a significant number of stars who had thus far been absent from the movement lent their support, including such prominent film actors as Cary Grant, Steve McQueen, Tony Curtis, and Gregory Peck. The committee also recruited admired television personalities such as Art Linkletter, Carl Reiner, Dick Van Dyke, and Mary Tyler Moore. Ironically, Brando did not actively participate in the Arts Division, apparently due to his film schedule.[32]

It is surprising that an issue described by *Time* magazine as "the most bitterly fought issue" in the nation, one that overshadowed even Lyndon Johnson's election campaign, would generate so much celebrity support, especially among first-timers.[33] Several complementary factors were at work. At the time of the stars' recruitment, the issue did not seem that controversial. CAP had been formed with Governor Brown's endorsement, and the Rumford Act had passed, albeit narrowly, with little fanfare. Furthermore, Prop 14 could claim few prominent allies. Most Republicans refused to support the measure, and, according to one historian, "The large majority of the state's political, civic, and religious organizations opposed the initiative."[34] Actor Ronald Reagan backed it, giving Prop 14 one celebrity friend, but he did not give it much lip service during the campaign. The celebrities who had participated in the March on Washington and in the NAACP "Freedom TV Spectacular" provided an established base of support for CAP. And the presidential race also likely had a spillover effect, as the Johnson administration had endorsed the Rumford Act.

Indeed, despite their wariness of controversial social causes, many celebrities had been involved in electoral politics throughout the 1950s. Belafonte and Heston, among others, had endorsed Democratic presidential contender Adlai Stevenson in 1956; President Dwight D. Eisenhower employed the Hollywood actor Robert Montgomery to help improve his television appeal; and the song and dance man George Murphy, known for his films costarring the child sensation Shirley Temple, in 1952 produced the first of several Republican national conventions with mass television audiences in mind.[35] After John F. Kennedy attracted unprecedented numbers of celebrity supporters in his 1960 presidential campaign, he tapped stars for presidential appointments, as with Belafonte's position on the Peace Corps Advisory Council, a practice President Johnson continued. By 1964, a number of Hollywood celebrities had political aspirations of their own, including Reagan. His electrifying televised speech on behalf of 1964 Republican presidential candidate Barry Goldwater generated $8 million for the campaign, its biggest

boon yet. The California GOP soon began priming Reagan for his 1966 gubernatorial race.[36] Murphy ran for the U.S. Senate in 1964, and easily defeated his opposition, former Kennedy aide Pierre Salinger. However,
Murphy avoided taking a stand on Prop 14, calling it a "moral question"
individuals had to decide for themselves. The California and national press
hailed the intersection of art and politics, and Murphy asserted that Eisenhower had encouraged him, saying, "People are getting tired of professional
politicians."[37]

The Arts Division capitalized on the stars' name recognition and
communication skills in setting its priorities, namely "to raise money to help
defeat Proposition 14, provide talent for producing television and radio
commercials and shows, and assist local groups in fund-raising activities
through personal appearances."[38] In fact, according to a report in *Variety*, by
September the "showbiz arm" was compelled to "take over" the fund-raising
for CAP because, perhaps in a foreshadowing of impending problems, "the
party's big donors, bankers, and savings and loan cos. haven't been able to
come thru on the campaign."[39] The Arts Division coordinated a letter-writing
campaign for which Lancaster and Frankovich signed direct appeals for funds.
The group also considered selling a television special to the networks and
making an album, but ultimately aborted these efforts due to lack of interest.[40]

The bulk of the organization's fund-raising energy went toward its
"Night of Stars" benefit at the Hollywood Bowl on October 4, 1964. Taylor
and Burton, Hollywood's hottest couple at the time, signed on as headliners.
Cole and his producer, Ike Jones, handled the musical program, and Judy
Franciosa and Milton Berle's wife Ruth arranged the rest of the production, which included Lucille Ball, Berle, Shelley Berman, Joey Bishop, Kirk
Douglas, and the Kingston Trio, as well as Lancaster, Peck, and Van Dyke.[41]
The executive committee used their show-business connections to maximize
profits for the benefit. The public relations coordinator, Maury Segal, made
arrangements with various publicity and public relations offices to donate
their services, and George Schlaff dealt with the tax procedures. It was arranged for all performers and musicians to play at scale, and that the rental
fee would be only 15 percent of the gross, which the Arts Division hoped
would be $115,000. They could then anticipate about $85,000 for their cof-
fers.[42] All told, they raised $104,457, about 20 percent of the $500,000 that
CAP raised overall.[43]

Its fund-raising success allowed the Arts Division to buy widespread
advertising that targeted fellow actors as well as the general public. The

group took out two full-page ads in *Variety* articulating their opposition to Prop 14.[44] They also produced a number of TV spots, again using their show-business connections to cut production costs, and employed "personalities like Art Linkletter in whom the public has a faith in matters of this kind."[45] Whereas the Hollywood Bowl benefit focused on glamour and entertainment to raise money, the TV spots played more like political ads. They increased the frequency of these spots in the last week of the campaign "to make full use of all the movie and television personalities who are working with us."[46]

The Arts Division also provided ways for the stars to talk directly with voters. It furnished fact sheets and set up speaking engagements with community groups, asking Peck to meet with a civic association in the Thousand Oaks neighborhood, for example. In a self-written speech, Peck told the audience that if a sense of "righteousness" did not convince them to oppose Prop 14, "then the practical side of discrimination and bigotry in the loss to the nation of the vast reserve of widespread talent, ingenuity, [and] genius" should. Other stars participated in radio call-in shows or made themselves available at designated times when citizens could call them at a phone bank. Wives of the stars, such as Marjorie Van Dyke and Rita Wade Davis (married to Sammy Davis Sr.) did door-to-door campaigning and distributed "No on Prop 14" literature.[47] This activity resulted in unprecedented grass-roots campaigning among the Hollywood set.

Going into election day, it seemed that CAP had the edge, one historian calling it "a mismatch of David and Goliath proportions."[48] However, 65 percent of California voters approved Prop 14, even as they voted for President Johnson in almost equal numbers. The reasons for Prop 14's stunning victory have been rigorously analyzed by scholars, and how the governor's office managed the Arts Division exemplifies the problems with CAP's overall approach. Following CAP's leadership, the Arts Division used increasingly moralistic language about Prop 14, eschewing the more logical approach it had emphasized early in the campaign. Its first *Variety* ad had focused on the proposition itself and had warned that its broad implications would "actually legalize housing discrimination" and "prevent the State and all Cities and Towns from ever passing any laws to prevent such discrimination." The second ad began much more dramatically: "The globe on which we spin needs a bath, an old-fashioned Saturday night scrubbing to cleanse it of the dirty stains of hatred and indecency that now despoil a planet." This approach annoyed voters, who were more interested in how fair housing affected them personally.[49] CAP had been concerned that specific references to racism or identification with minority groups would hurts its efforts, and thus focused on white voters in its campaign. Likewise, although the Arts Division included a number of African Americans on its committee, there was little outreach to black or Hispanic groups.[50] Finally, CAP had underestimated the reach of CREA and its vast network of developers, brokers, and other real estate partners, as well as its political sophistication. Instead of appealing to crass racism, CREA used civil rights language to frame the issue as one of "owners' rights," of a choice between "freedom of choice" and "forced housing."[51] By failing to address these problems, the Arts Division, while not causing CAP's defeat, reflected the missteps in its approach. However, two years later the California Supreme Court deemed Prop 14 unconstitutional (a decision affirmed by the U.S. Supreme Court in 1967).

Prop 14 marked a turning point in celebrity activism in the civil rights movement, allowing for a true cadre of star support when the Selma campaign for voting rights came to a head and ushering in a lucrative period for the NAACP, SNCC, and the SCLC as house parties and benefit shows became increasingly popular. At the same time, celebrities continued to apply civil rights gains to Hollywood. In 1966, civil rights organizations threatened lawsuits based on the Civil Rights Act's Title VII and made a breakthrough with the studios and unions to coordinate hiring and employment programs.[52] Sammy Davis Jr., Ossie Davis, and Poitier persistently moved into production as writers, producers, and directors in order to have more influence over their own films and to improve the portrayal of African Americans onscreen.

Prop 14 also highlights some of the advantages and drawbacks of celebrity activism. Its resounding defeat indicated that the state's liberal establishment, with which Hollywood celebrities would become increasingly associated, was somewhat disconnected from the priorities of everyday constituents. Journalist Tom Wolfe would famously excoriate wealthy liberals for their posh parties in support of the avowedly socialist and militant Black Panthers organization in his 1970 essay "Radical Chic," a negative characterization that has shaped contemporary attacks. For example, Ann Coulter recently dressed down jet-setting celebrities, like Leonardo DiCaprio, who live lavish lifestyles yet "hypocritically" support environmental causes.[53] However, even as Richard Nixon identified the Silent Majority as his natural constituency, he recruited a dazzling array of stars for his 1972 reelection campaign, including Sammy Davis Jr., who served on Nixon's National Advisory Council on Economic Opportunity and traveled to South Vietnam on behalf of the administration.[54] Indeed, Nixon recognized, just as activists and candidates before and after him, the potential favorability a celebrity can lend to a cause or campaign.

Most celebrities continued to delve into the political fray and embrace any number of controversial tactics and issues. Some celebrities became as well known for their politics as for their film roles, as with Brando's involvement in "fish-ins" with the American Indian Movement, Jane Fonda's support of the Black Panthers and traveling to North Vietnam as part of the antiwar movement, or Heston's involvement in a gun control task force before he deemed such legislation misguided and became a spokesperson for the National Rifle Association. Indeed, the civil rights movement had drawn celebrities back into politics, allowing them to comfortably take on a host of issues, whether liberal (as much of Hollywood now proved to be) or conservative.

CHAPTER 8

From "Faith in Facts" to "Fair and Balanced": Conservative Media, Liberal Bias, and the Origins of Balance

Nicole Hemmer

"There was a time in America—not very long ago—when only liberal voices were to be heard on the nation's communications networks, and most national debates were limited to options which often seemed to offer little choice," Phil Crane reminisced. It was the end of 1973, nearly a decade after Crane had written *The Democrat's Dilemma* for conservative publisher Henry Regnery during the Goldwater campaign. Crane, then a congressman, had wended his way through conservative media, organizations, and politics, and now, sitting before the *Manion Forum* microphone, recalled how different the landscape had appeared twenty years earlier. "Few indeed were the voices calling for national strength, limited government and fiscal integrity. Fewer still were the media outlets through which conservative spokesmen might reach a national audience and make available to that audience a viewpoint which not only represented a real choice but which, as we have seen, more recently represented the real views of the majority of Americans."[1]

Crane's language was revealing. Surveying midcentury media, he saw not an era of objective neutrality but a time "when only liberal voices were to be heard." He shared that perspective with the other conservative luminaries he had joined to celebrate the *Manion Forum*'s 1,000th broadcast. The weekly conservative radio program had been on the air since 1954, part of a network of conservative media outlets constructed in the postwar era. Spurred by a belief that mainstream journalism was not objective but intractably biased in favor of liberalism, these media activists sought to counter that bias with their own institutions, creating small, interlocking fields: conservative book publishing, conservative magazines and journals, and conservative broadcasting. So extensive were their efforts that by the end of the 1950s it was possible to talk about conservative media as a cohesive concept.

The modern conservative media establishment was a midcentury innovation, and the objectivity paradigm it was developed to combat was not much older. In the late eighteenth and early nineteenth centuries the United States, like Britain and many European nations, had an explicitly partisan press. Commercial incentives sometimes led papers to tamp down their overt partisanship in the late nineteenth century, but it was not entirely clear what, if anything, would replace the partisan model. Two alternatives emerged at the turn of the twentieth century: muckraking journalism and objective journalism. As advocacy journalists, muckrakers believed in the press's potential for social and political reform. They not only sought to expose corruption within the American political and economic systems, but pressed for a particular type of reform, usually requiring more federal oversight and regulation.

The muckrakers' advocacy journalism marked one of the new directions for news in the waning years of the 1800s, the strand from which founders of conservative media would draw. The other major development of the era came in direct response to tabloid-style journalism. In 1896, Adolph Ochs bought the *New York Times*. In order to differentiate the struggling newspaper from its more popular counterparts, he dedicated it to objective reporting. While the word "objectivity" wouldn't come into common use until the 1920s, its hallmarks—"accuracy, fairness, impartiality, independence, and responsibility to the public welfare"—were present in the *Times*'s reporting from the start of Ochs's tenure.[2]

As journalism professionalized in the first half of the twentieth century, those qualities of objectivity became central to newspaper, and later to radio and television, reporting. Reportage, analysis, and opinion became separate modes of journalistic writing, even migrating to different parts of the newspaper. It was in this era that the opinion and op-ed pages emerged. Papers were still known for their political leanings (often tied to the politics of their owners and publishers, a form known as "personal journalism"), but they were independent of political parties and, at least in theory, corralled their political preferences in the opinion section. The public appetite for political analysis gave rise, by the 1910s and 1920s, to in-house and syndicated columnists. This analysis was bylined, labeled, and generally confined to sections of the newspaper separate from reported pieces. Even as conventional just-the-facts reporting began to yield to more interpretive analysis, a process well under way by the end of the 1930s, interpretive journalism retained objective reporting's style: impersonal narration, an emphasis on fairness and accuracy, and deference to official sources and institutions. This objectivity standard defined mainstream newspaper reporting in the 1930s and 1940s.[3]

Objectivity defined not just a set of professional standards but a particular worldview rooted in factuality. The truth of reporting was best understood by its realism: How well did it conform to actual observable events? Moreover, journalists understood ideology as anathema to their work. Reporters interpreted facts and events, to be sure, but they were never to be driven by biases and partisanship, and they were expected to treat openly ideological agendas with suspicion. This set them apart from journals of opinion like *The Nation* and *The New Republic*, which were dedicated to advancing specific political agendas. There was still room for political debate in journalism, but in the 1940s and 1950s both the "sphere of consensus" and the "sphere of legitimate controversy," as Daniel Hallin famously labeled the zones of acceptable media coverage, were quite restricted, hemmed in both by anticommunism and by a bipartisan New Deal consensus.[4]

Early on, conservative activists advanced a different understanding of both media and knowledge, one that attacked the legitimacy of objectivity and substituted for it ideological integrity. Their doubts about objectivity came from a variety of sources. Some conservatives, like those who founded the newsweekly *Human Events* in 1944, came to doubt objectivity during World War II, when their opposition to American involvement pushed them to the outskirts of American political life. Others came around in the early 1950s, during the battles over McCarthyism, and still others during the civil rights movement, when journalists for northern and national newspapers betrayed sympathy for at least some of the aims of the black freedom struggle. Despite their varied origins, these critiques coalesced into cries of "liberal media bias," which disputed not just the content presented by mainstream journalists but also the claims they made about their journalistic practices. By the mid-1950s, belief in liberal media bias had becomes a constitutive part of modern conservatism.[5]

In their war on liberal media bias, conservative activists developed two main strategies. First, they created and promoted explicitly ideological media. In doing so, they provided their audiences—readers, listeners, and viewers—with an alternative to objectivity as a way of understanding the world: a different network of authorities, a different conception of fact and accuracy, a different set of values for evaluating truth claims. These values did not rest on impartiality; rather, they focused on the assumed biases of writers, editors, and publishers involved in any media enterprise. Media activists suggested to conservatives that they could discern the trustworthiness of the source by determining its ideological agenda rather than its track record of factuality and accuracy. Second, conservative media activists sought to expose the objectivity of mainstream media as a farce. Through anecdotal evidence, statistical studies, and media watchdog organizations, conservatives sought to convince Americans that objectivity was a mask mainstream media used to hide their own ideological agendas. These strategies combined, then, not only to offer a criticism of media practices, but to offer an alternative conservative epistemology, one that would remake the American media landscape by the end of the twentieth century.

Building Alternatives

"We might as well, as far as I'm concerned, get this off to a straight start. Objective reporting is nonexistent."

Fulton Lewis Jr. was in a playful mood. The panelists on his show, *Answers for Americans*, were considering the question, "How accurate is America's news?" William F. Buckley Jr., a practiced debater who had risen to national fame as author of a book on liberal bias at Yale, sat to his left, coiled and ready to strike. Arrayed against them were Charles Hodges, a journalist and professor of politics at New York University, and George Hamilton Combs, a New Deal Democrat and broadcast journalist. When Combs allowed there *was* bias in the media—bias against Democrats due to "a preponderantly, in fact almost an exclusively, Republican press"—Lewis laughed. "Oh, that breaks my heart!"

Buckley was far more focused. "Mr. Combs doesn't realize the extent to which he and people of his thinking run this country. The victory that has been won by Mr. Combs and by the liberals in this country has been so complete that people who want a genuine difference of opinion between the Republican party and the Democratic party are simply laughed off as extreme right-wingers." Liberals, Buckley contended, ran everything: the media, the universities, the political parties. Their control was so complete that it had become invisible. And worst of all, this happened with the public's consent. "The American people have become apathetic, supine, bored—with the result," Buckley concluded, "that outrage can be committed by the press or by the radio or by the intellectuals. They just don't care."[6]

When he launched *National Review* six months later, Buckley did so with the intention of making people care. He joined a group of media activists committed not just to capturing political power but to remaking American media. They founded their new enterprises on a critique of objectivity, yet could not quite give up the cultural power of the idea. Thus at the heart of conservative media was a tension between objectivity and ideology still present today. But that internal tension paled in comparison with the external one created by their alternative reading of mainstream media's hidden ideology. Believing established media were biased toward liberalism, conservatives viewed their own openly partisan media as a force of balance rather than a source of controversy. This led them into open battle with government regulators by the early 1960s, making it clear that for conservative media to truly flourish, public trust in objective media would first have to be dismantled.

*   *   *

Conservative media activism was born in opposition to mainstream journalism and its claims to objectivity. "I become increasingly impressed," book publisher Henry Regnery confessed to Buckley, "by the extent to which the liberals control the communication of ideas in this country which gives them, of course, rather complete control of just about everything else." Regnery was expressing a deep faith in the power of media: control the communication of ideas, he believed, and you would control the country. Believing conservatives should exercise that control, Regnery and others on the right constructed media institutions shaped by their assumptions about the power of the liberal media establishment.[7]

For instance, when Regnery founded his publishing company in late 1947, he structured it as a nonprofit organization. He argued that because he was issuing books that cut against "the reigning intellectual orthodoxy," he would have a tough time penetrating bookstores and reaching book buyers. And indeed, his first three books, works of revisionist history critical of Allied treatment of Germany and of the postwar order, did not sell well. But Regnery seemed not to mind. He chose the nonprofit model, he later wrote, "not because I had any ideological objection to profits, but because, as it seemed to me then and does still, in matters of excellence the market is a poor judge. The books that are most needed are often precisely those that will have only a modest sale." Markets could tell what people liked, but not what they needed. It was a much different philosophy than "the marketplace of ideas," which presumed that in an unrestricted system, the worthiness of ideas could be assessed by the number of adherents they attracted. As unprofitable as most early conservative media ventures were, Regnery's was a shared faith, though in tension with the free-market ideology to which most on the right adhered. (To Regnery's dismay, the IRS ruled the company was not entitled to tax-exempt status, since publishers welcomed profits even if they did not always find them.)[8]

In 1955, *National Review* emerged with a similar aversion to the marketplace's judgment and a similar critique of American media. Like Regnery, Buckley made clear from the start that he believed strongly in the ability of media to alter the political landscape. When he first proposed the magazine, he argued that it would "forthrightly oppose the prevailing trend of public opinion," but more importantly that "its purpose, indeed, is to *change* the nation's intellectual and political climate." Such a purpose contained an optimistic faith in the power of media to remake, rather than just reflect, public opinion.[9]

In the magazine's statement of intentions, Buckley further developed his view of American media and its effect on politics. Skewering the liberal conformity of the era—"Middle-of-the-road, *qua* Middle of the Road, is politically, intellectually, and morally repugnant," he wrote—Buckley laid the blame directly on the press. In introducing his project, he acknowledged that *National Review* would enter the world as "a minority voice." Yet he ascribed the minority status of conservative politics to the willful practices of liberal media. "America's 'respectable' press has ordained that such voices as ours are of the past, and are not worth serious attention. But," he rallied, "events in the very recent past positively establish that there is a widening gulf between the 'respectable' press and the American people, that they look upon each other, increasingly, as strangers." Enter *National Review*, a pugnacious journal of conservative opinion.[10]

Buckley saw *National Review* as a vehicle not only to strike back against liberalism in the press, but to uproot the "reprehensible journalistic trend

toward a genteel uniformity of opinion." As a natural contrarian, little
piqued Buckley's contempt as much as conformity. Derision dripped from
his descriptions of "that decadent, lukewarm mood of indifference which
permeates our Liberal press." Denouncing "sentimental uniformity," Buckley vowed his magazine would "never join that mutual-admiration society
of complacent American journalism," but would instead preside over "the
manly presentation of deeply felt conviction." Liberals might dominate the
press, but Buckley felt certain that once the battle was joined, committed and
virile conservatives would be well positioned for victory.[11]

Nor was *National Review* alone in dedicating a substantial portion of its
founding documents to attacking established media. A decade earlier, the
founders of *Human Events*, Felix Morley and Frank Hanighen, launched
their newsletter with a statement of policy that contained both their philosophy of politics and a critique of American journalism. Writing in 1944,
the founders charged that American journalists were shutting out alternative points of view, that they were "coloring, slanting, selecting and editing the news" in order to tamp down any criticisms of the war. Morley
argued that in trumpeting the official line doled out by government agencies,
journalists had played a role in the "subtle regimentation of public opinion."
Thus they dedicated themselves to "the reporting of facts that other newspapers overlook."[12]

This belief that established media echoed the official government line
spurred the founders of *Human Events* to start their own publication, one
dedicated to overlooked "facts." Yet while touting this fact-based approach,
the editors also promoted a distinct point of view. By the early 1960s, *Human
Events* arrived at this articulation of its mission: "In reporting the news,
Human Events is objective; it aims for accurate representation of the facts.
But it is *not* impartial. It looks at events through the eyes that are biased in
favor of limited constitutional government, local self-government, private
enterprise, and individual freedom." Distinguishing between objectivity
and impartiality, *Human Events* editors created a space where "bias" was an
appropriate journalistic value.[13]

The tension between those two ideas—between objectivity and ideology—
would become a defining feature of conservative media. On the one hand,
the editors insisted their work was objective. They understood the cultural
and political power of objectivity and were unwilling to relinquish all claims
to it. Yet they were also an ideological publication, dedicated to the propaga-
tion of conservative ideas. That contradiction was resolved—to the extent

it was resolved—in two ways. *Human Events* pledged to report, in a factual way, the stories and angles other media missed because of their liberal biases. In such news stories, selection, not content, would be biased. (*Human Events* also ran conservative columnists, opinion pieces, and analyses that made no pretense of content neutrality.) The editors also believed their ideological worldview was correct, and so they believed they did not need to sacrifice accuracy in order to be ideologically consistent. In other words, there was no contradiction to resolve.

As part of their belief that conservative media acted as a balance to liberal bias, media activists constructed their new outlets primarily as conservative-only spaces. They saw no reason to give airtime or print space to liberals. (This would shift some in the late 1960s with programs like Buckley's *Firing Line*, but the majority of right-wing media enterprises would remain conservative-only.) For instance, on his radio program, the *Manion Forum*, former Notre Dame law dean Clarence Manion clearly delineated his program as a liberal-free zone. "Every speaker over our network has been 100 per cent Right Wing," he told his audience in 1956, recapping the program's first two years of broadcasting. "You may rest assured, no Left Winger, no international Socialist, no One-Worlder, no Communist will ever be heard over the 110 stations of the Manion Forum network." Nor would those in the middle appear on the program. Not because, as Buckley believed, such a position was repugnant, but because it simply didn't exist. "No middle-of-the-roader will be heard—because there is no middle of the road. It is Constitutional government and states' rights—or slavery under Socialism, and then Communism."[14]

This view of conservative media as a counterbalance to liberal bias won considerable support within the conservative movement, where consumption of ideological media became a defining feature of the conservative identity. But it caused problems with those who didn't share this understanding of the media landscape—especially when those dissenters ran the Federal Communications Commission. Such was the source of conservative opposition to the Fairness Doctrine, the cause of a number of contentious battles with the FCC in the 1960s and 1970s.

The Fairness Doctrine, a regulatory requirement established in 1949, required broadcasters to cover controversial issues of "public importance" and present "both sides" of those issues. These requirements reflected the doctrine's twofold purpose. First, it was meant to guarantee important issues were covered—that is, that broadcasters didn't simply fill the airwaves with entertainment and commercial programming. Second, the FCC wanted to ensure that radio stations didn't become propaganda outlets for a particular viewpoint. So there was an affirmative obligation to cover controversy, as well as to provide multiple perspectives.

Beyond that purpose, however, there were no clear guidelines. A 1968 congressional report on the doctrine found that the central concept, controversial issues, "has not been defined in the statute or in any FCC regulation." Further, enforcement of the doctrine was "ad hoc" rather than following any "general rule or regulation." What counted as legitimate controversy? What counted as deviant and therefore unworthy of discussion? There were no set answers. For conservative broadcasters, whose programs were by definition controversial in an era of liberal consensus, the uncertainty and vagueness surrounding the doctrine fed their suspicions that it was a nefarious instrument of government suppression. In a newspaper column about the doctrine, Manion warned that only messages "approved by the Federal Government" would be heard on the air if the doctrine was fully implemented. "This is centralized censorship in its most reprehensible form."[15]

Nor were conservative broadcasters wrong to be wary of the FCC. The commission *did* have a bone to pick with them. Conservative media activists had repeatedly challenged the central assumptions the FCC made about journalism. The commissioners broadly accepted the journalistic assertion of objectivity. News reports, whether in print or on air, were assumed to be bias-free, unlike openly ideological programs like the *Manion Forum* or the *Dan Smoot Report*. Conservatives, of course, saw no such distinction between news reports and ideological broadcasting. As such, they understood right-wing broadcasts not as controversial anomalies in need of balance, but rather as answers to the slanted reporting that dominated every other sector of American media. For the right, fairness did not demand a liberal response to conservative broadcasters; conservative broadcasters *were* the response.[16]

The distance between the FCC and right-wing broadcasters widened even further thanks to another argument popular in conservative media: the values they broadcast were so broadly shared and so fundamentally American that to give voice to "the other side" meant giving voice to America's enemies. So Clarence Manion attacked Nikita Khrushchev and Fidel Castro—did he now have to make his program available to them for rebuttal? Dan Smoot spoke out against communism—did stations have to offer airtime to communists? Billy James Hargis, host of the conservative program

Christian Crusade, promoted Christianity and religious belief—did atheists thus deserve equal time?[17]

The FCC directly rebutted these interpretations in 1963 and 1964 notices to broadcasters. First, the agency made it clear that no station would have to give time to communists or atheists, as adherents to these views did not, in their judgment, meet the definition of "responsible groups." But neither could broadcasters hide behind labels of "anticommunism" and "Americanism" simply because the antitheses of these labels were "communism" and "anti-Americanism." There was, the agency held, significant room for disagreement on issues such as the best methods for fighting communism. Conservatives shot back with their contention that liberal anticommunism had more than enough spokespeople already.[18]

There were, then, core philosophical disagreements the FCC simply could not resolve, and that would remain the basis of conservative opposition to the Fairness Doctrine until it was abolished in 1987. Clashes with the FCC highlighted how important it was for conservatives not only to build alternative media outlets but also to dismantle public trust in the objectivity standards the FCC and established media worked so hard to defend. So long as Americans could view a network anchor like Walter Cronkite as the most trusted man in America, rather than as a mouthpiece of liberal propaganda, conservative media would remain a marginal presence.

But that was about to change.

Opposing Objectivity

On November 13, 1969, Vice President Spiro Agnew traveled to Iowa. Having recently made headlines by denouncing protestors calling for a moratorium in the war in Vietnam, he was in Iowa to deliver another barn-burner, this time focused on television news and public opinion. It began as an attack on instant analysis, the relatively new practice whereby newscasters, editorialists, and experts responded to speeches immediately after they occurred. President Richard Nixon loathed it. He believed instant analysis undermined his ability to control the administration's message. Two weeks before sending Agnew to Iowa, Nixon delivered a televised address on Vietnam and raged when stations cut to their studios afterward to question his claims and interview his critics. Fortunately, he had someone willing to hit back.[19]

Agnew easily stepped into the role of the administration's "bad cop," going after not just instant analysis but the entire news industry. A democratic society, he argued, could not function without an informed populace—a *well*-informed populace, not one misled by half-truths, obfuscation, and spin. Given that, Agnew questioned the wisdom of handing over so much influence to "a closed fraternity of privileged men, elected by no one." This select set of men, he argued, "perhaps no more than a dozen," determined the content of nightly news. In choosing the stories and writing the commentary, these anchors, producers, and pundits served up not objective analysis but the liberal pap of the New York–Washington echo chamber. And every night, forty million Americans tuned in, imbibing bias and mistaking it for neutrality.[20]

Like his moratorium speech, Agnew's Iowa diatribe grabbed headlines. Suddenly the question of media objectivity and liberal bias was part of the national conversation. Some in the media worried that it was the opening gambit in a crackdown on free speech. "My feeling is that the White House is out to get us," one CBS commentator fretted. "We're in for dangerous times." Others, though, cosigned Agnew's concerns. The editors at the *Washington Post* saw no signs of liberal conspiracy in news coverage, but they agreed that editorial news needed reevaluation. Tom Wicker, a reporter for the *New York Times*, delivered an address at the Massachusetts Historical Society in 1971 on the topic of journalistic objectivity. Though he dismissed Agnew as a "polyloquent pipsqueak," he agreed nonetheless that press values were problematic. "If I had been in Mr. Agnew's place and had been trying to make an intelligent, useful criticism of the American press, I would have said that its biggest weakness is its reliance on and its acceptance of official sources—precisely its 'objectivity' in presenting the news." Wicker called instead for journalists to take up the task of "journalistic muckraking," to "dedicate ourselves to the search for the meaning of things, and turn ourselves loose to be the true storytellers of our time, novelists of the age, rather than professional recorders of accumulated facts and authorized views." Support came from other unexpected quarters as well. Antiwar protesters, no great friends of Agnew, heartily approved of the view that the news was too controlled by establishment forces. Indeed, from the New Left would come a media critique to rival the conservative one, finding a mainstream voice in works like Edward S. Herman and Noam Chomsky's *Manufacturing Consent*, their 1988 book on the political economy of mass media.[21]

Objectivity was under attack from all sides. Yet it was conservative media activists who made the most of the bias charges. They didn't just laud Agnew—they loved him. They turned him into a touchstone, proof that theirs was a legitimate grievance. Six weeks after the speech, James J. Finnegan, chief editor for the *Manchester Union-Leader*, appeared on the *Manion Forum* to back up Agnew's claims. Conservative media, he argued, were "the only force standing between the liberal news media and the total monopolization of all news information available to the American people." A few months later, *Parade* magazine publisher Red Motley joined Manion to praise Agnew's indictment as "timely, and proper." And when it came time for the *Forum* to fund-raise in 1970, Agnew was front and center, symbolizing the call to balance established media's liberal tilt.[22]

Accolades for Agnew echoed through conservative media. Bill Rusher, the publisher of *National Review* who soon became friends with the vice president, described him as "a thoughtful, decent man" whose conservatism continued to develop while in office. His speeches provided regular content for *Human Events*, and his portrait graced the newsweekly's ads next to the question "How Much News Is Being Withheld from You?" So popular was the vice president in their offices that *Human Events* released five of his recordings as part of their Audio-Forum. (Audio-Forum recordings were classed by topic: conservative classics, politics, communism, foreign policy, economics—and Spiro Agnew, who rated his own category as a conservative field of study.) Less than a year after Agnew caught the right's attention with his Iowa speech, conservative publisher Arlington House released *The Enemies He Has Made: The Media vs. Spiro Agnew* (a book destined to reside on bookshelves next to a *Human Events* promotional offering, *Agnew: Profile in Conflict*).[23]

When it came to media bias, Agnew made the charge, but it was up to conservative media to make the case. At first they offered only anecdotal evidence, like an eleven-item list of liberal media infractions James Finnegan offered *Manion Forum* listeners. But soon they developed a more systematic approach. Hard numbers, rigorous tallying, percentages, and tables and charts: How better to prove liberal bias was not a figment of the paranoid conservative mind but an irrefutable fact?

One of the earliest efforts to provide support came from the Committee to Combat Bias in Broadcasting, an offshoot of the American Conservative Union. Inspired by Agnew, the committee set up a program designed to monitor television broadcasts for bias. In an effort to bring grassroots conservatives into their efforts (a way of keeping activists active between elections), the committee sent out letters from *Human Events* publisher Tom Winter along with Media Watch Monitoring cards. Want to expose liberal bias? Just rate the listed news commentators as "presents news accurately and objectively," "tends to be liberal in his presentation," or "goes all out to distort facts and to discredit conservatives." (Note the committee didn't expect their watchmen to find conservative bias in the nightly news broadcasts.)[24]

The heavy lifting, though, fell to Edith Efron, a writer for *TV Guide*. Efron had caught media activists' attention in 1964 with an article criticizing the Fairness Doctrine. A former student of John Chamberlain at Columbia University's School of Journalism, she leapt into the media bias fight soon after Agnew's speech. Her article "There *Is* Network News Bias" first ran in *TV Guide* and then in *Human Events* two weeks later. For the piece, she interviewed Howard K. Smith, the self-proclaimed "left-of-center" ABC News anchor. Smith turned out to be the perfect subject. Though far across the political spectrum from Efron, he too believed journalists wore liberal shades that blinded them to improvements in the South, military successes in Vietnam, and the appeal of conservatives and Middle America. If even a leftist could see it, Efron reasoned, liberal bias must be real.[25]

Efron remained interested in the subject of media bias long after the Smith interview, and in 1968 she determined to make a more systematic study of it. She set about analyzing election coverage from September 16 through Election Day. Armed with thousands of hours of videotape and a grant from the Historical Research Fund (of which Buckley happened to be the Projects Chair), she plucked out a hundred thousand words on Nixon and Humphrey from each of the Big Three's nightly newscasts.

Then she started counting.

For and against: tick, tick, tick, until Efron had tallied every favorable and unfavorable word spoken about the candidates. Crunching the numbers, she found about half of all words spoken about Humphrey were positive. For Nixon? A paltry 8.7 percent. No wonder she concluded that network news followed "the elitist-liberal-left line in all controversies."[26]

In the lead-up to the book's publication, Efron turned to Buckley and the network of right-wing media to get out the word about her work. She laid out a seven-item plan to use *National Review* and its stable of writers to advertise *The News Twisters*. For the magazine: "some splendid outburst" in September. For Buckley himself: a syndicated column, a book blurb, and an episode of his television show *Firing Line*. For Rusher: a debate on *his* television show, *The Advocates*. For the Conservative Book Club: selection of the month. Even James Buckley, then the Conservative Party senator for New York, got a request: "Would you ask your brother-of-the-exquisite-dimples to walk around Washington . . . ostentatiously clutching a copy of my book?" Buckley happily forwarded the letter along to his colleagues, encouraging them to add in their ideas. *National Review* would, of course, make "a special splash" when the book came out. "But," he added, "this is too good to preempt just for ourselves."[27]

Conservative media weren't the only ones interested in making sure Efron's book made a splash. The White House instantly understood the importance of a book that broke down, in hard numbers, the extent to which the media were biased against the administration. After all, as John Chamberlain wrote in *National Review*, the book was science, not art. The charges of liberal bias were more than just "Mrs. Efron's say-so"—her quantitative tabulation proved her point. Such evidence (no matter how questionable the methodology might have been) appealed powerfully to Nixon. So he ordered Special Counsel Charles Colson to get the book on the *New York Times* best-sellers list. Not an easy feat, but Colson, who had a nose for gaming the system, figured it out. He ferreted out which stores' sales were used to determine the list, and bought up every copy they had. For years Nixon staffers stumbled upon boxes crammed full of *The News Twisters*. But it worked: Efron's book became an official *New York Times* best-seller.[28]

Statistics were part of the right's attempt to bring the media bias argument to a broader audience; the development of media watchdog groups was another. Conservatives sought to police mainstream media outlets in order both to provide evidence of bias and to "play the refs," to convince mainstream media outlets that they were unfairly excluding conservative viewpoints. In 1969, Reed Irvine founded Accuracy in Media for just this purpose. Outraged at media coverage of the 1968 Democratic convention that he felt favored the protesters, Irvine, an economist with the Federal Reserve, established Accuracy in Media as a watchdog organization that would "investigate complaints, take proven cases to top media officials, seek corrections and mobilize public pressure to bring about remedial action" on behalf of "the consumers of the journalistic product and not the producers." The name was important: Accuracy in Media. It betrayed no ideological bent, reflecting instead a core value of objective journalism. As Irvine told Manion, "We felt that since the journalists all profess devotion to accuracy, we would be able to work wonders by simply pointing out to them cases in which they were inaccurate." But soon AIM was filing Fairness Doctrine complaints against programs they felt were "one-sided and biased."[29]

The use of Fairness Doctrine complaints was relatively new for conservative media activists, who during the 1950s and 1960s had their hearts set on repealing the doctrine. AIM advocated that conservatives instead use the doctrine against nonconservative broadcasters, publicizing their lack of balance. In his appearance on the *Manion Forum* in 1975, Irvine explained how to register a complaint, including the address of the FCC. He also updated *Forum* listeners on a Fairness Doctrine complaint the group had leveled against ABC, in which the FCC had agreed that the doctrine had been violated before being overturned by an appeals court. This use of the Fairness Doctrine reflected an understanding that the FCC was an ideological institution, one that, with Nixon in the White House, could be used effectively by conservatives. At the time, that was their only option. The Nixon administration strongly opposed the repeal of the Fairness Doctrine, seeing in it a powerful tool for managing the press.[30]

Initially Irvine used direct mail, letters to the editor, and Fairness Doctrine complaints to call attention to what he saw as biased reporting. As its budget grew, exploding to $1.1 million in 1981 from $5,000 a decade earlier, AIM would be able to engage in major campaigns. But even on a shoestring budget it had an impact. In 1971 it organized against *The Selling of the Pentagon*, a CBS documentary on the military's public relations tactics that led to conflict between the White House and the network. Agnew delivered a lengthy diatribe against the documentary, denouncing it as "a subtle but vicious broadside against the nation's defense establishment." Meanwhile, Chuck Colson pushed for an equal-time response from the administration to combat the documentary. Irvine joined that battle, detailing the documentary's inaccuracies in a seven-page report and explaining the controversy to conservatives in *National Review*.[31]

AIM and the Nixon administration were ideologically aligned on issues of media bias, but their ties did not end there. As historian Chad Raphael detailed in his book *Investigated Reporting*, "the White House helped expand the group's funding and coordinated many attacks on media bias with AIM." Colson in particular saw AIM as a helpmate for the administration's media-bias battle. When the Nixon administration put together a plan to scale back the Public Broadcasting System, Colson urged the use of AIM to funnel FCC complaints about the broadcaster. Colson worked behind the scenes to get big-name board members, advertisers, and funding for the organization. The appeal of AIM was, as one Nixon aide put it, its usefulness as "a mechanism under which private non-governmental pressures can be brought to bear on the three networks."[32]

AIM also found a champion in Clarence Manion, who hosted Reed Irvine on his show and regularly touted the *AIM Report*, the group's newsletter, and its investigations. In a 1975 "Footnote" (one of the *Forum*'s five-minute radio snippets), Manion displayed how effective the many organizations and activists working on media bias could be in creating a self-referential realm of information and authority. Edith Efron, writing for *TV Guide*, penned an article on the anti-American biases of TV news. The *AIM Report* publicized Efron's conclusions, then added its own evidence of TV news bias—all of which Manion presented to his audience. Thus, three centers of authority—Efron, AIM, and Manion—worked together to disseminate and legitimize a conservative interpretation of biased news. Manion continued to burnish Irvine's reputation as a defender of "true, accurate and unbiased reporting" throughout the 1970s.[33]

AIM was not the only media-watchdog organization of the 1970s. The National News Council, founded in 1973, was a mainstream organization intended to investigate complaints against the media (and to forestall greater government regulation). Populated mostly by liberals, the NNC board invited Bill Rusher to join in order to provide some ideological balance. The existence of the NNC came, Executive Director William B. Arthur said, at a time when the country was undergoing "a degree of self-examination and self-criticism on the part of the media without precedent in our nation's history." Wary of government interference with the press, Arthur argued that American journalism needed an independent body that could shore up public confidence in the news without inviting government regulatory bodies into the debate. Yet a number of outlets, most notably the *New York Times*, refused to deal with the NNC, limiting its effectiveness and ultimately leading it to shutter operations in the early 1980s.[34]

Nonideological watchdogs like the NNC were the exception. Much more common were groups like the Foundation for Objective News Reporting, established in 1975. Tom Winter of *Human Events* served as the chair; conservative journalist Stan Evans and *Human Events* editor Allan Ryskind sat on the board. Like AIM, FONR was an ideological organization that emphasized objectivity in reporting, acting as the guardian of fairness. Both groups did so not because they believed conservatives should be objective, but because they believed mainstream media, having proclaimed themselves to be objective, had to be held to that standard—or else be exposed for the liberal media that conservatives were convinced they were. Though their work was conceived in opposition to the notion of objective journalism, conservative media activists found objectivity remained a vital conceptual tool for undermining mainstream media.[35]

*   *   *

In the wake of Agnew's speech and conservative efforts to discredit media objectivity, conservatives sensed a climate change in American media. Manion pointed to the 1971 launch of *Spectrum*, a sort of op-ed page for the CBS morning news. Debuting first on radio, the show trotted out commentators, many of them conservative, to offer news analysis. With the right-wing viewpoint now prominently featured on national television, *Spectrum* constituted "the greatest boon to our cause that has ever happened on 'air.'" And it wasn't the only place conservatives were popping up. Elsewhere on CBS, *60 Minutes* pitted conservative columnist James J. Kilpatrick against liberal Nicholas von Hoffman in a regular segment called "Point/Counterpoint." These shows joined Buckley's *Firing Line*, which first went on air in 1966, and Rusher's debate show *The Advocates*, conservative-centered programs that highlighted and legitimated the conservative perspective. Kilpatrick mused that "a great sea change came over my friends in New York" after Agnew's speech. "And all of a sudden they began to think, my gracious there is another point of view in this country after all . . . and maybe it ought to be heard on our networks."[36]

That impulse toward ideological balance grew throughout the 1970s. The elimination of the Fairness Doctrine in 1987 removed the regulatory requirements for editorial fairness and balance, but it did not weaken the power of those claims. "Balance" still carried the promise of objectivity, or at least journalistic integrity. A claim to balance was a claim to credibility—which is not to say that conservatives were happy with the new balance promoted by the networks and cable news channels like CNN. Invariably, they felt, conservative pundits were outnumbered by liberals or treated as outsiders, labeled as right-wingers while the liberals were treated as politically neutral.[37]

Fox News Channel, which went live in 1996, offered an alternative. The new channel was neither exclusively nor explicitly conservative, though it would evolve in that direction over time. Instead, the channel carried the tagline "Fair and Balanced," a phrase capacious enough to contain the ambiguities still unresolved after decades of conservative media activism. On the one hand, it proclaimed a devotion to some of objectivity's central values: fairness and evenhandedness. "We report, you decide," as another Fox News slogan declared. Yet there was a second, contradictory meaning behind "fair and balanced": As an explicitly conservative network, Fox News balanced the liberal bias of established media. Like *Human Events* before it, Fox News thus carved out a space to be both objective and biased, arguing that it should be trusted because it was right, and because it was right-wing. Thanks to the efforts of conservative media activists over the past half century, both in building an audience for conservative media and in challenging the trustworthiness of established media, not only has that formula brought Fox News substantial profits and loyal audiences—it has helped remake American news media.

CHAPTER 9

Abe Rosenthal's Project X: The Editorial Process Leading to Publication of the Pentagon Papers

Kevin Lerner

In late January of 1971, A. M. Rosenthal, the editor of the *New York Times*, began keeping a journal. The timing of Rosenthal's journal-keeping was serendipitous, since the spring and summer of 1971 would present Rosenthal with the chance for his newspaper to publish a potentially cataclysmic set of government documents that had come into the possession of one of the paper's Washington reporters. Large parts of the story of the publication of what came to be known as the Pentagon Papers have been told before. Daniel Ellsberg, the government contractor and military historian who gave the *Times* access to the 7,000 pages of the classified report, told his story in a memoir, which focuses on smuggling the papers out of his office and on the political change that Ellsberg hoped would come from their release.[1] Neil Sheehan, the *Times* Washington reporter and former Vietnam correspondent whom Ellsberg entrusted with access to the papers, has never publicly talked about the process of obtaining the papers, saying only that he obtained them.[2] Besides the cloak-and-dagger story of Ellsberg, histories of the Pentagon Papers incident tend to focus on the legal wrangling that resulted in a Supreme Court victory for the *New York Times*.[3] This is somewhat ironic, given that legal historians tend to see the *New York Times Company v. United States* decision not as a great precedent-setting decision for freedom of the press, but rather as "a First Amendment fizzle."[4] The Supreme Court did decide in favor of the newspapers, but the decision was limited in scope to the case at hand. Future newspapers seeking to publish classified information have no basis in the decision for determining whether or not their stories would be similarly protected.

The Rosenthal journals do not contradict the main thrust of the story as it has been told. But they do add depth and insight into the decision-making processes of Abe Rosenthal as a fundamentally cautious, pro-institutional editor seeking to maintain a down-the-middle approach for his paper. The Pentagon Papers troubled Rosenthal, and the editorial decisions that led to the eventual presentation of the stories have affected how the papers were received. Abe Rosenthal, faced with his own somewhat conservative beliefs and that down-the-middle attitude, served as the fulcrum between a rabidly aggressive editorial team (Sheehan, Max Frankel, Scotty Reston) and a thoroughly skeptical publisher. Rosenthal knew that any doubt he expressed to Arthur Sulzberger would give the publisher the opening he needed to scuttle the publication of the papers, but he also knew that publication would rile the Nixon administration and cast a negative light on the Kennedy and Johnson administrations, with which the *Times* had had a close relationship. The paper would be rocking the establishment at a time when it still thought of itself as a part of the establishment. In the end, Rosenthal's sense of a story prevailed, and he held firm in support of the Washington bureau and his top editors, persuading Sulzberger to defy his newspaper's law firm, no matter what the consequences. Rosenthal, for reasons both noble and selfish, had to make the case to publish, and in doing so, he began the paper's shift to the left.

Rosenthal and the Counterculture

The *New York Times* of 1971 was still very much the Gray Lady, a smart but conservative paper—conservative in the sense that it was slow to change and dedicated to principles of fairness that made the editorial stance of the paper as frustrating to the left as it was to the right. The paper covered the news, and was reluctant to make news itself. This was not a paper that was particularly interested in rocking the boat, and its editor was the conscience for the news staff of the paper.

But the leadership of the paper was also quite politically conservative. Harrison Salisbury, who was then an associate editor at the paper, and who would go on to be the founding editor of the op-ed page, recalled the politics of the paper's executives and top editors in his 1980 memoir. The publishers, he wrote, were at best traditional southern Democrats, comparable to middle-of-the-road conservative Republicans.[5] None of the editors could "have won a prize in a flaming liberal contest" either, he wrote. Scotty Reston was "an essentially conservative man who grew steadily more conservative as the years passed," and despite being "the darling of liberal professors and do-good elements," he was "the amanuensis of the Establishment," counting Henry Kissinger among his most trusted sources. Salisbury describes Washington bureau chief Max Frankel as an establishment man, too, an immigrant who did not want to rile the country that had welcomed his family.[6] Abe Rosenthal was similarly a European Jewish emigrant, and while his family and educational background might have pegged him for a "typically radical Jewish emigrant" like his family, he was in fact "the most conservative editor on the paper."[7] According to Salisbury, Rosenthal chafed at the counterculture, and positioned himself "firmly against what he saw as shapeless anarchy swirling up from the streets."[8]

Rosenthal had the political left on his mind when he began keeping his journal. In its first pages, after noting the funeral of a friend, he confesses that something else had been on his mind, "and perhaps more the reason that I am writing this journal than Manny's death: the incessant attacks on The Times from the left and the liberal community."[9] He writes that attacks from the right have never bothered him, since he expects that conservatives have never liked what the paper was trying to do. Attacks from the far left never bothered him either. But now—as he perceived it—those attacks had begun to infect the leaders of the center-left, and he found those to be particularly stinging. He even admits in the journal that he sees attacks on the *Times* as attacks on him personally, since he identified so much with the paper. The radical left had become an institution in itself, and was seeking to destroy the establishment left, including the *Times*, which Rosenthal suggests would be the second institution to be taken down if there were a real revolution in the United States. The previous week, the press writer and critic Edwin Diamond had written a piece for *New York* magazine that called the *New York Post* a better newspaper than the *Times*. "The man knows better," Rosenthal wrote: "But he is so seized with hatred—of The Times, of me, and probably of himself—that he twists, distorts, omits and prostitutes himself.

The Newfields and the Hentoffs and the Powledges and Halberstams—all of whom could not live without The Times—are filled with hatred. Why?"

Jack Newfield, Nat Hentoff, Fred Powledge, and David Halberstam were all vocal critics of the *Times* (some of whom had worked there) in a period when a younger generation of reporters had entered the newsroom with university educations and a generational identification with the counterculture, and these younger reporters found themselves stifled by the sort of dry objectivity that a paper like the *Times* required of them. There was sex appeal in attacking the *Times* because of its power, Rosenthal wrote. "You get attention when you attack The Times. There is also an enormous amount of penis envy involved." Presumably he meant something about measuring manhood, not the more Freudian connotations of that term.

For Rosenthal, the key to publishing a paper like the *Times* was to maintain a sense of decorum. The *Times*, he wrote, had to stand for "honest values as we see them." The antiestablishment left had begun to take on a tone that Rosenthal found antithetical to the reasoned tone of discourse that he felt was necessary for the proper conduct of public affairs. "When a society does that," he wrote, "it destroys itself." But the *Times* men he supervised would strive to tamp down their own human impulses: "We try to create in The Times something better than ourselves."[10]

The Meeting in Scotty's Office

In 1971, Abe Rosenthal both was and was not the top editor at the *New York Times*. He held the title of managing editor instead of executive editor, but there was no executive editor serving above him. James "Scotty" Reston had been the exec from 1968 to 1969, but he had never really left, taking on the title of vice president of news operations and serving as a sort of buffer between Rosenthal and Sulzberger, the publisher, who had not quite decided to trust Rosenthal with complete command of the paper. James Goodale, who in 1971 was a young chief counsel for the *Times*, described Rosenthal as being "in purgatory of sorts" until Sulzberger could decide whether or not he trusted the irascible Rosenthal.[11]

Rosenthal first heard of the existence of the Pentagon Papers in a roundabout way. Neil Sheehan, who has never named his source, got access to them from Daniel Ellsberg, the military historian who had been trying to get attention for the documents for some time. Ellsberg approached Sheehan, a reporter in the *Times* Washington bureau, because Sheehan had covered the war more skeptically than many other reporters, and may even have worked with Ellsberg before, with the historian as a confidential source.[12] What is clear, however, is that Sheehan did not immediately tell Rosenthal, the managing editor, about the trove. He did not even go directly to his bureau chief, Max Frankel, with whom he had had some disputes in the past.[13] Frankel felt that Sheehan was equal parts tenacious and dawdling.[14] Eventually, though, once Frankel had found out about the papers, Rosenthal had to know too, since he was running the paper. However, neither Sheehan, Reston, nor Frankel brought them up with Rosenthal directly. Instead, word leaked from Ivan Veit, a vice president at the *Times*, who had found out about the papers because Ellsberg had suggested getting the newspaper's book publishing imprint, Times Books, involved.

Max Frankel recalls getting a panicked phone call from Rosenthal when he found out about the papers. "What's all this about? What's going on? What's Ivan Veit got to do with the news? What the hell is Reston up to now?" Frankel remembers him asking.[15] Rosenthal wrote in his journal that Veit had casually mentioned some kind of book project to him, and that it was a couple of days later that he finally called Frankel to ask about what was going on.[16] But Frankel and Rosenthal's accounts agree that there was not much that could be said on the phone, given the paranoid atmosphere in Washington. Sheehan and Frankel both suspected that the *Times* Washington bureau might have been bugged by the government.

So Frankel brought documents—which Sheehan had obtained from a source other than Ellsberg, apparently—to New York to show them to Rosenthal and two other editors: James Greenfield, the foreign affairs editor, and Seymour Topping, who was assistant managing editor. These documents appeared to be genuine, and if they were a small part of Ellsberg's archive, they would constitute a major story. Sheehan set about obtaining the documents from Ellsberg in an often-told story that had Sheehan coming and going from Ellsberg's Boston-area apartment to read the documents, possibly with a tacit understanding that he would be allowed to ferry them to a copy shop in order to produce his own collection. Sheehan finally gained access to the documents in mid- to late March.

Topping called a meeting to be held in Scotty Reston's office for 11:00 a.m. on Wednesday, April 21. Max Frankel and Neil Sheehan had brought the photocopied Pentagon Papers to New York and "The Washington proj-

ect" had "reached a point where decisions must be made."[17] In Reston's office, the editorial team met to discuss how to approach the story. They met
without Sulzberger, but James Goodale, the in-house counsel, was present to
advise them.[18] Goodale had come to understand his role at the paper as a facilitator whose brief was not to tell Rosenthal whether or not he could publish, but rather *how* he could publish.[19] This was in stark contrast to the role
of Lord, Day & Lord, the external firm that counseled "Punch" Sulzberger
not to publish at all.

The first reference to the Pentagon Papers in Rosenthal's journals came
on April 23, 1971, about a month after Sheehan obtained the papers. Apparently unable to control his emotions about the project that his editors and
writers were working on, he noted that the *Times* was "involved in one of the
biggest, most voluminous and probably one of the saddest and most damaging stories it has ever confronted journalistically." That phrase "saddest and
most damaging" hints at his own feelings, and he would expand on his reasoning and his emotions in his journal again, after the publication of the
Pentagon Papers. But his newsman's instinct also shows through, and appears to win out, even as early in the process as late April. Rosenthal might
be expected to be most worried about breaking the law by publishing the
papers, but this seems to be almost the least of his worries. He acknowledged
that the documents "are of the highest degree of government security classification," but having worked as a reporter and editor covering government
affairs, he had realized, as many other reporters had, that government officials often use the classification system to hide embarrassing details rather
than to protect true national security secrets. He had no qualms about publishing for that reason: "I do not really feel that we have a moral dilemma
here. I believe that the public's right to know what took place is of a far higher
order of priority than the protection of the reputation of the statesmen and
politicians involved."[20] Then, despite noting the need to maintain the secrecy
of the files and of the people working on them, he goes on to describe the
"vast collection of documentation relating to the decision and conduct of the
war" and the team that had been assembled to parse it. He names the members of the early working group explicitly, and says that he and Seymour
Topping would oversee it more directly in its last stages. He also notes that the
team was working not in the 43rd Street offices of the *Times*, but in "a New
York hotel." That was a three-room suite at the New York Hilton, the largest
hotel in New York City, big enough to hide a team of reporters and editors

working on a momentous study among the conventioneers and tourists. Rosenthal called it "Project X."

The Editorial Policy Takes Shape

Rosenthal did not mention the Pentagon Papers again in his journal until June 13 (though he did bind in a few memos that had been sent in the office). Two days later, on the night of the 15th, Rosenthal could finally catch his breath again and reflect on what had happened over the course of three days of publication. That day, the Nixon administration had succeeded in winning a temporary injunction against the *Times*, so the mad rush to get the Pentagon Papers into print had to end, at least until the Supreme Court would rule two weeks later. That night Rosenthal dictated ten single-spaced pages of memoirs about the previous night. This represents the most direct, contemporaneous account of what happened in the newsroom during the first fevered days of publication, reaction, and legal action.[21] In July he returned to his journal to detail the process leading up to those first days of publication.

From the beginning, Rosenthal realized just how important the handling of the Pentagon Papers would be to the *New York Times* and for the country. "Just about everything important to all of us involved was wrapped up in the decision to publish the Pentagon Papers—and the decision as to how to publish them. And just about everything important was at stake."[22] The huge bundle of papers—and they literally came to New York tied in a bundle, with string—challenged the very core of Rosenthal's pro-institutional, pro-stability worldview. In his July journal, Rosenthal ruminated on his loyalty to the *Times* and the risk that publishing the Pentagon Papers might damage or even destroy the paper: "What was the true meaning of loyalty? Loyalty to an institution—did it lie in trying to protect the institution from trouble, or insisting on exposing its troubles in the belief that unless it faced the trouble and overcome it, it would become a second-rate institution?"[23] But the *Times* was not the only institution that might be damaged by publication. The reputation of the entire nation was at stake, and this caused Rosenthal to worry even more than protecting the paper. He wondered if loyalty to country lay in "adhering to a set of long accepted rules and laws, designed not only to protect politicians in general but, to the minds of many, to protect the country itself? Or did it lie in facing a decision to break those rules and laws?"[24] Rosenthal, Sulzberger, and the editorial team decided that risking damage to an institution would, in the end, make the institution stronger. It was a principle rooted in the First Amendment, which principled newspaper people hold even stronger than their personal political beliefs.

One topic that never bothered Rosenthal was the issue of breaking the classification of the documents. "As a matter of fact, it bothered damn few newspapermen,"[25] he wrote. Rosenthal knew that reporters would often come into the possession of documents that were nominally classified, but that had been leaked to them by government officials for political purposes. The magnitude was different for the Pentagon Papers, but that seemed to give Rosenthal fewer qualms than his anti-institutional concerns.

One of these concerns seems implausible and amusing in retrospect, but also speaks to Rosenthal's fear of attacks from the left. In his journal, he writes of fears that the 7,000 pages of documents were faked, an elaborate hoax to fool the *Times* into publishing a ridiculous report on faked government malfeasance. Who could have had the resources to fake such a voluminous study? Maybe, Rosenthal mused, it was a group of members of Students for a Democratic Society who got together and concocted the whole thing. He wrote about the fears in his Westport journal, but recalled them several years later. In a 1975 memo to Charlotte Curtis, a *Times* editor, Rosenthal responded to what must have been similar concerns—perhaps joking concerns given how late they came: "'Listen, the greatest nightmare I had when I first saw the Pentagon Papers was that they were written by a thousand SDS kids in some loft at Harvard. You know—one of them would say—I'll be McNamara and you be the Chairman of the Joint Chiefs.' But believe me, they're real, they're real, they're real."[26] The SDS hypothesis seems to have legitimately troubled Rosenthal, and given his concerns about the radical left and the high educational attainment of many SDS members (hence the Harvard reference), perhaps this was a plausible origin story for the papers. It did not take him long to see all of the internal connections, though, and Sheehan and Frankel assured him that the papers jibed with other government documents that they had seen in the course of reporting on the war. Rosenthal came out of the meeting in Reston's office convinced that they were genuine.

At the meeting in Reston's office, Rosenthal began to shape the editorial approach to the documents that Sheehan and Frankel had been working with: "I insisted—and there was no objection—that what we had to do was to stick to the story of the Pentagon study itself. I said that there had been hundreds of books and series written about the war from the viewpoint of various individuals or publications. This was not what we were doing, this was not what we had in hand. What we had was something quite unique—the Pentagon's own version of the war—or at least the study made within the Pentagon by Pentagon experts. I said that in every single story, this is what we should tell."[27]

This became Rosenthal's guiding principle for shaping the editing of the papers, and this principle is largely responsible for the memory of the Pentagon Papers that we have today. First: this had to be the government's own story. Rosenthal believed that was what made this a story. In other words, the papers themselves had to be the story, not just a major new source for a new history of the war. That would come, Rosenthal thought, but the discovery of the papers themselves and the story they had to tell would be the focus of the *Times* report. To that end, Rosenthal forbade his editors and writers to add too much context or weave together the threads into a new tapestry. The *Times* would be presenting the raw materials, as much as possible. This turned out to be more difficult than Rosenthal expected: "There were not whole neat sections that we could simply print and say this is the Pentagon study. Furthermore, one section of the study was not necessarily related in the knowledge of the author to another section. Therefore the reporters had to face a momentous job—not faced even by the authors of the study themselves—of mastering the entire study. . . . They also had to master the public record as against the private record and we had a chronology drawn up for that purpose."[28] Rosenthal used two different metaphors to describe the process. One was a jigsaw puzzle, the other a tapestry. Journalists, he wrote, were conditioned by their work to weave tapestries. But he hoped that instead he could insist that they put together the pieces of the puzzle, even if there were still missing pieces. And since the papers were largely drawn from the records of one man—Secretary of Defense Robert McNamara—there would be large gaps. Rosenthal and the editors particularly lamented the absence of President Johnson's perspective on the war.

Rosenthal was in touch with the editorial team at the Hilton almost every day, but for the most part he kept himself aloof from the day-to-day writing and editing. He did, after all, have a newspaper to continue putting out. But when he did check in, or when the editors or reporters came to him, he continued to enforce his single editorial guideline:

More than halfway through the project, Jimmy Greenfield, who was in the middle taking the pressure from above and below, came to me and said that the crew was cracking up under the pressure of the guideline and was trying to break away from it. He said it was time for me to step in. I went to the Hilton, gathered the group together, and listened to them talk. . . . I realized there might have been times when we had stuck too rigidly to the letter instead of the spirit of the guideline, but that on the whole, this was a small price to pay for telling the Pentagon story instead of our story.[29]

Rosenthal also managed the working conditions of the writers and editors, who, in their three-room suite, had started to get on each other's nerves. One morning Neil Sheehan came to Rosenthal's house, nervous that the interpersonal dynamics of the group would bring the project down. Rosenthal told Sheehan that his main job was to give the team working conditions suitable for the production of the story. He rented another suite at the Hilton and separated the editors from the writers, calming Sheehan.[30]

Advocate for the Editorial Team

When Rosenthal came to the conclusion with a heavy heart that he would have to publish the Pentagon Papers and risk the future of The *New York Times* and of the United States, he knew that his biggest barrier would be Arthur Sulzberger. According to Rosenthal's journals, Sulzberger "never evinced any great enthusiasm for the project."[31] He knew that it was a story, but he could never understand why it was as big a story as his editors thought it was. He also made it clear to Rosenthal that he would be the one making the final decision as to whether or not to publish. While it is unusual for a publisher to take this control away from his top editor, Sulzberger did have the survival of the newspaper and issues of national security to worry about, so Rosenthal "agreed entirely." That meant, however, that Rosenthal would have to be a fulcrum of sorts, having to persuade Sulzberger to publish, and having to persuade his editors and writers to shape the story in such a way that it would be acceptable to Sulzberger. In the end, both sides made compromises, but Rosenthal clearly had more work to do as his editors' advocate.

Sulzberger remained even more aloof from the process than Rosenthal did, though he seems to have nursed his doubts about publication right up until almost literally the last moment. Rosenthal never wavered in his support in front of Sulzberger. Meanwhile, Punch was consulting his own group of advisers, including senior executives at the *Times* and the law firm of Lord, Day & Lord. The last angered Rosenthal, who felt that this blue-chip Wall Street law firm was not sufficiently advocating for the *Times*. He much preferred the point of view of James Goodale. So these were the angels and devils sitting on Sulzberger's shoulders, giving him conflicting advice: "His editors were telling him that if we failed to publish we would be doing a disservice to the country, and jeopardizing The Times. His lawyers and some of his confidants were telling him that if we did publish, we would be endangering the country and jeopardizing The New York Times."[32] Rosenthal appealed to Sulzberger's sense of duty as the keeper of his family's newspaper. Arguments about integrity and truth might not have worked as well if Rosenthal were presenting them to a president appointed by a board of directors. Rosenthal said that if the paper did not publish, then "we would be admitting to ourselves that we were a second-rate newspaper, unable to face the real test of confidence in our function and in our integrity when it came." "I also told him that if we could not do this, it would make a mockery of everything we ever told reporters, because how could we possibly ask them to go out in search for the truth when at a time when the ultimate truth, the biggest story ever presented to The Times, had been placed in our laps and we turned away from it out of fear of the consequences of publication."[33] Rosenthal pushed on these two arguments right up to the point of publication.

Meanwhile, Sulzberger began to request some changes. Greenfield and the editorial team came up with a plan to run nine stories at between ten and twelve pages per day, including photographs, historical context, and biographies of some key players, as well as the stories themselves and the verbatim documents that Ellsberg had allowed Sheehan to access. Sulzberger was not impressed enough with the stories to authorize that much space, so he and Rosenthal agreed eventually on six pages per day, cutting out almost all of the photographs and charts. In his journal, Rosenthal writes that these changes actually helped the news presentation: "Pictures would have added superficially to the appearance, but in the end the sheer overpowering weight of column after column of type gave the whole project a documentary look which it really should have had. I liked it far better without pictures than with pictures."[34] This reads like rationalization after the fact, so it's not clear that Rosenthal really did agree with the changes. He did fight for more room for the stories after the court's injunction had been lifted, weeks later.

Sulzberger's other main point of worry was whether or not to print the actual documents. For Punch, this meant that the *Times* might be exposing itself to more legal battles than it would if it were merely reporting on them. Accessing classified material seemed like it would be far less of an infraction than actually reprinting the documents. But Rosenthal insisted that if the *Times* did not publish the documents, readers—and particularly those antithetical to the *Times*—might speculate that the documents contained far worse than they actually did, and that the paper was protecting the government—or the opposite. Sulzberger held out on this issue until the very last day before typesetting had to begin.

On June 1, Rosenthal finally made his pitch to Sulzberger, outlining the stories that the team had decided to run. He believed that the story that had emerged from the Hilton suite had jelled enough that he could submit the material to the publisher for his approval. The other was that the *Times* was paranoid about being scooped by other papers, or even by Congress. In fact, the order of story publication was determined in large part by which material they believed to be in the hands of others. The first three days of publication (which turned out to be the three days before the injunction) would cover the most scoop-sensitive material. Then, with day four of publication, the paper would circle back to the beginning of the story. Once again, Rosenthal articulated the editorial rationale that he had first formulated during the meeting in Scotty Reston's office in April: "This is not The New York Times history, I emphasize, but The New York Time's [*sic*] report on the Pentagon's history—and this is what makes it far different and far more significant, in my opinion, than previously published material."[35]

On June 10, more than a week later, Sulzberger sent back his response, authorizing publication. He had three stipulations:

1. The *Times* would honor any injunction against publication.
2. Senior executives would be allowed to read all of the stories before publication for one last check that no military secrets would be printed.
3. The stories needed to be edited one more time for clarity and simplicity.

But Rosenthal and his editorial team had finally prevailed. The Pentagon Papers would be published. Rosenthal asked Max Frankel to write an overview story introducing the papers and some of their highlights—a story that was put off until the last week before publication. Sheehan did a rewrite of it. Then it was time to set the type.

Rosenthal was still reluctant to make too big a splash with the publication, which shows in the headline that ran on the first day's story, one that was chosen to be deliberately bland: "Vietnam Archive: Pentagon Study Traces 3 Decades of Growing U.S. Involvement." The headline took up two lines and three columns, but it was neither the lead story nor even the "off-lead," or second most important story. That was a report on Tricia Nixon's wedding. By contrast, when the Supreme Court ruled a little more than two weeks later to allow the *Times* to resume publication, the headline ran across all six columns and filled three lines. The first day's story was clearly deliberately underplayed. And in a sense, it worked. Reaction was quiet on the first day of publication.

By Monday, though, Attorney General John Mitchell requested that the *Times* cease publication and threatened legal action if they did not. Rosenthal had to persuade Sulzberger to continue. "The Publisher was miserable," Rosenthal recalled in his journal. "He had never wanted any part of this. He had taken our judgment, he had known he would get into trouble but when the trouble came, naturally enough, he didn't like it."[36] Rosenthal knew that the top executives of the paper were pushing Sulzberger—who was in London that day—to stop publication and wait for the legal go-ahead. But Rosenthal consulted with his editors to agree on a common position, and to appeal to Sulzberger with the support of other publishers and editors who had contacted the *Times*. "Look, you are off in London, it's in the middle of the morning, you don't know what's going on, all you can think about are the threats you're receiving but I want to tell you that this is a great national issue," Rosenthal recalled telling Sulzberger: "The country is aroused by it, there are a lot of people on our side. . . . If we back down now, we'll be cowards. If we go ahead, we'll show ourselves as strong and true men. It's not all black, Punch. There are a lot of people for you. And for us." Sulzberger agreed. *The Times* published for a third day.

After the Decision

While the legal team toiled to win the right for the *Times* to resume publication, the editorial staff regrouped and took stock of the direction of the Pentagon Papers stories. The lull gave Rosenthal and his group a chance to rethink the scope of the story, and the response gave him ammunition for pushing Sulzberger for permission to expand the coverage. Sulzberger had limited the team to six pages per day for seven days, a reduction from Rosenthal's original request for ten pages per day for ten days, which would have given more room for unabridged documents and for more photographs and illustrations. On June 21, about a week after the series had begun, Rosenthal sent a memo to Sulzberger with a revised story list attached. Rosenthal pitched his argument as one that seemed inherently obvious. He peppered his memo with phrases such as "I'm sure you will agree," and signed off "Yours in brotherhood," allying the editorial side and the publishing side in the same mission. After all, since Sulzberger had already agreed to publish at this point, had already agreed to defy the attorney general, had already taken his newspaper to court, shouldn't he at least go the whole measure and publish the whole story as it was meant to be told? Sulzberger, Rosenthal seems to be saying, should trust his editors at this point. "Journalistically, I think we would be hardput [sic] to explain why we killed a couple of good stories at a time when the whole world wanted information about the Pentagon papers," he wrote. "I think it would be too bad if we laid ourselves open to criticism of not telling the whole story by taking a decision to lop off two days for no discernible journalistic principle."[37]

Rosenthal also took the opportunity of the break in publication to rename his series. The *Times* had originally published them under the rubric "The Vietnam Archives," which Rosenthal admitted was intentionally bland. "Nobody calls them the Vietnam Archives. They call them the McNamara papers or the Pentagon papers or the Vietnam papers or the Pentagon study or something," he wrote in a memo to Greenfield. His suggestion, however, is not the one that took: "How about Vietnam Papers?" Apparently Rosenthal did not have an ear for alliteration.

Conclusion

The former *Times* editor John Hess argues in his memoir that the Pentagon Papers was a courageous coup by a group of reporters, editors, and executives who he didn't believe would have had the moxie to pull off such a huge and disruptive project. But Hess argues that they were an aberration, and that the only real change that the publication of the Pentagon Papers brought about was to drive Richard Nixon into the paranoid cover-ups that eventually brought about his downfall. But the *Times* hadn't changed its mostly pro-establishment, pro-institutional outlook enough to pick up on the Watergate story.[38] The Pentagon Papers did not change the course of the Vietnam War, which was already winding down, and they did not change the *New York Times* either. Arthur Gelb characterized the publication differently. For him, the Pentagon Papers were clear proof of "how far *The Times* was from being in the government's pocket."[39] The truth lies somewhere in between Hess's and Gelb's readings. While the *Times* was certainly never "in the pocket" of any administration, it was, as of 1971, certainly a tactful and cautious paper when it came to openly criticizing the government. In the end, the Pentagon Papers changed the *New York Times* more than they changed anything in the external political world.

Change would have come eventually to the paper, as it does to all institutions, but the change would have been even more incremental than it was with the Pentagon Papers. The Pentagon Papers fell into the lap of the newspaper just after the height of the counterculture, at a time when the paper represented the institutional center-left, and at a time when its top editor was constitutionally opposed to printing anything that might seem impolite. They were the proverbial bombshell story that broke through the editorial staff's inherent conservatism owing to the revelatory nature of their contents. But an intentional downplaying of the news presentation blunted their impact, and if it were not for the fact that the government sued for an injunction to halt their publication, the dull headlines and lack of illustrations may have consigned them to a smaller place in political history than they have. And no one story, even one that filled fifty-some newspaper pages over nine days of publication, can be expected to change the entire management culture of a newspaper. More than forty years later, the *Times* held reporter James Risen's story on the National Security Agency's warrantless wiretapping program, bowing to concerns of high-level Bush administration officials, and top editors routinely consult with administrations about national security issues to this day.

But the Pentagon Papers stories were an early eruption on the road to some reforms, many of which happened under the leadership of Abe Rosenthal, including expanded arts and cultural coverage, better treatment of women's issues, and accountability measures such as a daily corrections box. The *Times* did eventually publish the NSA wiretapping story, too, and was the main U.S. publication partner for Wikileaks. Rosenthal recognized that as times change, so too must the *Times*. It had to change to survive, and its survival kept him up at night.

In the first entry of his journal, Rosenthal wrote: "Years ago I used to have a dream, a recurrent dream. In my dream, I would wake up on a Wednesday morning and there was no New York Times and there was a terrible grayness, and people went around asking, 'Where is the Times? Where is the Times?'"[40]

CHAPTER 10

"Ideological Plugola," "Elitist Gossip," and the Need for Cable Television

Kathryn Cramer Brownell

In 1968, feelings of persecution by the media establishment animated both an individual's and an industry's pursuit of vindication. Convinced that the press had "kicked him around" all his career, Richard M. Nixon relied on staged television productions and entertainment forums to circumvent the power of network news programs and communicate his message directly to voters.[1] The cable television industry also felt that the Federal Communications Commission (FCC) and broadcast networks had mistreated it over the previous two decades. But by 1968 the president of the National Cable Television Association, Frederick Ford, proudly declared to fellow cable operators that "we are a stable industry. Our property is secure. Our business is a full-fledged member of the mass media complex. Our faith justified. Our reputations vindicated. We have arrived."[2] Formerly conceived of as merely a rural delivery system for broadcast signals, cable television burst on the scene as a seemingly revolutionary technology that year. Scientists, engineers, journalists, and policymakers debated not *if* the electronic wiring system would transform American society, but *when* and *how*.

Though unconnected in their respective triumphs in 1968, the "New Nixon" and a "new" cable industry arrived on the national stage together, and the former would be integral to the expansion of the latter as they both challenged the authority and power of the "Eastern establishment" and the dominance of network broadcast television. While a history of regulation had limited the cable industry's growth and potential since the 1940s,

Nixon's election coincided with a flood of excitement over the political possibilities of cable television in solving social and economic problems. A 1970 report from the Alfred Sloan Foundation's Commission on Cable Communications highlighted the fierce urgency that policymakers faced to influence its technological trajectory, because now "it remains possible by government action to prohibit it, to permit it, or to promote it almost by fiat."[3]

The future possibilities of cable captured the interest of liberal and conservative activists alike, and during Nixon's administration a battle ensued over the regulatory, economic, and political structure that would coalesce. Cable television presented an opportunity to expand and remake the public sphere, and debates about its future reflected the broader political battles about the failures of post–World War II liberalism and the possibilities of free-market conservatism. The growth of cable and rise of satellite technology in the 1970s created a "constitutive moment," which media scholar Paul Starr defines as when "constellations of power" meet with cultural beliefs and political biases to reshape basic assumptions and regulatory practices in the communications infrastructure.[4] As someone who felt that media institutions were unfairly under the control of a "privileged class of individuals" who engaged in "elitist gossip," Richard Nixon took advantage of this moment to shape the future of the media landscape.[5] Using the muscle of the Executive Branch, and its newly created Office of Telecommunications Policy, Nixon saw cable television as a powerful way to wage his ideological war against the "liberal media" and his economic pursuit of market-based solutions for public policies.

Historians have documented the bitter relationship Nixon had with the press and how a "politics of clean and dirty" set the standards for investigative journalism in the wake of the Watergate scandal.[6] And yet, Nixon's influence in media policymaking was equally transformative and influential. Through the Office of Telecommunication Policy (OTP) and its director Clay "Tom" Whitehead, Nixon's administration expanded the legislative role of the president in ways that advanced his economic, political, and ideological beliefs while also pursuing his personal vendetta against network television, which both Nixon and conservatives in general agreed had undermined their respective messages. Technological change begun in Nixon's administration made "cablemania" a defining hallmark of the Reagan era. Hinging on the privatization of public services, deregulation, and a discrediting of and even apathy toward broadcast news programming, the triumph of the free-market reality for cable television emerged because of dramatic policy

shifts and powerful rhetoric surrounding those shifts in the Nixon White
House, ultimately illuminating how presidents can influence the media
environment in which they lead by shaping policy discussions.

It started with organizational changes in the Nixon White House. The
Communications Act of 1934 outlined broad structural mandates and responsibilities for telecommunications policy, splitting authority between
the Federal Communications Commission (FCC), Congress, and the Executive Branch. In August 1967 Nixon's predecessor, Lyndon Johnson, asked
Congress to establish a presidential task force to reevaluate this telecommunications organization in the federal government. Under the leadership
of Under Secretary of State for Political Affairs Eugene V. Rostow and Director of Telecommunications Management James D. O'Connell, the Task Force
on Communications Policy outlined the history of telecommunications
policy in the government and debated possible reorganization structures.[7]

With the final recommendations of the "Rostow Report" circulating
in December of 1968, the incoming president, Richard Nixon, would set
parameters for its application. Lyndon Johnson never released the Rostow
Report, instructing his staff instead to inform the transition team of its
recommendations. Though Nixon agreed with the broad conclusions on
the need to reorganize the bureaucracy and develop a coherent policy to
grapple with technological changes, his staff made very clear his unwilling-
ness to give any weight to the Rostow policy conclusions, especially those
regarding the development of domestic satellite initiatives. While the report
advocated a government-regulated multipurpose pilot program to pursue
a commercial satellite for communications, the Nixon administration stood
firm in its promotion of deregulation and the free market, two staples of
Nixon's telecommunications policy.[8]

For all the legislative muscle he flexed during his presidency, Lyndon
Johnson did not pay much attention to telecommunications policies, and
in fact, as the director of telecommunications management, James D.
O'Connell never even personally met the president after his swearing-in
ceremony.[9] Johnson, like Kennedy before him, appointed FCC members who
shared a commitment to advancing the interests of the broadcasting industry, and then generally allowed commissioners to develop their own relationships with broadcasters. Friendly collaboration between network television
presidents and the FCC had resulted in twenty years of favorable regulatory
structures to protect the monopoly the "Big Three"—the National Broadcasting Corporation (NBC), Columbia Broadcasting System (CBS), and

American Broadcasting Corporation (ABC)—held over the airwaves.[10] Richard Nixon, however, brought a different philosophy to the White House. For Nixon, deregulation and the encouragement of new forms of television would be good politics in two ways. It promoted economic development and consumer choice for constituents while also dismantling the influence of national reporters who set the news agenda.

By December 1969, visions for a new agency began to formalize within the administration. Given the name Office of Telecommunications Policy and situated in the Executive Office of the White House, it would connect qualified, yet loyal, aides to Nixon while also representing the president's policy stances and imperatives to the FCC, Congress, and the public. Officially, the White House repeatedly affirmed that the OTP would not infringe on Congress's policymaking function or the regulatory decisions of the FCC, but would simply allow the Nixon administration "to speak with a clearer voice and to act as a more effective partner in discussions of communications policy with both the Congress and the FCC."[11] Private discussions about the office's functions were more direct. Tom Whitehead, Nixon's special assistant who would soon head the office, told a longtime supporter of the president, "much good can be done without formally 'taking over' the FCC responsibilities" because the FCC "cannot by itself fully consider the broader implications of its actions and is too much caught in the reconciliation of disputes among competing interests and firms."[12]

Finding a director with the partisan, educational, and professional qualifications to fulfill such an important and controversial position proved difficult. In the end President Nixon decided on the person who designed the OTP from the beginning: Tom Whitehead. Born in Neodesh, Kansas, Whitehead received his B.S. and M.S. in electrical engineering and a Ph.D. in management from the Massachusetts Institute of Technology. Along with his impressive education, Whitehead also had communication industry credentials from his undergraduate work with Bell Telephone Laboratories and then as an analyst for Rand Corporation. A lifelong Republican, Whitehead worked for Nixon during the 1968 campaign and then joined him in the White House that following January as a "Special Assistant to the President." While his responsibilities ranged from space to maritime affairs, Whitehead quickly became Nixon's "go-to" person for communications policy. In 1969, he put his doctoral training to use as he formulated the reorganization of the Executive Office, which resulted in the creation of the OTP the following year. Though only thirty-one years old when he was sworn in as the first director of the Office of Telecommunications Policy, Whitehead garnered the respect of industry leaders, researchers, and politicians, with the chairman of the Senate Subcommittee on Communications, John Pastore (D-R.I.), calling him "one of the most brilliant young persons who has come to Government in a long-long time."[13]

By September of 1970, the OTP, with Dr. Whitehead at its head, began its mission to coordinate, research, and streamline telecommunications policy in the White House. Whitehead clearly articulated to the public that "whatever his office said would have the weight of the President behind it."[14] Expanding the bully pulpit into communications policy began what *Television/Radio Age* called a possible "era of White House domination of the FCC." Over the past decades the White House had been "chary of meddling in FCC affairs," noted the magazine. "But, it is now a new decade and many of those old Administration fears have disappeared." What would happen, the publication wondered. "Partisan manipulation is imaginable, and so is a badly needed vigor in communications policy—and elements of the two together may be more likely still."[15] For the television industry, partisanship, vigor, and ideology would bring dramatic transformations.

With a radically different shape than any telecommunications agency before it, the OTP focused on fostering the development of satellite technology and the expansion of cable television. Its approach toward cable television digressed not just from the current FCC policy, but also from government attitudes toward the industry since the 1950s.[16] Beginning in the late 1940s, community antenna television (CATV) provided broadcast service to small rural towns in the mountains of Pennsylvania, the river valleys of the Northwest, and the hollow spaces of western frontier towns. Entrepreneurial cable operators like George Gardner of rural Pennsylvania traveled with heavy equipment up and down Jacks Mountain, to capture the broadcast signal from Johnstown, a local station almost a hundred miles away.[17] Friends and family also wanted access to these broadcast signals, providing the demand that Gardner met with his homemade system of running antenna wires down a mountain and into homes throughout rural Lewistown. Community television was just that: a service to provide a community with television when they could not access the airwaves from the local broadcasting station because of distance or terrain. In 1950, a mere seventy communities relied on such hand-rigged systems, but as television gained popularity over the next decade, so too did the demand for cable. To fend off the IRS and copyright battles, cable operators repeatedly claimed that they merely offered a service; CATV simply constituted a "passive antenna" that extended the reach of the airwaves.[18] While Hollywood studios saw an opportunity to regain audiences during the 1950s with the idea of "pay TV" using coaxial cable technology, the FCC and Justice Department restricted this venture, instead providing a more profitable business environment for the broadcast networks by limiting competition.[19]

Subscriptions continued to grow, nevertheless. Small operations merged into regional "multiple service operators" (MSOs), creating lucrative businesses across the Midwest and the West. In 1966, eager to gain leverage against broadcasters and to potentially expand services, the National Community Television Association shed the name CATV and renamed itself the National Cable Television Association. In a symbolic move to declare itself a "new kind of business and a new kind of technology," cable operators positioned themselves as not merely an extension of broadcast television, but a new medium altogether. [20] And the broadcasting industry took notice, especially of a range of articles that surfaced that same year declaring how cable television could "revolutionize concepts for television programming." Using their deep connections and influence with the FCC, broadcasters successfully convinced the regulatory commission to introduce a new set of restrictions on cable television, shutting out the top one hundred television markets to CATV operators. The cable industry failed to alter the FCC's new freeze on its growth. But, its definition of cable television as a new technology with an ability to alleviate social ills—a utopian rhetoric that became known as "blue skies" for the open, far-reaching possibilities of cable—permeated university lecture halls, elaborate research labs, crowded meeting rooms of the Americans for Democratic Action (ADA), national newspapers, the chambers of Congress, and the halls of the White House.

Over the next five years, a diverse coalition of individuals and organizations on both sides of the political spectrum joined together with a common belief that an imminent communications revolution hinged on cable television.[21] New York City Mayor John Lindsay commissioned a task force on cable's potential to solve the urban crisis, and celebrated the "glittering possibilities" of the "new" technology. Engineers at Rand Corporation and researchers at the Ford Foundation produced studies that reinforced these visions, giving optimism to minority activists, consumer groups, the ADA, and the ACLU on how cable television would provide meaningful social change. The Democratic senator from Utah, Frank E. Moss, celebrated how "cablecasting" (or program origination for dissemination on cable systems) "promotes democracy" by enabling individuals to have a media presence. "Cablecasting gives people in communities of this type their only opportunity to originate programs about their local affairs—to discuss local bond issues, to hear debates about local political candidates and to celebrate local events," Moss argued.[22] As Lyndon Johnson left office with many of his Great Society programs in turmoil amidst growing racial unrest in cities at home and a controversial war abroad, liberal policymakers wondered: Did the expansion of cable provide the missing link to liberalism's success?

Ralph Lee Smith thought so. Cable television had the potential to transform public and private services, the writer prophesied as he popularized the "blue sky" vision in a 1970 article in *The Nation*. "The cable" will provide "newspapers, mail service, banking and shopping facilities, data from libraries and other storage centers, school curricula and other forms of information too numerous to specify. In short, every home and office will contain a communications center of a breadth and flexibility to influence every aspect of life."[23] The subsequent "wired nation" could solve problems of urban decline, educational inequality, and unemployment. Fueled by research at the Sloan Foundation, the Ford Foundation, and in the popular writings of figures like Smith, the progressive possibilities of the industry's future captivated public attention and spurred massive interest into "wiring" cities for cable.

The hope for a technological solution to rectify the failures of Johnson's liberal agenda drove the intense anticipation of the Rostow Report, and explains Richard Nixon's reluctance to release its findings. The Rostow Report did not just advocate for an organizational restructuring in the telecommunications sector of government. It also promoted a "big government" view of technological innovation, as did many other advocates for the "wired nation." Ralph Lee Smith argued that the federal government needed to invest in wiring the country for cable television as they had in the post–World War II infrastructure to promote suburban development. "In the 1960s the nation provided large federal subsidies for a new interstate highway system to facilitate and modernize the flow of automotive traffic," explained Smith. As such, during the 1970s, "it should make a similar national commitment for an electronic highway system, to facilitate the exchange of information and ideas." This view, which was reinforced in much of the blue skies literature and the Rostow Report, required substantial government support to develop a communications infrastructure that promised to alleviate the social problems of the post–World War II infrastructure—a New Deal for the Information Age. This last gasp of postwar liberal policy, however, became the first step in Nixon's communications agenda. Excitement for cable television became a way to undermine further New Deal unity and the prominence of the Eastern establishment.[24]

Though blue sky advocates and the Nixon administration could agree on the functions of cable—creating programming diversity, opening access to media outlets, promoting engagement, expanding local services—the reality of these ideas took shape very differently under the blue skies progressive view versus that of the White House. The OTP concluded that Nixon needed to set forth a policy to link the development of this new technology to the president's larger domestic agenda. In June of 1971, Nixon established a special cabinet committee to explore the current status, potential, and policy implications surrounding cable television. Delegating Whitehead as chair, Nixon then asked Len Garment (his media advisor during the 1968 campaign and current legal counsel) and Herb Klein, a journalist turned director of presidential communications, to join Secretary of Health, Education, and Welfare Eliot Richardson, Secretary of Housing and Urban Development George Romney, and Secretary of Commerce Maurice Stans to form a committee that would "take full account of the wide range of social, economic, and political considerations involved" in cable television's development and how White House action could influence policies surrounding its future.[25]

With the creation of the Presidential Cabinet Committee on Cable Television in 1971, the Nixon administration committed to working with cable operators, interest groups, researchers, activists, and the FCC to develop a new policy toward cable television and to negotiate between their conflicting interests. Each committee member received a background report from the OTP that outlined how cable could solve current problems in broadcasting, especially the lack of diversity in programming and the denial of facilities to "minority, civil rights, and political groups."[26] Moreover, the report highlighted how the sheer number of channels available on the cable dial made the contemporary debate about the Fairness Doctrine obsolete. The FCC had deemed the airwaves a public commodity, and thus had instituted regulations to ensure political candidates had equal access to broadcast television and programs presented both sides of controversial issues. With more channels, cable television offered an easy point of access for anyone, regardless of political party or ideological perspective, to find distribution space—they just needed viewers. But the industry's expansion required the committee to grapple with other pressing questions about contentious legal and economic issues, notably questions of copyright and regulatory

structures, concerns about ownership across media (current FCC regulations forbade network television ownership of cable systems), and congressional versus FCC power to shape communications policy.

In short, the committee had the responsibility of negotiating the current
debates with the FCC and Congress, while also working with the OTP in
developing long-term options for the industry's development. The committee hoped to conclude its recommendations within the next six months. But
though it worked successfully to negotiate a short-term compromise, which
resulted in the 1972 FCC Third Order, it would take two more years to develop a more comprehensive vision for cable that fit the mandates of President Nixon, who Whitehead later argued "cared more about it than anybody
on his White House staff."[27] The first decision would appease lobbyists in
1972, while the second effort would shape the trajectory of the modern cable
industry over the next decade.

On February 3, 1972, the FCC released a report of over three hundred
pages outlining the new policy, which rescinded the 1966 freeze and pushed
for the immediate exploitation of cable's potential. It opened the top one
hundred markets to cable infiltration, required copyright payments, permitted the importation of distant signals, set mandates for public service
channels, and capped local franchise fees. Nevertheless, the new order still
protected broadcast interests, and thus constituted what Whitehead characterized as a "messy stew of forced compromises."[28] Public reaction was
mixed. But the OTP did not bear the brunt of the criticism, and instead highlighted its role in "seeking to act as mediator in the dispute."[29]

The cabinet committee and the OTP more broadly served as facilitator
between what it saw as "a whole business [that] crackles with crisis."[30] Recognizing that struggles would develop between the OTP, FCC, congressional committees, and a range of industry advocates, the cabinet committee
focused first and foremost on "the political aspects of the matter," leaving
"long term policy and trends" to future discussions. Why? One White
House memorandum of recommendations reminded the committee of an
important external factor: "the communications business will be even more
important in the coming year to us."[31] Notably, after Nixon's successful
reelection bid, cable television became a central and explicit tool in Nixon's
war on the press and his campaign against the liberal slant of network news.
While the White House reminded the OTP of the need for support from the
communications industry during the campaign season, once Nixon won
reelection, his and the OTP's approach to cable television took shape quite

differently. While the OTP initially negotiated compromises between inter-est groups, in the final years of the Nixon administration it became a pub-lic and private tool to wage direct war on what Nixon saw as the monopolistic, undemocratic, and biased power of network television.

Changes in two reports on cable policy from 1970 to 1972 illustrate this broader shift in the Nixon administration. In 1970, economist Bruce Owen penned a cable policy analysis for the newly formed OTP staff. Within it, one paragraph stood out as an implicit critique of the problem of liberal bias in the news. The report digressed briefly to distinguish "between freedom to hear (select) a wide variety of programming sources, views and opinions, and the putative right to be informed in the passive sense."[32] Calling the latter freedom "both paternalistic and antithetical to the spirit of the First Amendment," the report reminded the OTP staff that cable television would "provide the public with the opportunity to hear what it wishes without Federal regulation or private barriers to access."

Two years later, Owen outlined a more targeted mission for cable tele-vision called "Project B.U.N. (Break Up the Networks).[33] This project delin-eated the agenda which the OTP, with direct White House collaboration and support, would pursue over the next two years. The central problem in mod-ern communications, argued the report, hinged on the fact that "three na-tional networks dominate television." Viewers had only three options to hear the news. Advertisers and program producers had only three choices to sell their products on television. This economic power, as a result "yields high prof-its for the networks, as well as freedom to make what are essentially political and social decisions without market discipline." The political power thus gar-nered concerned the OTP because the networks had "the ability to control the flow of information and of ideas to the people." Moreover, they "can signifi-cantly mold public opinion" and quash diversity and freedom of expression. This power, wrote Owen, "is unacceptable in the United States, whether it is viewed from antitrust or First Amendment perspectives."

"Politically, economically, and philosophically," concluded the OTP in December 1972, the concentration of power in network television consti-tuted the central barrier to the Nixon administration's pursuit of objectivity in news programming and its effort to reverse "the growth of regulatory intervention in the private enterprise broadcasting system."[34] The OTP recog-nized that the "network triopoly was created by technology, demographics, and policy," but this trifecta could also provide alternatives to combat the networks' power, notably in two areas: "cable television and encouraging new networks."[35] The expansion of cable television offered the first and "probably the most effective and most lasting approach." Though the report surmised that cable's effectiveness in combating the networks' authority would take at least ten years, promotion of favorable regulatory policies for cable was essential. The deregulation of cable television thus became a way to show the merits of the marketplace in promoting technological innovation, diversity in programming, and true freedom of speech, upon which network dominance currently infringed. News programs had become "cliquish, if not incestuous," but "if properly structured" cable television promised to bring alternative news programming and help new regional and national television networks develop.

Project B.U.N. and Whitehead's subsequent, formal report to the president about integrating these OTP initiatives into his forthcoming programs illustrated how combating network power would depend on the technological expansion of cable television, deregulatory policies that promoted the free market, and an intensive publicity campaign that derailed the authority and credibility of networks as a harbinger of the public good. Economically, this approach promoted Nixon's effort to restructure government to "let the private sector play its role."[36] Politically, it afforded Nixon the opportunity to place his imprint on launching the "information age." Nixon would determine "the extent to which the benefits the communications revolutions are realized by the public and by industry—and whether communications regulation by the Federal Government will be locked into the same kind of morass as transportation and power or whether a more competitive free-enterprise framework is created."

With support from Nixon, the OTP appealed to conservatives across the country who had campaigned against the liberal bias of universities and mainstream media since the 1950s.[37] With Spiro Agnew as his vice president, Nixon had a vocal "attack dog" on liberal bias in the media who had battled with the press during his first term. But during the president's second term, Whitehead urged Nixon to link his critique of network power directly with concrete telecommunications policies. "The Administration's image on communications matters has been colored by the network news battle," the OTP director wrote John Ehrlichman. "We need a more statesman like record of policy development and advocacy to stand on."[38]

As the cabinet committee continued its work, Whitehead began this effort to integrate communications policy into the president's broader political agenda, stressing the importance of cable television and pressuring local broadcasters to push back against national network bias. To launch this mission, Whitehead traveled to Indianapolis and gave a speech that would be quoted extensively in the press and even during congressional testimony the following year. In a bold address, Whitehead assailed the bias in news management and threatened the licenses of local broadcast stations that did not meet FCC standards of objectivity and fairness. At a time when the majority of Americans turned to national news shows for information and facts, news programming, argued Whitehead, had failed the American people. Their programs conveyed "ideological plugola," by which reporters stressed or suppressed "information in accordance with their own beliefs."[39] As a result, contended Whitehead, the First Amendment had unwittingly produced "a privileged class of men called journalists, who are immune from criticism by government or restraint by publishers or editors." These men confused "sensationalism with sense" and "dispense elitist gossip in the guise of news analysis." Whitehead's unflinching language captured the headlines across the country. Reporters charged that he waged an "attack on the TV industry" by threatening licenses of local stations that aired "biased" network news programs.[40] Charging "onto the playing fields last week with all the sis-boom-bah of a linebacker kept too long on the bench," wrote conservative columnist James Kilpatrick, Whitehead "had come to replace Vice President Agnew, who has turned demure in recent months, in the Administration's great body contact game with badgering the TV networks."[41]

Whitehead responded to public criticism with extensive radio and press interviews, taking the publicity as an opportunity to explain the president's communications agenda in more detail. He diligently replied to critical letters from network executives with a sales pitch about how broadcasters should favor the president's policies. Sure, the speech used strong language, admitted Whitehead, "but those who have twisted an appeal for the voluntary exercise of private responsibilities into a call for government censorship—that they can now denounce—have abandoned reasoned debate in favor of polemics."[42] Whitehead attempted to highlight the hypocrisy of Nixon's and his critics in the press with the fact that the White House was proposing to "diminish government's power to control broadcast content." Demonizing the White House's political philosophy toward the media ignores Nixon's efforts to "begin to take these tools from the hands of government" and place them in the hands of the marketplace, contended the OTP director.

The incendiary rhetoric aroused the attention and publicity both Nixon and Whitehead had planned. Even though both men had different motivations, they shared a common vision, thus the speech became an opportunity to move forward with Project B.U.N., the OTP's plan for comprehensive communications reform, while launching a new stage of the Nixon administration's attack on network television's authority. Originally, Whitehead had drafted a speech that included moving forward on cable television and that discussed logistical operations of the OTP. After sending a draft of the speech to the White House, he had received a dramatically revised speech from Nixon's close aide Charles Colson, who explained that Whitehead's version was "too obtuse."[43] In response, Whitehead eliminated the discussion of cable television and repackaged the main point of the speech. Rather than simply focusing "attention on the responsibility of local stations and network managements or the balance and objectivity of network news," as he originally planned, Colson pushed him to include a more poignant criticism of the mainstream press and the need for alternative media.[44] Nixon cleared the final version, which Whitehead anticipated would "get a lot of attention." When it did, the president and his staff wrote the director letters of support for handling the aftermath of the speech with poise.

"The Speech" set the stage for the next year and the various communications policies set forth by the OTP and the Nixon administration. The next month, Whitehead met personally with the president to discuss both the messaging and the specific policies. Nixon expressed admiration for how Whitehead "had been handling his job, particularly with respect to the problem of the networks and broadcasting."[45] Though he knew the "formidable adversaries" that the White House faced in pursuing this battle against the networks, Nixon reminded Whitehead of the need to continue to pursue it "vigorously." Moreover, if any staffer in the White House did not share this view of the network problem, Nixon would "reorder" them. It was imperative that everyone in the administration be "on board," the president explained, because "we could not afford to appear indecisive to the outside world." The president supported the recommendations about using cable television to solve "many of the problems brought by the current network dominance of broadcasting" and Whitehead's proposal to "insist on broadcast industry support in improving network news in return for our vigorous pursuit" of extending the licensing agreements.

Whitehead traveled across the country to deliver a similar version of the speech to broadcasters, cable operators, and newspaper organizations. He frequently deployed this contentious rhetoric to drive passions, which he hoped would encourage discussions of policy. Following Nixon's directions, his speeches specifically adhered to the White House–approved rhetoric, so that in all appearances and discussions of the White House and the media, the administration spoke with "one voice." During an appearance on *Firing Line*, a political talk show hosted by conservative icon William Buckley Jr., Whitehead joked about the meaning of "ideological plugola" and "elitist gossip" while highlighting deeper regulatory problems of the FCC and its Fairness Doctrine.[46] The solution to these communications issues, both men agreed, rested in cable television. Buckley asked Whitehead if he would be "100 percent sympathetic to anybody who wanted to start to program by cable." When Whitehead enthusiastically concurred, the host proclaimed, "Let's do it." The cabinet committee on cable, assured Whitehead, would soon recommend policies to ensure that "good old free enterprise" would triumph. After all, Whitehead reminded his conservative host, the current FCC structure was developed during the New Deal era, before the free market economic ideas of Milton Friedman had gained acceptance.

With cable heralded as the "savior" to problems of diversity, bias, and the regulatory state, anticipation built around the release of the cabinet committee's report to the president. Finally, on January 14, 1974, Whitehead submitted the final 117-page report to Nixon. In the introduction, the committee expressed that it did not look to cable as a "modern day Rosetta stone capable of unraveling the complex problems facing this society."[47] Rather, the committee emphasized that cable "has much to offer and it should be given an opportunity to prove its worth to the American people in the marketplace of goods and services and in the marketplace of ideas." The report reflected the belief that permeated OTP discussions: cable development began with the assumption of First Amendment rights, similar to the printed press. The government would not force political or news judgment or commentary on programs, but would simply ensure that choice and competition triumphed. The market, thus, would determine which ideas, perspectives, and biases people believed, not the "elitist view" of what broadcasters thought constituted news and suitable entertainment. The importance of cable, emphasized the committee, rested in how the medium "offers countless Americans a chance to speak for themselves and among themselves in their own way, and a chance to share with one another their experiences, their opinions, their frustrations, and their hopes."[48]

The report argued for deregulation of the industry—especially eliminating the current FCC classification of the medium as an extension of the broadcast industry—while also emphasizing the need to separate ownership of operating systems and program producers (a controversial recommendation which would ultimately be ignored). Following its release, over fifty cable leaders met in Washington to discuss the report's findings, which cable advocate Sol Schildhouse summed up as "bullish." Though the report had several recommendations with which he disagreed, the former head of the CATV division of the FCC celebrated how the report, as a result of "presidential jaw-boning," produced the first "long-range planning" document that "contemplates an industry that will amount to something in its own right and not just something that will exist to protect and enhance broadcast television."[49] The report's promotion of deregulation for the industry and its belief in the future expansion of the industry immediately boosted confidence in and stock prices for cable television.

Despite the politicized rhetoric Whitehead advanced in press appearances over the past year, the director argued that the policy recommendations did not have a liberal or a conservative slant, nor did it benefit one industry at the expense of the other.[50] Nevertheless, the Watergate investigation interfered with any real presidential or congressional engagement with it. Whitehead openly acknowledged that the president should not give the report "a great push" because of the "reverse effect of such an endorsement under the circumstances of the Administration's reverse Midas touch in matters of media."

That being the case, Whitehead argued that the real impetus for change "will have to come from public opinion," and he believed a "national consensus" surrounding cable's future would emerge even when his proposed cable legislation went nowhere in Congress.[51] Thus, the public relations campaign that Whitehead pursued, during which he offered a political understanding of the possibilities of cable, mattered as much as the internal policy debates. A decade later, Thomas Whiteside observed in an article in the *New Yorker* how this new view of cable resonated especially with "young congressional-staff mavericks who were the kids of the sixties" and pushed to "let this baby loose."[52] OTP staffers—from Brian Lamb, who founded C-SPAN five years later, to future Supreme Court Justice Antonin Scalia, to Whitehead, who soon moved into the private sector as the founder of Hughes Communications and the international Galaxy satellite system—left the OTP eager to pursue alternative ways to promote cable distribution, programming, and legal copyright clearances that paved the way for the industry to explode over the next decade.

While the Watergate scandal forced Nixon's resignation and marked a decisive victory in the press's battle with the president, Nixon won the war against media institutions that he launched through cable television. By 1975, blue skies advocates wondered what happened to the progressive visions they had articulated for the cable industry. Less than five years ago, observed the University of California law professor and former member of the Sloan Commission, visions for cable television's "panaceatic" possibilities abounded, shaping the construction of the 1972 cable television rules under the FCC.[53] After all, wrote Dr. Monroe Price, "one was either in favor of the wired nation, or against progress." Yet, in less than half a decade, the hopes for the "wired nation" had "diffused." Someone, wrote Monroe, "pricked the bubble." The former blue skies believer, and many of his contemporaries, felt that the excitement surrounding the utopian vision oversold the potential of cable, and in fact the "cable fable" that offered possibilities for change that was just that: a fable.[54] But what progressive activists and liberal policymakers lamented as a failure in 1975, Nixon aides and conservatives classified as the origins of a successful embrace of market-based solutions to public problems and an effective step in combating network television's political and economic dominance.

Over the next two decades, the basic pillars of Nixon's cable vision would find supporters across the next four presidential administrations. His Republican and Democratic successors, Gerald Ford and Jimmy Carter, respectively, both advocated for deregulation of the industry, even as they each tempered the polarizing rhetoric of the Nixon administration surrounding these policy changes. In Congress, Republicans like Arizona's Barry Goldwater joined with Democrats like California's Lionel Van Deerlin to support the basic findings of the committee and even to declare by 1979 that communication matters had "no room for partisanship."[55] Nixon's media obsession and economic agenda met with Whitehead's firm commitment to deregulation, private enterprise, and strong First Amendment protection for the electronic media that, with the cable industry's success in the early 1980s, became a "proof of concept" of the effectiveness of the marketplace in American life.[56] As Americans subscribed to cable by the millions over the next decade, they turned the dial from network entertainment and news to channels filled with nonstop sports, music videos, or old Hollywood films. Nixon's political attitudes and biases shaped the expansion of cable television, but his Republican successor would face the challenge of how to govern in the age of cable television.

CHAPTER 11

How Washington Helped Create the Contemporary Media: Ending the Fairness Doctrine in 1987

Julian E. Zelizer

The news media has become as polarized as our elected officials. When a person turns on a television or radio news show, they are almost certain to hear a host who is explaining the news from a particular political perspective. Americans now consume the news the same way they watch football, baseball, or even professional wrestling. They tune in to cheer their favorite host or to hiss at the person reading the teleprompter as they explain what happened on a given day in Washington.

The journalistic professional norm of objectivity that was forged at the turn of the twentieth century has all but vanished. There was a period in the mid-twentieth century, as the authors in this volume show, when news reporters insisted on presenting the facts without opinion and without interpreting the story from any particular political perspective. To be sure, as the essays in this volume also demonstrate, that ideal was never a strict reflection of reality. The roots of divisive journalism run deep. But in terms of scale and scope, the situation has changed. These days, almost everyone who is on the airwaves comfortably expresses their political points of view. Journalists are no longer fearful of expressing where they stand. Indeed, the network brass encourage them to do so.

There are many explanations for how this happened—how we moved from the era of Walter Cronkite to the era of Bill O'Reilly and Rachel Maddow. Most importantly, technological changes that started with the advent of cable television and accelerated with the emergence of the Internet ended the monopoly on political news that a handful of television and radio stations had enjoyed for decades. With the proliferation of media sources that covered political news, most of which were not subject to older federal regulations that had been imposed in the 1930s and 1940s, it became easier for producers and editors to allow more opinions to be heard.

There have also been important commercial changes that explain what happened. The breakdown of the strict division between the business and news divisions of television and radio stations has created greater incentives to publish and broadcast news that will attract as many viewers as possible. This has often meant providing news stories through a colorful and combative political lens. People like to tune in and see a fight. More hyperbolic and opinioned news attracts more eyeballs.

In addition, there are also broader cultural changes that help us to understand why this shift took place. As Americans became more polarized in all aspects of life, it is natural that we see the same phenomenon take place within the news.

One area that has not received as much attention is the realm of public policy. This is the focus of the following pages, with special attention to the history of television and radio. The essay builds on the work of historians who have been paying closer attention to the ways in which public policy has shaped the evolution of the news media. In his account of nineteenth century, for instance, Richard John provided a fascinating history of how communications developed in response to local regulatory policies.

Changes in federal public policy during the 1980s played an important role in creating our current polarized media environment. In 1987, the Federal Communications Commission, with the strong support of the Reagan administration and Republicans in Congress, abandoned the Fairness Doctrine, which had been in place since 1949. The Fairness Doctrine had required radio and television stations to provide contrasting views representing all sides of an issue that was relevant to the public interest. When Democrats tried to pass legislation to formally implement the Fairness Doctrine in the late 1980s, they failed. President Reagan vetoed their legislation. This decision by the FCC, and then Reagan, had a huge impact since the regulation had provided the policy foundation for the norm of objectivity.

The Fairness Doctrine was based on the fact that broadcasters needed to obtain a license from the federal government to be able to use the airwaves. The first medium that was subject to these types of restrictions was radio.

Congress had retained the authority to grant licenses to radio stations only if they served the "public interest." In 1927, Congress had articulated this principle through the Radio Act. The legislation provided Congress with leverage in terms of shaping what kinds of journalism would be legitimate for broadcast. Then the Communications Act of 1934 created the Federal Communications Commission, the agency that was to be responsible for regulating the airwaves.

The battle over the right to editorialize had been intensifying. Commercial broadcasters had undertaken a fierce war to overturn the "Mayflower Doctrine," a regulation imposed in 1941, which prohibited any kind of editorializing on the airwaves. Liberals feared that if commercial broadcasters were successful in overturning this regulation, they would flood the airwaves with conservative shows, as there was a rightward drift in American politics taking place after World War II. Unions complained that without the Mayflower Doctrine radio would turn into a forum for probusiness views. "I hesitate to think what would happen when the bars are lifted and a few men in key positions are given the power to beam their views to America's radio audience . . . radio is a business, a big business, and as such is bound to represent that viewpoint," wrote a group of labor leaders.[1] Liberals tried to fight back against the campaign, warning that overturning the Mayflower Doctrine would open the airwaves to right-wing propaganda. The broadcasters won the war, and the doctrine was overturned.

Despite the victory for commercial radio, the FCC did offer liberals a compromise, a much weaker measure that would provide some obligation to the public interest and balanced reporting—within the context of an unfettered commercial industry.[2] The FCC released a report in 1949 stating that radio and television stations receiving licenses had to provide equal time to different political perspectives and to deal with issues of public concern. According to the doctrine, broadcasters had to "devote a reasonable portion of broadcast time to the discussion and consideration of controversial issues of public importance" and "that in doing so [the broadcaster must be] fair—that is must affirmatively endeavor to make . . . facilities available for the expression of contrasting viewpoints held by responsible elements with respect to the controversial issues presented." They based this rule on the argument that since access to the airwaves was limited, the federal government had the authority to impose certain requirements on those companies to which they granted the right to broadcast.

The Fairness Doctrine was a modest regulation. It didn't provide much enforcement power, and it depended on the government checking into what stations were doing at the time of the renewal of their license. Dealing with violations depended on individuals bringing complaints to the government.

Though it was not nearly as strong as the Mayflower Doctrine, the regulation still mattered within the industry and provided a check against how far major stations were willing to go in allowing for openly biased shows to reach the airwaves. The FCC strengthened the Fairness Doctrine in 1967 with two new decisions. The first was the "editorial rule," which stipulated that if a station broadcast an editorial against a specific candidate, that candidate was to be given twenty-four hours' notice and allowed to provide a response. The second rule stipulated that a station must provide notice to an individual whose personal character was maligned and to offer them ample time on the airwaves to respond to the charges.

Conservative radio talk show hosts hated the Fairness Doctrine. Conservative voices, for instance, found a greater number of opportunities to make their way onto the airwaves through religious broadcasting, which often eluded the regulators.[3] During the 1950s and 1960s, there were a growing number of these right-wing radio broadcasters who were taking to the airwaves and openly challenging the FCC regulation. The rules were not well enforced, so there were a number of opportunities for opponents to get on the air. In 1963, Myer Feldman reported to the president, in a secret study of right-wing movements, that conservative philanthropists were spending between $15 and $25 million every year to provide support to conservative broadcasts that aired on one thousand stations all over the country.[4]

In a dramatic surge of right-wing talk, conservatives were openly flouting the Fairness Doctrine. There were over a thousand shows by 1964 broadcasting all over the nation, funded by wealthy conservative philanthropists like H. L. Hunt and Howard Pew, which were sound pieces for the right. The *Twentieth Century Reformation Hour* featured Reverend Carl McIntire of New Jersey, who called civil rights a movement "working for a Socialist order in this free land," and whose show played every weekday in forty-five states, and the *Manion Forum*, hosted by the former dean of the Notre Dame law school, Clarence Manion, who had a huge following on over 261 radio stations.[5]

During a fifteen-minute show that aired on the *Pennsylvania Christian Crusade Radio Hour* (on a station owned by the Red Lion Broadcast

Company), Reverend Billy James Hargis delivered a blistering speech in which he attacked everything that he felt was liberal, from UAW President Walter Reuther to the United Nations. In this particular broadcast, Hargis charged that a well-known investigative journalist named Fred Cook, who had published hard-hitting books about the FBI and Barry Goldwater as well as a controversial article in *The Nation* entitled "Radio Right: Hate Clubs on the Air,"[6] had written for a communist publication and had defended Alger Hiss. Hargis also charged that Cook had attempted to bribe New York officials. Cook was a well-respected print journalist who had been receiving information about conservative talk radio from the Democratic National Committee, which had been increasingly concerned about right-wing organizations that were sprouting up around the country.[7]

Listening to the show from his home near Asbury Park, New Jersey, Cook was furious when he heard the charges that Hargis was making about him. As soon as the show ended, Cook sent a letter to the owners of the station saying, "I shall expect you to grant me equal time, at your expense, as provided in FCC regulations, to answer in appropriate fashion this scandalous and libelous attack." Executives at Red Lion sent him back a notification that included the costs for airtime, asking him what he wanted to purchase.[8] In their minds, they owed him nothing.

Cook believed that the company was violating the FCC regulation. The FCC concurred with Cook. Red Lion still resisted and took the case to court. The Court of Appeals for the District of Columbia upheld the decision of the FCC. "The requirement that a broadcaster seek out any person who is alleged to have been personally attacked, furnish him a script, tape or summary of the broadcast, and grant him free time to reply, irrespective of ability to pay, places an obvious and unreasonable burden on the exercise of free speech," complained Reverend John Norris, who owned Red Lion. "I don't feel this is a fair decision. I won't take it." He challenged the decision.

The case ended up in the Supreme Court. As the justices were reviewing the case, many network leaders were saying that the regulation should be eliminated. "The decision will have a major impact not only upon the entire broadcasting industry but upon the vigor and quality of the discussion of public affairs in the United States," claimed CBS, NBC, and the Radio-Television News Director Association.[9]

In 1969, the Supreme Court issued, in a unanimous decision, *Red Lion Broadcasting Co., Inc. v. Federal Communications Commission*, in which they upheld the constitutionality of the Fairness Doctrine. The Court said that the

FCC had the right to uphold the regulation, though it was not required to do so. Equal time had survived. The Court ruled that the FCC had the authority to impose these kinds of requirements in exchange for granting a license. The doctrine, the Court said, followed the wishes of Congress, which had decided that the public interest should be a guiding principle in determining who gained access to the airwaves. The FCC had very clearly defined the public interest as meaning "ample play for the free and fair competition of opposing views," and the decision on this conservative broadcaster fit those guidelines. The Court rejected the claim that the broadcaster had made in saying that this regulation violated free speech. At the heart of the Court's decision was the "scarcity rationale." According to the Court, given that there were a limited number of radio frequencies, Congress had the right to maintain certain requirements in determining who would be granted a license. Free speech, the Court said, was "the right of the viewers and listeners, not the right of the broadcasters."[10]

Although enforcement of the Fairness Doctrine had been spotty, the existence of the federal rules, with the potential of court action, had created ongoing pressure against the political presentation of news. The rules also helped to support the kind of journalistic norms that Michael Schudson has written about, which made objectivity a goal of everyone in the news business.

Emboldened by the Court's decision, two years later the FCC further strengthened the provision by putting in place a new procedure called the "Ascertainment of Community Needs." The process stipulated that stations would have to provide a report each time they renewed their license, explaining how they were helping to discuss issues that were of concern to the communities that watched or listened to them. In 1974, the FCC released a report in which they said that the Fairness Doctrine was "the single most important requirement of operation in the public interest—the sine qua non for grant of renewal of license."[11]

Conservatives as well as broadcasters who opposed the doctrine did not give up. Despite their disappointment with the *Red Lion* case, the Supreme Court had offered them some solace in 1974 with a ruling in *Miami Herald Publishing Co. v. Tornillo*, which said that newspapers could not be subject to the same rule, since in the case of print journalism it could stifle free speech. In the decision, Chief Justice Warren Burger wrote, "Government-enforced right of access inescapably dampens the vigor and limits the variety of public debate."

Opponents of the regulation gained strength after the 1980 presidential election. President Ronald Reagan strongly supported repeal as part of his broader effort to promote deregulation. Like many other conservatives (though not all), Reagan believed that, notwithstanding claims of objectivity, the media clearly leaned to the left. Opening up the airwaves would provide the right with more opportunities to communicate their message to voters.

Not all Republicans agreed with the president. As Nicole Hemmer shows in this book, some figures on the right saw the Fairness Doctrine as a way to go after the existing network structure. There were some Republicans in Congress, including a young Republican firebrand from Georgia, Newt Gingrich, and Mississippi Republican Trent Lott, who believed that the Fairness Doctrine provided an important check against the liberal bias in the media. They agreed on the problem but differed on the policy solution. The grassroots activist Phyllis Schlafly, for instance, disagreed with the administration. Since the doctrine had not been perfectly enforced, there was still more than enough room to broadcast rightward-leaning shows. Gary Bauer, who worked for Reagan's Office of Policy Development, warned in a confidential memo to the White House that without the Fairness Doctrine "the networks are under no serious imposition to present both sides. It is the only 'stick in the closet' to ensure a fair hearing." Given that, in their minds, the ideological bias of the networks was liberal, he believed that repeal would hurt the right.[12]

Notwithstanding the splits that existed, Republican supporters of the Fairness Doctrine were overshadowed by conservatives who wanted to rules to be jettisoned. As Clarence Brown of the Justice Department argued, "Broadcasters are subject to a different set of rules in this regard from those applied to print journalists: there is no Federal Newspaper Commission second-guessing the editorial decisions made by newspaper editors, and attempts to impose similar restrictions on newspapers have been struck down by the courts."[13]

Dramatic technological changes were also rendering the policy more difficult to defend. Cable television started to undermine the rationale of scarcity that the Supreme Court had outlined as a basis for the doctrine. With satellite technology, the space available for broadcasting was proliferating at a rapid rate, so there was less need for the government to decide who would be able to broadcast. In June 1980, CNN had launched its twenty-four-hour cable news network. As Brown argued in his memo, "the presence of a large number of free broadcast voices is the best guarantee that the public will have full access to the information necessary to reach their own conclusion on any given issue. . . . Since 1969, the number of broadcast outlets has grown more than 30 percent and the number of cable TV subscribers from seven to more than 40 million."[14]

The federal courts created another chip in the regulatory armor of the government in 1984. In the *FCC v. League of Women Voters*, the D.C. Circuit of the U.S. Court of Appeals reexamined a 1959 amendment by Congress that had been said to provide legislative support for the Fairness Doctrine. But, the court ruled, legislators had only clarified the communications issue rather than officially legitimating the doctrine. In a 2–1 decision, the court, with Robert Bork and Antonin Scalia writing the language, ruled that "we do not believe that language adopted in 1959 made the Fairness Doctrine a binding statutory obligation." They concluded that the FCC had the right to enforce the rule but were not required to do so.[15]

Reagan's strategy to push back against existing regulations was to staff bureaucracies and commissions with civil servants who opposed the mission of their organizations. This was the case with the FCC. In 1985, under Chairman Mark Fowler, the FCC announced that it would conduct another detailed investigation into the doctrine to see whether it was still constitutional given the changes that had taken place in the market, and what effect the regulations had on free speech.

Fowler was a well-known opponent of the Fairness Doctrine who had been working with Reagan since he ran for the presidency in 1976. When the Supreme Court issued its *Red Lion* decision, he had published an article in the *Texas Law Review* arguing that the constitutional basis of the doctrine— spectrum scarcity and the absence of a chilling effect—were no longer true. "We've got to look beyond the conventional wisdom that we must somehow regulate this box," said Fowler, who had worked as a lawyer for the broadcast industry.[16] He believed that television was "just another appliance—it's a toaster with pictures," and he had concluded that "the perception of broadcasters as community trustees should be replaced by a view of broadcasters as marketplace participants." Fowler, whose opponents called him "Mad Mark," believed that the Fairness Doctrine violated the First Amendment rights of stations and stifled debate. The federal government under the current laws had the power to exercise editorial control over the media. In a profile for the left-wing magazine *Mother Jones*, the reporter claimed that Fowler was "on a mission to return broadcasting to an imagined forest primeval, where brave entrepreneurs are free to fight it out, unburdened by government regulation." Fowler announced that he pledged to "take deregulation to the limits of existing law. We should let the marketplace work its will."[17] The well known consumer advocate Ralph Nader would call him the "most damaging appointment Ronald Reagan ever made."[18]

Fowler was not alone. A number of other members of the administration in the Justice Department and the Department of Commerce agreed. Bruce Fein, the general counsel to the FCC, had been arguing for years that changes in electronic technology had rendered the doctrine meaningless. When the Communications Act passed, he wrote in one memo, there had been 583 broadcast stations serving a population of 126.4 million. By 1984, there were 234.2 million people served by 4,736 AM radio stations, 4,671 FM radio stations, and 1,414 television stations. Almost 37 percent of households, he added, had cable television, while there were video delivery services like MDS and DBS that offered even more choices. "The competitive state of the electronic media marketplace assures that without content regulation the First Amendment's goal of 'the widest possible dissemination of information from diverse and antagonistic sources'" will still be achieved. To further complicate matters he added that electronic and print media were converging. Papers like *USA Today* and the *Wall Street Journal* sent news from their national headquarters to local printing plants via satellite, while teletext services were expanding. "Thus I believe that there is no meaningful basis upon which to differentiate the print and broadcast media in terms of the constitutional protection accorded to their content."[19]

With Republicans in control of the Senate, Congress responded to the court decision by instructing the FCC to hold hearings and produce a report on the doctrine and what kinds of alternatives might be used instead. In their final report on the Fairness Doctrine, released in August 1985, Fowler's commission detailed a number of problems with the doctrine, including that it was fundamentally a subjective process to decide what was of public importance and how to determine what views deserved to be heard on any given issue. The doctrine, the report said, violated free speech.[20]

Moreover, the FCC pointed out that the regulations imposed on radio and television were not required of the print media, where the Supreme Court had deemed them to be unconstitutional. The conclusion of their report was that the Fairness Doctrine should no longer stand since it constrained free speech and no longer served the public interest. Their report mentioned a number of instances when broadcasters didn't even air certain stories for fear of legal retribution. "The potential of a chilling effect . . . is not restricted to the fear by a broadcaster that the Commission will find a violation of the fairness doctrine and impose sanctions on the licenses. A licensee may also be inhibited from presenting controversial issue programming by the fear of incurring the various expenses and other burdens which may arise in the context of fairness doctrine litigation regardless of whether or not it is ultimately found to be in violation of the doctrine." The FCC also claimed that the scarcity rationale was no longer applicable to the modern media: "the information services marketplace has expanded markedly, thereby making it unnecessary to rely upon intrusive government regulation in order to assure that the public has access to the marketplace of ideas." The number of radio stations had jumped from 2,564 in 1949 to 9,766 in 1985; there had been 51 television stations in 1949, increasing to 9,766 in 1985, along with 6,000 cable stations.[21]

Sensing that victory was at hand, the National Association of Broadcasters mounted a massive public relations and lobbying campaign to kill the provision. Its president, Edward Fritts, argued that if the provision was repealed television and radio stations would actually be able to offer more diverse views. *Chicago Tribune* columnist Stephen Chapman wrote that "A free press doesn't mean requiring that every newspaper present all points of view. If you don't like the conservative slant of The Wall Street Journal, fine—buy the New York Times instead. But don't expect the government to force the Journal to publish opinions it finds repugnant. The right answer to network TV bias is the one provided by Sen. Jesse Helms (R-N.C.)—get your own network and run it according to your own political beliefs. Then let viewers decide which version of the news they want to see. If Dan Rather is really out of step with mainstream America, CBS would prosper with a more conservative tilt."[22]

There were groups such as Morality in the Media in Massachusetts that desperately urged the administration to stop moving toward deregulation. They warned the president in November 1986 that the "American sense of fair play" was threatened.[23] There were other supporters of the Fairness Doctrine who joined them, including companies like Mobil, that feared that abandoning the provision could create too many opportunities for voices critical of the corporate world. That, however, was not their formal justification, which rested on constitutional arguments. "Whatever its shortcomings," the company said in a full-page ad, "the Fairness Doctrine preserves a level playing field in the market place of ideas. To abolish the doctrine, the company said, would weaken the oversight over a special class of monopolists—and diminish the First Amendment rights of the rest of us."[24]

Most Democrats in Congress opposed eliminating the Fairness Doctrine. The party claimed that it had been good for broadcasting and that the rules provided the government some authority to make sure that the networks devoted time to the news. "Unlike the print media," said Oklahoma Democrat Mike Synar, "broadcasters have a license, something no one else can have. With that license comes responsibility."[25] House Democrats argued that without the doctrine the owners of stations would have little interest in continuing with serious newscasts. The Democrats had the support of a coalition of good government organizations such as Common Cause and Ralph Nader, who warned that "The fairness doctrine is not only constitutionally permissible, it is constitutionally required." The repeal, he said, would mean that broadcasters could "ignore crucial issues or present only one side" of debates. Liberal organizations such as the American Civil Liberties Union, the AFL-CIO, and Americans for Democratic Action, all core liberal groups, wanted to codify the doctrine. In an unusual alliance, these liberal groups were joined by conservative organizations like the Eagle Forum and the Conservative Political Action Committee.

When Democrats attached a provision requiring the Fairness Doctrine to a $600 billion spending bill. Republicans tried to rebuff their efforts. "It's absolutely contrary to the First Amendment for us to make a law that intends to control or inhibit freedom of expression," claimed Iowa Republican Tom Tauke.[26] Despite their best efforts, Congress passed legislation formalizing the regulation.

The next step was to veto the bill. Kenneth Cribb, Reagan's domestic advisor, urged the president to veto the bill on the grounds that the doctrine was unconstitutional. Reagan vetoed it with a message that Fowler had written. The latest doctrine from the FCC, he said, "strongly suggests that the Fairness Doctrine is at best unnecessary and at worst actually results in less diversity of speech than would obtain if there were a total free market."[27] Within the administration, the White House Counsel's office, the Justice Department, the Commerce Department, and the Office of Management and Budget all wanted the president to veto the bill. As Kenneth Cribb wrote advisor Rhett Dawson, "the Fairness Doctrine in Broadcasting Act is itself unconstitutional because, in violation of the First Amendment, it requires the private owners of television and radio stations in every state to publish statements by members of the general public that they do not agree with, under the threat of criminal penalties to be imposed by a five member Commission of the Federal Government." Cribb called the Fairness Doctrine an "abomination." He complained that some conservatives "dislike the big media so much that they would rather trust their fate to a five member Federal Commission than rely on decentralized competitive market forces to preserve their access to the public. This is the height of folly."[28]

The opponents of regulation called on the president to veto the bill. The National Association of Broadcasters and the Radio-Television News Directors Association called on the president to take action. So too did the editors of the *Washington Post*, which on June 10, 1987, published an editorial calling for veto of the bill.[29] "Ignoring the fact that there is nothing 'fair' about the so-called 'fairness doctrine' with which government can control the broadcasting of ideas in this country, Congress has voted to convert this chilling federal regulation into a full-blown law. . . . It is a dangerous government control of free, independent, *responsive* broadcast journalism," the editors warned.[30]

Upon issuing the veto, Reagan said:

> Quite apart from these technological advances, we must not ignore the obvious intent of the First Amendment, which is to promote vigorous public debate and a diversity of viewpoints in the public forum as a whole, not in any particular medium, let alone in any particular journalistic outlet. History has shown that the dangers of an overly timid or biased press cannot be averted through bureaucratic regulation, but only through the freedom and competition that the First Amendment sought to guarantee. . . . S. 742 simply cannot be reconciled with the freedom of speech and the press secured by our Constitution. It is, in my judgment, unconstitutional. Well-intentioned as S. 742 may be, it would be inconsistent with the First Amendment and with the American tradition of independent journalism. Accordingly I am compelled to disapprove this measure.[31]

Regulation supporters on Capitol Hill failed to override the president's veto. Republican Robert Packwood warned that the Fairness Doctrine was a "terrible power to put in the hands of government in this country, any government, conservative, liberal or otherwise." Observing these events in Washington, columnist Clarence Page wrote that,

> Constitutionally, the doctrine stood on Jell-O, unless I missed something in my readings of the Bill of Rights, like a footnote where the

Founding Fathers said, "This does not apply to television and radio. Perhaps even in this enlightened age too many of us still tend to regard that boob tube as some sort of witchcraft, a magic genie filled with treachery and mischief who must somehow be kept corked up in the lamp or, at least, kept on a short leash. Leave it to the administration of former broadcaster Ronald 'Dutch' Reagan to try to cut through the witchcraft and strike the doctrine down."[32]

Soon after the veto, the FCC announced that it would no longer enforce the Fairness Doctrine. The Syracuse Peace Council filed a complaint that a local television station had broadcast an ad supporting nuclear power without giving them equal time. The FCC refused to take up their case and then went even further by getting rid of the doctrine altogether. In doing so, the FCC proclaimed that: "The intrusion of government into the content of programming . . . actually inhibits the presentation of controversial issues of public importance to the detriment of the public and the degradation of the editorial prerogative of broadcast journalists." Dennis Patrick, the chairman of the FCC who had replaced Fowler, explained that, "We seek to extend to the electronic press the same First Amendment guarantees that the print media have enjoyed since our country's inception." The general counsel for the commission added that with 1,300 television stations and 10,000 radio stations in the United States, "numerical scarcity simply cannot justify different First Amendment treatment" for print than radio and television. The counsel of the FCC said that the rule had created an atmosphere "under which they [broadcasters] have shied away from covering controversial issues in news, documentaries and editorial advertisements. . . . [This] completely frustrate[d] the goal of the doctrine to foster robust debate and diversity of views."[33]

The decision was huge. Radio and television broadcasters understood that the regulatory obstacles toward politicized news had been dramatically lowered. The end of the regulation, combined with changing media opportunities resulting from the advent of cable, had created a new atmosphere. Among the first to take advantage of the new policy were conservative talk radio hosts, whose numbers expanded rapidly all over the country, with broadcasts by extraordinarily political and pointed right-wing broadcasters railing against liberalism, Democrats, and all of their opponents. Later the left would mimic what the right had done by establishing a number of outlets (rarely as successful) where the news could be presented from a liberal perspective. As print journalism felt intense pressure to survive the growing popularity of broadcast news, many outlets replicated the contentious style of television and radio (and later the Internet).

Future efforts to reinstate the doctrine never succeeded. Politicians who wanted to bring back the Fairness Doctrine used a number of rationales, ranging from the fact that the political economy of broadcasting meant there still was scarcity in the ability to produce news, to the argument that newscasters still needed to serve the public interest. The recent victory of net neutrality rules within the FCC, which opponents called the Fairness Doctrine of the Internet, gave some potential for regulatory bite even if the production of news was now virtually limitless in the era of streaming broadcasts. But thus far the idea of enforcing balance seems quixotic to most observers of contemporary journalism.

Without federal restraints and with unlimited access to broadcasting, the nation moved deeper and deeper into an age of polarized news without anything to hold these forces back.

CHAPTER 12

The Multiple Political Roles of American Journalism

Michael Schudson

American journalists often profess to stand outside of politics. And yet they also hold that no institution is more essential to constituting democracy than the press. This is not a contradiction. An umpire or referee stands outside of the game of baseball or football, soccer, or basketball, and yet the games would be difficult or impossible without them—and difficult or impossible if the players or the viewers did not have faith in the referees' essential fairness and consummate professionalism.

But the metaphor of the umpire does not quite fit journalism. In sports, the responsible referee does not ever enter into the game. The responsible journalist does, sometimes. Some journalists of high professional standards and standing may even enter into the game of politics regularly. The professional bodies that formally or informally represent journalists may on occasion enter into the game. The most prestigious journalists in Washington, who talk to government officials and publish information they relay, recognize that the information the source provides in an interview may be a "leak," or it may be an authorized "plant," or it may be what David Pozen has dubbed a "pleak"—something ambiguously in between an authorized plant and an unauthorized leak.[1] The reporter here is not necessarily playing the same game that the official is playing—politics—but is playing a game of his or her own, proving their journalistic skill and advancing their career by publicly demonstrating intimacy with government officials. This is not necessarily politics, but it is not not-politics, either.

There is value for journalism and, I think, for democracy when journalists assert their neutrality or professionalism. But from the viewpoint of a historian or social scientist analyzing the press, there is no virtue in taking these pronouncements at face value. In a recent episode, NBC news anchor Brian Williams backpedaled from, and apologized for, his statement that in covering the Iraq war he had flown in a helicopter that was hit by RPG fire. The military newspaper *Stars and Stripes* quickly and correctly reported that this never happened and that Williams had puffed up his own risk-taking and heroism. In his apology, Williams said, "In the midst of a career spent covering and consuming news, it has become painfully apparent to me that I am presently too much a part of the news, due to my actions."[2] This is an awkward adaptation of the self-defining, self-protecting, and self-legitimating trope among journalists, the distinction between "covering" news as a neutral bystander and becoming "a part of the news," a dangerous, prohibited practice. But it is not, in fact, prohibited in practice, even though it is denied in professional self-presentation.

What I want to do in this paper is to offer categories of instances when journalists enter into political activities they claim to stand apart from. These are important elements in what journalists do, but I caution readers that this does not mean that professionalism does not exist. It does not mean that "objectivity" is a patently false ideology. It means that life in a democracy close to the centers of political power is very complicated, that journalists can and often do wear multiple hats at once, and that, leaving aside the occasional saint, purity of motive and action is impossible.

I am going to give a few examples here, primarily from the era since 1945, by which point an ideal of objectivity and professionalism was regnant in American journalism. If we look back to the nineteenth or early twentieth century, politicized journalism was so much taken for granted that fastidious efforts of journalists to demonstrate their political neutrality were not a fundamental element in the image journalists projected.

This is not a general historical narrative. It is simply a list, illustrated with historical examples, of ways in which the U.S. press has acted politically, or at least has acted politically in this democracy at a particular moment.

The Press as Partisan or Advocate

This is simple, obvious, and important, and I have nothing to add to what everybody knows: almost all daily newspapers have an editorial page where they advocate public policies, endorse candidates for office, and otherwise express opinions on public affairs that the owner of their news organization approves or, at least, does not actively disapprove.

The editorial page, with its direct attempt to persuade rather than to report, is a journalistic practice of long standing. It is a political intervention. And for the ideologists of professionalism in journalism, it is invariably ignored. More than ignored, it may even be shunned. Former *Washington Post* editor Leonard Downie Jr. (a friend and sometime coauthor of mine) told me that as executive editor he never read his paper's editorial page. The editorial page was as much a separate department as advertising or home delivery— and Downie did not want the news pages to be inadvertently influenced by advocacy positions taken in editorials.

Journalists have also been advocates outside the editorial pages but without the same legitimacy. The opinion columnist is granted a longer leash to be a party or candidate or policy advocate, although not in the mandarin fashion of Joseph Alsop or Walter Lippmann in the past. Those gentlemen did much more than advocate in their columns. They also advised presidents behind the scene. Lippmann was all over politics. He advised Republican presidential candidate Wendell Willkie in 1940. Also in 1940 he worked out with the British ambassador to the United States a plan to get around isolationist opposition to providing aid to Britain, enlisted General John J. Pershing to make the case to the public, and wrote Pershing's speech. He worked with a Roosevelt aide to draft what would become the Lend-Lease Act. And he was still at it in 1945 when he teamed up with *New York Times* correspondent James Reston to convince Republican Senator Arthur Vandenberg to abandon his isolationist leanings. The two journalists then wrote a speech for Vandenberg that he delivered in the Senate to great acclaim. Among those giving the speech public praise were Reston, who wrote in a news story in the *Times* that the speech was "wise" and "statesmanlike," and Lippmann, who used his column to praise Vandenberg's turnabout.[3]

The Press as Lobbyist

News organizations in the United States are almost all private businesses, and they sometimes have important financial interests at stake in government actions. Sometimes they advocate for their business interests by, say, testifying before Congress, or advocating in the hallways of Congress for favorable postal rates, or urging upon the Federal Communications Commission a ruling they believe would best serve their private financial advantage. Sometimes the news media take positions on behalf of their professional, rather than their strictly economic, interests, and this cuts closer to matters that make journalism professionals squeamish. Here the press advocates for public policies not as corporate entities but as professional entities, and the most active effort comes not from publishers but from professional associations of working journalists.

Let me offer an extended example. The Freedom of Information Act (FOIA) became law in 1966. It became a much more effective law in 1974. But it began with a hard-working California congressman named John Moss. In 1953 Moss was a freshman congressman and innocently asked the Civil Service Commission for data on dismissals of government employees for disloyalty. He did not want names, he wanted numbers. The Civil Service Commission said no. "Well, the Commission refused to supply the information requested by the committee," Moss later recalled. "This was my first experience with an agency refusing to respond to the legitimate demands of the legislative body. . . . It was the case of a freshman member being somewhat outraged over Executive arrogance." It took Moss a decade to move the Congress from the individual outrage of one man to collective action. It was the first freedom of information act since Sweden instituted one in 1766. It was the first in the world with significant influence. It had no public support—and no public opposition. No one much cared outside Congress. FOIA does not cover Congress itself, nor the courts, nor the president, but only the executive agencies. It became law as an effort of Congress to hold the executive to account. It is used frequently by journalists and historians, among others.

How did it pass? How did it pass when the Eisenhower, Kennedy, and Johnson administrations showed little interest in it and when, in the end, every single executive agency head who testified before Congress testified against it? It passed with the help of the news media, not in covering it but in advocating for it in the halls of Congress.

In 1955, organized groups in journalism cheered the establishment of the subcommittee on government information that John Moss chaired. James S. Pope, who had served on and chaired the American Society of Newspaper Editors' (ASNE) Freedom of Information Committee in the early 1950s, recalled that the establishment of the Moss committee came as a welcome surprise to journalism's leaders. "We had not really expected to get such political clout so early; it was like gaining a fleet of nuclear subs."[4]

Moss committee staffers early on consulted with James Russell Wiggins of the *Washington Post*, then head of the ASNE Freedom of Information Committee; Lyle C. Wilson, United Press vice president and Washington bureau manager; Bill Beale, Associated Press Washington bureau manager; and a dozen reporters who could testify to specific instances of government suppression of the news. Media leaders backed Moss from the beginning, and Moss encouraged their support. "I hope more of you will bring your complaints to the Subcommittee," he told a meeting of news executives in 1957. "By demanding your right of access to Federal information—and by bringing the case to the attention of the Subcommittee if your right is disregarded—you can help reverse the present Federal attitude of secrecy."[5]

ASNE, founded in 1923, had taken no interest in government secrecy until World War II, and then only as a problem in other countries; ASNE took it for granted that Americans could and should instruct the rest of the world in press freedom. Only as the Cold War developed did journalists become concerned about press freedom at home.

ASNE created its first committee on freedom of information—the Committee on World Freedom of Information—in 1948. In the same year, Sigma Delta Chi, the national journalism honor society, created a Committee on Advancement of Freedom of Information—likewise with a global, not a national, focus. The ASNE and Sigma Delta Chi both moved toward a domestic focus by 1951.[6]

A freedom of information movement also developed at state and local levels as at the national level—which is to say, journalists were by no means exclusively preoccupied with secrecy related to national security. A 1952 *Indiana Law Journal* article on "Access to Official Information" opens with three examples, only one of which was about national security—a New Mexico newspaper reporter was denied permission to witness a U.S. Navy rocket testing at the White Sands, New Mexico, proving grounds. The other examples are about the confidentiality of federal tax collectors' actions in levying fines on Albany, New York, taverns for adulterating liquor, and Oregon's state board of education's secret meetings about separating the state university's dental school from its medical school.[7] Sigma Delta Chi, the AP managing editors, ASNE, the National Editorial Association, and state press associations all promoted state open meeting and public records laws.[8]

This freedom of information movement in journalism proved a natural ally for Moss—and he was equally an ally for the movement. Sometimes "the Moss Committee staff wrote the press organizations' freedom-of-information annual reports—which were in turn widely reproduced in the press in terms laudatory of the Moss Committee."[9] The committee's investigations were organized in consultation with key leaders in the press, and Moss employed a staff dominated by former newspaper reporters, including his chief of staff, Sam Archibald, a former *Sacramento Bee* reporter. Moss spoke all over the country—often to journalism schools and press associations. Journalists testified before his committee and offered him useful examples of government suppression of the news.[10]

Communications scholar Jim Carey wrote, in one of his last publications, that journalists are obliged to abandon their objectivity in exactly this domain—they "can be independent or objective about everything but democracy," he wrote. "About democratic institutions, about the way of life of democracy, journalists are not permitted to be indifferent, nonpartisan, or objective. It is their one compulsory passion, for it forms the ground condition of their practice."[11] American journalists and journalism organizations had come to the same conclusion in practice, if not in theory, fifty years before Carey wrote those words. This chapter in the history of American journalism is, as Carey intimates, inconsistent with general professions of political detachment, but it needs to be incorporated into how we think about the institution of journalism in democracy.

The Editor as National Security Executive

American journalists act in ways that express obligation to and affiliation with the nation-state. When they have their hands on a story they think may reveal secrets that bear on national security, they customarily notify the government ahead of publication and even negotiate the content of the story with the White House, Defense Department, or other relevant agencies. This was the case when the *New York Times* learned of the impending Bay of Pigs invasion of Cuba and voluntarily modified its story at the strenuous urging of the White House.[12]

The same thing happened in 1986 when the *Washington Post* learned of a secret U.S. underwater mechanism code-named "Ivy Bells" that had successfully tapped Soviet cable communications. The *Post* also knew that the operation had been compromised by Jack Pelton, a low-level technician for the National Security Agency (NSA), who sold information to the Russians. Newsroom executives at the *Post* met with the NSA director, Lieutenant

General William Odom, who urged them not to publish anything. Odom contended that any story about Ivy Bells would be dangerous to the country, revealing to the Soviets something they did not know.

But, editor Ben Bradlee objected, Pelton had spilled the beans, the Soviets already knew about Ivy Bells! Nevertheless, General Odom responded, which Soviets know? There might have been internal Soviet secrecy. There might have been a cover-up. A story in the *Post* would set off a general alarm in the Soviet Union, building pressure for the Soviets to increase anti-espionage measures. Odom's protest was cogent enough to give the *Post* pause. Successive drafts were written, each less detailed than the one before. Bradlee repeatedly asked his colleagues, "What is this story's social purpose?" In the end, the *Post* published the story—over the objections of the administration—after a back-and-forth that went on for months.[13]

The *Post* made similar decisions in 2009 when longtime investigative reporter Bob Woodward received a copy of a confidential report produced by General Stanley McChrystal about the war in Afghanistan. The *Post* informed the Pentagon and the White House about what was coming. The secretary of defense, the national security advisor, and the vice chair of the Joint Chiefs of Staff each asked the *Post* to reconsider. Editor Marcus Brauchli, speaking of the incident later, observed proudly that, in the American system, the government could ask, but not command, the paper not to publish; the decision was in the end the editor's, not the government's.[14]

In these cases and in many others, editors for commercial news organizations voluntarily assume the mantle of secretaries of defense, acting—ultimately on their own—as stewards of public safety.

In 2003, Dean Baquet, today executive editor of the *New York Times*, then managing editor at the *Los Angeles Times*, was involved in a decision about whether to publish a damaging story about Arnold Schwarzenegger, then a leading gubernatorial candidate in California. The paper had gathered a half-dozen credible allegations by women in the movie industry that Schwarzenegger had sexually harassed them. With the story ready to print just days before the election, the editors wondered if they should delay running it until after the election. Would the article not seem to be a "hit piece" sprung on Schwarzenegger? Would the timing not make it difficult for him to respond? Baquet later told a reporter (after the *Times* went ahead and published the story), "Sometimes people don't understand that to not publish is a big decision for a newspaper and almost a political act. That's not an act of journalism. You're letting your decision-making get clouded by things that have nothing to do with what a newspaper is supposed to do."

Baquet's statement is a revealing and representative example of professional news ideology: journalism is journalism, not politics, and it should stick to that role. Journalism is making information public; choosing not to publish for any reason—except, in Baquet's view, insufficient journalistic quality or the possibility that publishing could endanger a life—abrogates one's professional responsibility.

That's not hogwash, but neither is it an accurate representation of what journalists do. Now that Mr. Baquet is the top editor at the *New York Times*, he surely finds himself on occasion in the same position as others before him—engaging in "almost a political act," conscientiously placing national security ahead of the journalistic responsibility to raise hell, come what may. Nowhere, to the best of my knowledge, have these dramatic and wrenching moments been reconciled with the notion of journalism's "outsider" standing. Indeed, nowhere, so far as I know, have these moments become a central part of the way U.S. journalists discuss their own history or construct their own identity. They are just too uncomfortable and too deeply at odds with how journalists like to see themselves.

The Journalist as Government Insider

Journalists have often been employed in American government. They have been appointed to office. They have been elected to office. They have been friends and confidants of presidents. They have routinely served as press secretaries, of course, and media advisers, but they have also served in a variety of other staff roles. Collectively, the fact that journalists move into government, imbued with a professional ideology alien to most of the lawyers and others who inhabit the world of public officialdom, helps orient government to keeping its publics in mind and strategizing how to appeal to them. I will highlight just one instance here. This concerns reporter Richard Conlon, who became staff director of the Democratic Study Group, a pioneering caucus in the House of Representatives. Through Dick Conlon, journalism played a key role in making Congress a more public and democratic institution. Let me go back a step:

Congress in the 1950s and 1960s was stunningly undemocratic. It was undemocratic when John Moss arrived in 1953. It was still undemocratic when Tom Foley, a Democrat from Washington, arrived as a freshman in 1965. Foley recollected how Agriculture Committee chair Harold Cooley (D-N.C.) addressed him and other freshman members at the committee's first meeting: "I hate and detest, hate and detest, to hear senior members of this committee, of either party, interrupted by junior members of this committee, of either party. You new members in particular will find that you will require some time, some of you months, others of you regrettably probably years, before you develop sufficient knowledge and experience to contribute constructively to our work. In the meantime, silence and attention, silence and attention is the rule for new members of this committee."

From 1959 on, liberal Democrats grew more and more frustrated—despite having a majority in the Democratic Party, they could not get any initiatives past the southern conservative committee chairmen.

By a practice dating to the first Congress, amendments to bills before the House were discussed and voted on when the House convened itself as the so-called committee of the whole. All members of the House are members of the committee of the whole, but the committee of the whole can convene with a much smaller quorum than the House in ordinary session. This affords it a great deal of flexibility. Moreover, individual votes in the committee of the whole normally went unrecorded. Often voting was by unrecorded "teller vote."[15] In this practice, each member of the House, one by one, walks up to a "teller" and votes. The total count—so many yeas, so many nays—then became part of the public record. *What was not public is which representatives voted which way.*

This meant that all votes on amendments to bills taken up in the committee of the whole that were defeated would be forever shielded from the public eye; constituents would never know if their representatives had supported or opposed key amendments on critical legislation if the amendments went down to defeat. Only amendments that the committee of the whole approved would be voted on publicly when the bill came up for final passage after the House resolved itself back into the House of Representatives.

This changed in 1970 with the passage of the Legislative Reorganization Act. That act opened up committee deliberations to the public, allowed television coverage of deliberations on the House floor, made committee votes public, and ended the unrecorded teller vote in the committee of the whole. What enabled these reforms to triumph?

They were made possible in no small measure by the efforts of the Democratic Study Group. The DSG was the first enduring, formally organized "caucus" in the history of the U.S. Congress, established in 1959 by Eugene McCarthy, then a representative in the House, later a Senator, and in 1968 an antiwar aspirant for president.

A Minnesota reporter, Dick Conlon, became the full-time staff director of the DSG in 1968. He quickly turned the DSG into a crackerjack research outfit. He did so by insisting that it live up to his journalistic values—give both sides of a story, and write clearly and lucidly for people with very short attention spans—which is to say, members of Congress. The DSG fact sheets and reports, and their own research on voting in the Congress, are brilliant pieces of analysis, summary, and condensation. Conlon was effective not only because he was a very accomplished writer himself but because he was a perfectionist with others, too.

Liberals in the House in 1969 had begun working on procedural reforms to make the House responsive to its own liberal and moderate majority. The DSG became especially interested in ways to make the workings of Congress more publicly visible and, in particular, to make votes in the committee of the whole available to the press and the public. Conlon called attention in the DSG executive committee to the possibility that they could sell the procedural reforms they favored, including ending the unrecorded teller votes, by packaging them as "anti-secrecy" amendments to the pending reform bill. He thought this would attract news media interest, a notion that arose for him in a conversation with a reporter friend. In 1970, the DSG produced several brief reports on secrecy and unrecorded teller voting. Secrecy, according to one of the reports, reduces the effectiveness of the House, inhibits the press in its responsibilities, and denies the public the "information to which it is entitled in a democratic society."[16]

The Democratic Study Group decided to promote their anti-secrecy amendments to the general public, believing that the topic of antisecrecy would catch on with journalists. "Secrecy was just a magic button with the press," Conlon recalled later. "As a trained journalist myself I know what made me salivate when I was reporting and I know that an editorial writer in particular sitting there behind a desk, frustrated as hell and not being able to get out and get at things is always railing against government secrecy and it was just the magic button that turned a shower of things on."[17] DSG chair Donald Fraser wrote hundreds of letters to editorial page editors and columnists, and he got support from the University of Missouri's Freedom of Information Center, which contacted 770 newspapers and hundreds of radio and television stations, as well, to support the amendment.

DSG efforts produced results in newspaper editorials and opinion columns around the country. What the newspapers found irresistible was not simply the idea of antisecrecy measures, but also the delicious irony that the vote to lift the veil on unrecorded voting in the committee of the whole would be taken by an unrecorded vote in the committee of the whole. One editorial or column after another delighted in the irony. It allowed the press to support an important but obscure reform and to ridicule Congress at the same time.[18] It was no accident that so many publications noticed the irony—the Democratic Study Group told them about it in DSG chair Donald Fraser's "Dear Editor" letter June 30, 1970.[19]

Democracy is a matter of the public's being oriented to government, but also orienting government to the public. In orienting government to the public, journalists inside government have made a difference.

Journalism as Agenda Advocacy

Partisan advocacy in print or electronic or digital journalism has a deep history.[20] As journalism became professionalized in the twentieth century and overt partisanship in the news columns became more rare, journalists nonetheless on occasion have self-consciously promoted attention to specific public issues.

Some of this is obvious and widely noted. The news media collectively embrace a "watchdog" role. They not only report on what government officials say and do but on what they promise—and whether they make good on their promises, and on what their sworn obligations are—and whether they live up to them. Academic studies offer abundant evidence that when the press covers politicians well, politicians become more responsive to public needs. (One especially convincing study of how well and how quickly different states in India respond to food shortages demonstrates that where media are plentiful and active, politicians have been more responsive than where media are scarce or supine.)[21]

If the general "public guardian" role of the press is much noted, there is less attention to acts of journalistic advocacy on specific topics a reporter or editor deems worth covering. It would be hard to deny that mainstream U.S. news organizations today should cover the issue of same-sex marriage—the issue has been joined, in state after state, as a legitimate public controversy. But at what point did this issue, in recent memory too touchy for even many liberal Democrats to embrace (Barack Obama found it too hot to handle in his 2008 campaign for president), come to routinely command mainstream news attention?

In the 1970, Philip Shabecoff, a *New York Times* correspondent, newly assigned to the Washington bureau, asked to be on the "environment" beat full-time. His editors said no. When he did an occasional environment-related story, he recalls that the general response he got was, "What, another story about the end of the world, Shabecoff? We carried a story about the end of the world a month ago."[22] Did Shabecoff show the better news judgment— or was his a personal or political judgment that he placed before his news sense? Or were his editors insensitive to a major new public policy issue that required a good newspaper to rethink its priorities? And was it their news sense that was more politicized than his? How far ahead of public opinion or Washington opinion is it appropriate for a news organization to be? How far behind general opinion can it afford to be? There is no answer to these questions, only the recognition that these decisions are not made in some journalistic ivory tower but in a real world where political judgment necessarily enters.

Journalism as the Medium for the Formation of Political Culture

Journalism as a Medium Through Which Politics Flows

So far, I have discussed ways in which specific reporters, editors, and organizations of reporters and editors make political choices and political decisions. But journalism also plays a political role in a far more collective fashion, shaping, constituting, coordinating, and legitimating specific ways of doing politics and specific ways of thinking about politics. It is possible to see this if we look at the changes wrought in journalism and in American public culture broadly speaking between 1960 and the end of the twentieth century.

Consider the work of Steven Clayman and his colleagues in their brilliant study of presidential news conferences, and how reporters' questions during them changed from 1953 through 2000. They find a marked increase in the aggressiveness of questioning. The biggest change came in the late 1960s. While assertive questioning had both ups and downs in the 1980s and 1990s, it never dropped to the low levels of the 1950s and early 1960s. As Clayman and his colleagues conclude, "Sometime around the late 1960s, the tenor of Washington journalism began to change. A growing body of research converges in its portrayal of a shift toward increasingly vigorous and in some respects adversarial treatment of government officials, political candidates, and their policies."[23] Journalists themselves have placed so much emphasis on Watergate (1972–74) as a turning point that they sometimes forget that the big change in the news culture began before Watergate, and they rarely acknowledge at all that the growth of contextual journalism, a term I will explain in a moment, represents a much larger change in the character of news than a reallocation of effort to investigative reporting.

Today, essentially no one defends the journalism of the 1950s. Journalist Paul Duke remembered the Washington press corps after World War II as "rather sleepy" and "content to report from handouts and routine news briefings."[24] Reporters and politicians were frequently "pals," as political scientist Larry Sabato observes.[25] In 1959 veteran journalist Douglass Cater criticized "objective" or "straight" reporting and judged objectivity to be a "worn-out concept."[26] Cater urged that reporters be free "to contribute an added dimension to reporting which is interpretive not editorial journalism."[27]

Journalism moved exactly in the direction of the "added dimension" Cater urged. Katherine Fink and I have charted the growth of what we call contextual reporting. We looked at two weeks' worth of front pages of the *New York Times, Washington Post*, and *Milwaukee Journal* for 1955, 1967, 1979, 1991, and 2003. Contextual reporting—a broad category that includes explanatory reporting but much more—barely turned up in our 1955 sample—8 percent of all front-page stories. By 1991 it represented half of what one finds on the front page of all three of the newspapers we studied. The notion that the news media are dominated today by "he-said-she-said" stories that write themselves is not a valid critique of leading U.S. newspapers, nor has it been for several decades.[28]

What accounts for the change? Clayman, in trying to explain the stunning rise of a more critical and aggressive tone in the questions reporters asked at presidential news conferences, throws his hat in with a change in the culture, norms, and values of journalism. The plausibility of this explanation grows when we recognize that European journalism moved at about the same time in the same direction, even without Vietnam and Watergate.[29]

This lends credence to Clayman's conclusion that a change in newsroom culture is key. But what caused *that*? My hunch is that a substantial part of the answer is that more journalists came to their work with a college education and, simultaneously, college education had become much more an education in critical thinking. Academic culture itself adopted more "adversarial" habits—not so much politically adversarial as intellectually adversarial. Students were expected to learn to "read against the text" in courses in the humanities, not simply to absorb accepted canons of high culture. And in the sciences and social sciences, students were increasingly encouraged not to memorize textbooks but to imagine themselves fledgling scholars, moving on to a next level of insight by criticizing the assumptions, methods, or reasoning of the exemplars whose work they were assigned to read. This was especially true in the research universities and the small liberal arts colleges that dedicated themselves to the same critical ideals and to grooming students to go on to graduate education.

Hisotrians have not yet integrated their own story—the story of higher education—into the broader history of modern American society. Like journalists, academics have come to believe their own public relations literature—that they are outsiders looking in. They—we—are insecure in thinking of our own corner of the world as having actually made a difference.

Journalism as a Matrix in Turning Language into Action

I have been puzzling over a paper by Lynton Keith Caldwell in *Public Administration Review*, published in 1963. Its title was "Environment: A New Focus for Public Policy?" In a scant ten pages or so, Caldwell, a political scientist at Indiana University, proposed that, yes, the environment should be a focus for public policy. What puzzles me about it is that it was so well received, that it is much honored to this day, that there is a serious biography of Caldwell just published last year, and that students of Caldwell's collected his papers and published them as a volume many years later called *Environment as a Focus for Public Policy*. No question mark.

My puzzlement is that, in my opinion, it's not a very good paper. The writing is pedestrian, at best. It is not well argued. When it offers a name for what to call this new "focus," it offers not "environmental policy" or "environmental studies" or even "ecology" but "ekistics," and, needless to say, this did not catch on. What caught on (and certainly not because of Caldwell alone) is the first word of the title of the paper—"environment." It came to be the taken-for-granted watchword of a new consciousness, institutionalized in a new department that *Time* magazine inaugurated in 1969, "The Environment." How on earth did that happen when the term as part of public thinking simply did not exist before 1963?

Now, maybe it doesn't matter. Maybe "conservation" was a perfectly serviceable term. But "conservation" is an action people may take toward the natural world; "environment" is the natural world itself. "Environment" thus shifts the focus from human agency to, in a way, the context in which humans make their lives as having agency of its own, its own demands, its own vulnerabilities, its own retribution if we fail to give it its due. With "conservation," humans look large and the world around us small; with "environment," humans are put in our place.

Does that make a difference? I cannot show exactly how. But we do know that words matter, that catch phrases matter, that rubrics matter, that language carves up the world in one way and not another, and that journalists, among our leading meme-makers, matter. The linguist Charles Hockett argued against the view that language determines how and what humans think. Instead, he suggested, "Languages differ not in what *can* be said in them, but rather as to what it is *relatively easy* to say in them."[30] That is one of the best sentences I have ever come upon in the social sciences, and it has just the subtlety required for thinking about the role of journalism in society. Journalists are in the business of knowing what can be communicated easily. This places them in the public business of politics. They are not there alone. Others in the same business include the President's speechwriters, the advertising executives and media consultants presidential campaigns employ, the directors of topically themed films and documentaries, the writers of gags and monologues for late-night television, the makers of political satire or political polls, and other forums in which the task of reducing the complex to the simple and the prosaic to the memorable is preeminent. But journalists are near the point of origin of the whole machinery of political language, and they often provide the primary forum in which political language takes shape.

Journalists wear political hats. They do so sometimes avowedly (in editorials or opinion columns or as their principal objective in advocacy publications), sometimes under extreme situations that make them uncomfortable (in negotiating with the government to sometimes withhold information from the public to protect national security), sometimes as insiders or people very close to insiders in ways that they prefer not to discuss (except perhaps in memoirs), and sometimes in the course of trying to provide fair-minded and thoughtful leadership in reforming reportorial conventions to adapt to changing social norms and values, either a step behind or a step ahead of public opinion.

To acknowledge all this is not to declare it good, nor to declare it bad, but to declare it, plain and simple. To acknowledge this longstanding and continuing feature of how journalism operates may provide an improved foundation for sorting out what kind of political journalism, or political journalism beset by what sorts of circumstances, we should see as desirable, or as necessary, or as requiring criticism and reform.

NOTES

Introduction

1. See, for example: Paul Starr, *The Creation of the Media* (New York: Basic Books, 2004); Michael Schudson, *Discovering the News* (New York: Basic Books, 1981); Michele Hilmes, *Radio Voices* (Minneapolis: University of Minnesota Press, 1997); David Greenberg, *Republic of Spin* (New York: W. W. Norton, 2016); Kathryn Brownell, *Showbiz Politics* (Chapel Hill: University of North Carolina Press, 2014); Susan Douglas, "Presidents and the Media," in Brian Balogh and Bruce J. Schulman, eds., *Recapturing the Oval Office* (Ithaca, N.Y.: Cornell University Press, 2015); and Lawrence and Cornelia Levine, *The People and the President* (Boston: Beacon Press, 2002).

2. Michael Schudson, "News, Public, Nation," *American Historical Review* 107 (April 2002): 481.

3. Chris Daly, "The Historiography of Journalism History, Part 1: An Overview," *American Journalism* 26 (Winter 2009): 141.

4. John Nerone, "Does Journalism Matter?" *American Journalism* 28 (Autumn 2011): 7.

5. Robert W. McChesney, "Communication for the Hell of It: The Triviality of U.S. Broadcasting History," *Journal of Broadcasting and Electronic Media* 40 (Fall 1996): 540–52.

6. See for example, Starr, *Creation of the Media*; Richard R. John, *Spreading the News: The American Postal System from Franklin to Morse* (Cambridge, Mass.: Harvard University Press, 1995); Richard R. John, *Network Nation: Inventing American Telecommunications* (Cambridge, Mass.: Belknap Press of Harvard University Press, 2010); Chris Daly, *Covering America: A Narrative History of a Nation's Journalism* (Amherst: University of Massachusetts Press, 2012); Michele Hilmes, *Network Nations: A Transnational History of British and American Broadcasting* (London: Routledge, 2011); and Allison Perlman, *Public Interests: Media Advocacy and Struggles over U.S Television* (New Brunswick, N.J.: Rutgers University Press, 2016).

1. Proprietary Interest

1. Francis B. Thurber, "The Right to Combine," *Journal of Social Science* 37 (December 1899): 225–26. For assistance, I am grateful to Elizabeth Benn, John Evans,

Nancy R. John, Heather Cox Richardson, Bruce J. Schulman, Mark Wahlgren Summers, Julian E. Zelizer, and two anonymous referees.

2. Thurber, "Right to Combine," 215.

3. 15 U.S.C. §§ 1–7 (1890).

4. "Records," vol. 1, Boston Wholesale Grocers' Association, October 26, 1905, Baker Library, Harvard Business School, Boston, Massachusetts. I am grateful to Mookie Kideckel for bringing this document to my attention.

5. The concept of "big business" has long been a favorite of historians, even though it is notoriously hard to define. The phrase itself only rarely appeared in print before 1900; a Google NGram search reveals that its occurrence spiked up rapidly between 1900 and 1920. For a recent overview, see Youssef Cassis, "Big Business," in Geoffrey Jones and Jonathan Zeitlin, ed., *Oxford Handbook of Business History* (New York: Oxford University Press, 2007), 171–93.

6. Not all merchants, of course, were men. Yet, since the wealthiest and most powerful merchants *were* men (as well as all the most prominent merchant-antimonopolists), it makes sense to use the male pronoun here to describe the group.

7. David Paul Nord, "The Urban Newspaper and the Victorian City," in Richard R. John and Jonathan Silberstein-Loeb, ed., *Making News: The Political Economy of Journalism in Britain and America from the Glorious Revolution to the Internet* (New York: Oxford University Press, 2015), 73–106; Richard R. John, "Markets, Morality, and the Media: The Election of 1884 and the Iconography of Progressivism," in Gareth Davies and Julian E. Zelizer, ed., *America at the Ballot Box: Elections and Political History* (Philadelphia: University of Pennsylvania Press, 2015), 75–97.

8. Lee Benson, *Merchants, Farmers, and Railroads: Railroad Regulation and New York Politics, 1850–1887* (Cambridge, Mass.: Harvard University Press, 1953); George Hall Miller, *Railroads and the Granger Laws* (Madison: University of Wisconsin Press, 1971); Scott C. James, *Parties, Presidents and the State: Electoral College Competition, Party Leadership, and Democratic Regulatory Choice, 1884–1936* (Cambridge: Cambridge University Press, 2000).

9. Richard R. John, "Robber Barons Redux: Antimonopoly Reconsidered," *Enterprise and Society* 13 (March 2012): 3–5.

10. Richard R. John, *Network Nation: Inventing American Telecommunications* (Cambridge, Mass.: Belknap Press of Harvard University Press, 2010), 124–26, 175–76.

11. Charles Postel, *The Populist Vision* (New York: Oxford University Press, 2007). See also Norman Pollack, *The Just Polity: Populism, Law, and Human Welfare* (Urbana: University of Illinois Press, 1987).

12. John, *Network Nation*, chap. 11.

13. The long and deliberate campaign to legitimize the managerial corporation, including, in particular, the key role in this development that was played by specialists in corporate public relations (a profession called into existence to perform precisely

this task), has been explored with insight and wit in Roland Marchand, *Creating the Corporate Soul: The Rise of Public Relations and Corporate Imagery in American Big Business* (Berkeley: University of California Press, 1998).

14. John, *Network Nation*, chap. 4.

15. The unnatural monopoly argument has inspired three notable books on the history of the transcontinental railroad: Robert William Fogel, *The Union Pacific Railroad: A Case in Premature Enterprise* (Baltimore: Johns Hopkins University Press, 1960); Robert W. Fogel, *Railroads and American Economic Growth: Essays in Econometric History* (Baltimore: Johns Hopkins University Press, 1964); and Richard White, *Railroaded: The Transcontinentals and the Making of Modern America* (New York: W. W. Norton, 2011).

16. John, *Network Nation*, 156–70.

17. Bellew's visual rendering of Uncle Sam depicted him as the weak and ineffectual rival of John Bull, a stand-in for the British government. John Bull supported granting subsidies to the Cunard Steamship Company to carry the transatlantic mail; Uncle Sam refused to lavish an analogous privilege on Edward K. Collins, Cunard's American rival. Frank Bellew, "Collins and Cunard: Raising the Wind; Or, Both Sides of the Story," *Lantern*, March 13, 1852.

18. For more on the visual iconography of antimonopoly, see John, "Markets, Morality, and the Media."

19. Online galleries of antimonopoly cartoons can be found at websites hosted by National Humanities Center and Smith College economics professor Mark Aldrich: http://nationalhumanitiescenter.org/pds/gilded/power/text1/octopusimages .pdf; http://sophia.smith.edu/~maldrich/home.htm. Another resource is the innovative online cartoon archive "Politics in Graphic Detail," curated by the Historical Society of Pennsylvania: https://hsp.org/history-online/historic-images-new -technologies.

20. Frank Bellew, "The Cephalopod, or Terrestrial Devil Fish—A Monster of Centralization," *Daily Graphic*, March 4, 1873.

21. Frank Bellew, "The American Frankenstein," *Daily Graphic*, March 18, 1873.

22. Frank Bellew, "The American Frankenstein," *Daily Graphic*, April 14, 1874.

23. Frank Bellew, "The Modern Laocoön," *Daily Graphic*, April 25, 1874.

24. Ida M. Tarbell, *The History of the Standard Oil Company* (New York: McClure, Phillips, 1904).

25. John, *Network Nation*, 146.

26. Henry Demarest Lloyd, *Wealth Against Commonwealth* (New York: Harper & Brothers, 1894), 512, 532.

27. Ibid., 535.

28. Ibid.

29. Ibid., 506.

30. Ibid., 533.

31. Richard L. McCormick, "The Discovery That Business Corrupts Politics: A Reappraisal of the Origins of Progressivism," *American Historical Review* 86 (April 1981): 247–74.

32. Lloyd, *Wealth Against Commonwealth*, 507.

33. Ibid., 534.

34. Francis B. Thurber, "Steam and Electricity," *International Review* 2 (September 1875): 633.

35. Ibid., 631.

36. *Justice*, September 2, 1882.

37. Frank Bellew, "Upon What Meat," *Justice*, November 11, 1882, 1; "Comparative Bigness," *Canard*, October 28, 1882, 7. Bellew drew his Vanderbilt cartoon for *Canard*, a short-lived humor magazine, where it appeared, sans caption, on page 4. To help interested readers who might not quite get the point, the cartoon was accompanied by a brief explanation along with an invitation to check out the accompanying article on page 7; this article was entitled "Comparative Bigness." Given the limited familiarity of today's audience with the Shakespearean allusion ("Upon What Meat") that the editors of *Justice* hit upon as a title for Bellew's hitherto untitled cartoon, as well as the likelihood that Bellew had nothing to do with its selection, "Comparative Bigness" would seem to be the better title for the cartoon, even though it did not run on the same page on which the cartoon had originally appeared.

38. Bellew, "Upon What Meat."

39. Francis B. Thurber, *Democracy and Anti-Monopoly* (Brooklyn: n.p., 1883), 13.

40. John, "Robber Barons Redux," 16–20.

41. Lloyd, *Wealth Against Commonwealth*.

42. *Justice*, April 4, 1885, 11.

43. Thurber, *Democracy and Anti-Monopoly*, 9.

44. Ibid., 15.

45. Ibid., 14, 15.

46. John, "Markets, Morality, and the Media," 75–97.

47. "The Standard Oil Octopus," *Daily Graphic*, February 4, 1879; Frank Beard, "The Monster Monopoly," *Judge* 6 (July 9, 1884): 16.

48. "Hooper," "A Horrible Monster," *Daily Graphic*, July 19, 1880.

49. Ibid.

50. Joseph Keppler, "Consolidated," *Puck* 8 (January 26, 1881): centerfold.

51. Joseph Keppler, "In Danger," *Puck* 8 (February 9, 1881): centerfold.

52. Joseph Keppler, "The Monster Monopoly," *Puck* 10 (January 25, 1882): centerfold.

53. "O. K.," "Puck's Perplexing Position—Between Two Evils," *Puck* 10 (October 12, 1881): 1.

54. G. Frederick Keller, "The Modern St. George," *Wasp* 6 (April 9, 1881); Keller, "The Coming Man," *Wasp* 6 (May 20, 1881); Keller, "The Curse of California," *Wasp* 9 (August 19, 1882).

55. John, *Network Nation*, chap. 8.

56. James A. Wales, "The Best Kind of Monopoly," *Judge* 2 (October 7, 1882): 1.

57. Keppler, "In Danger."

58. Joseph Keppler, "The Bosses of the Senate," *Puck* 24 (January 23, 1889): centerfold.

59. Grant E. Hamilton, "In the Clutch of a Grasping Monopoly," *Judge* 14 (April 7, 1888): 16.

60. Joseph Keppler Jr., "Next!" *Puck* 56 (September 7, 1904): centerfold. Joseph Jr. was originally known as Udo; he changed his first name to honor the memory of his father shortly after his father's death in 1894.

61. Frank A. Nankivell, "The Infant Hercules and the Standard Oil Serpents," *Puck* 59 (May 23, 1906): 1.

62. "Not Business, but Monopoly," *Daily Graphic*, October 11, 1884.

63. Benson, *Merchants, Farmers, and Railroads*; Miller, *Railroads and the Granger Laws*; James, *Parties, Presidents and the State*.

64. Rebecca Edwards, Richard R. John, and Richard Bensel, "Forum: Should We Abolish the 'Gilded Age'?" *Journal of the Gilded Age and the Progressive Era* 8, no. 4 (2009): 461–85. See also James Livingston, "The Myth of a 'Second Gilded Age,'" *Chronicle Review*, January 31, 2016, accessed May 2, 2016, http://chronicle.com/article /The-Myth-of-a-Second-Gilded/235072?cid=cpl.

2. Progressive Political Culture and the Widening Scope of Local Newspapers, 1880–1930

1. Robert Ezra Park, "The Natural History of the Newspaper," in Robert Ezra Park, Ernest Watson Burgess, Roderick Duncan McKenzie, and Louis Wirth, ed., *The City* (Chicago: University of Chicago Press, 1925), 85.

2. Ibid.

3. Alfred McClung Lee, *The Daily Newspaper in America: The Evolution of a Social Instrument* (New York: Macmillan, 1937), 323.

4. For example, see "New York Now Has Seven Levels of Transit," *New York World*, March 14, 1909, cover of special "Transformation of New York" section. As reprinted in Nicholson Baker and Margaret Brentano, eds., *The World on Sunday: Graphic Art in Joseph Pulitzer's Newspaper 1898–1911* (New York: Bulfinch Press, 2005), 113.

5. Louis M. Lyons, *Newspaper Story: One Hundred Years of the Boston Globe* (Cambridge, Mass.: Belknap Press, 1971), 113.

6. *New York World*, June 17, 1906, magazine section, 2, as reprinted in Baker and Brentano, eds., *The World on Sunday*, 88.

7. *Chicago Daily News*, July 16, 1885, 2.

8. *Milwaukee Free Press*, September 25, 1906, Sunday magazine section, 1.

9. *New York Tribune*, July 8, 1883, 4; *New York Sun*, January 2, 1889, 5; *New York World*, October 27, 1889, 15; *New York Sun*, July 24, 1881, 6.

10. Theodore Dreiser, "Out of My Newspaper Days, II: St. Louis," *The Bookman* 54, no. 5 (January 1922): 431.

11. *New York Times*, November 13, 1904, magazine section, 7.

12. *New York World*, June 6, 1897, main news section, 8; *New York World*, June 13, 1897, 38.

13. *The Journalist*, January 26, 1889, 2.

14. William R. Scott, *Scientific Circulation Management for Newspapers* (New York: Ronald Press, 1915), 167–68; Robert L. Perkin, *The First Hundred Years: An Informal History of Denver and the Rocky Mountain News, 1859-1959* (Garden City, N.Y.: Doubleday, 1959), 414; *Philadelphia Record*, May 14, 1945, 12.

15. *New York World*, June 6, 1897, main news section, 6.

16. Irving Dillard, "Foreword," in John M. Harrison and Harry H. Stein, ed., *Muckraking: Past, Present, and Future* (University Park: Pennsylvania State University Press, 1973), 4.

17. Jason Rogers, *Newspaper Building: Application of Efficiency to Edition, to Mechanical Production, to Circulation and Advertising* (New York: Harper & Brothers, 1918), 126.

18. *Collier's Weekly*, September 2, 1911, 23.

19. *Collier's Weekly*, October 14, 1911, 35.

20. The Fresh Air Fund first campaigned in the *Brooklyn Daily Union* in 1877, and moved to the *Tribune* in 1882. On the Fresh Air Fund, see Julia A. Guarneri, "Changing Strategies for Child Welfare, Enduring Beliefs About Childhood: The Fresh Air Fund, 1877-1926," *Journal of the Gilded Age and Progressive Era* 11, no. 1 (January 2012): 27–70.

21. *Philadelphia North American*, October 9, 1921, 4.

22. *Editor & Publisher*, December 21, 1929, 9–10.

23. *Collier's Weekly*, September 30, 1911, 34.

24. For examples, see the *New York Tribune*, August 11, 1890, 6, and August 8, 1902, 9.

25. *New York Times*, December 15, 1918, 75.

26. *New York Times*, December 14, 1924, Section 8, front page.

27. Statistics come from the Tribune Fresh Air Fund's annual reports, New York Public Library.

28. *Collier's Weekly*, August 19, 1911, 18.

29. *New York Herald Tribune*, August 23, 1927, late city edition, Section 5, 2–7.

30. *Philadelphia Inquirer*, May 15, 1895, 8; *Chicago Tribune*, April 10, 1888, 10.

31. Baker and Brentano, eds., *The World on Sunday*, 196; *Chicago Tribune*, March 12, 1884, 2; *Chicago Tribune*, March 13, 1884, 7. The story of this first express train appears in William Cronon, *Nature's Metropolis: Chicago and the Great West* (New York: W. W. Norton, 1991), 333.

32. A yearly subscription to the 1896 *Chicago Tribune*, for example, cost country readers six dollars, only twenty-eight cents more than the same subscription cost in the city.

33. Lee, *The Daily Newspaper in America*, 280.

34. Ibid., 281.

35. *Chicago Tribune, Pictured Encyclopedia* (Chicago: Tribune Company, 1928), 195–97.

36. I am gauging this using the city/suburban/country circulation breakdowns of these papers and their competitors in *Editor & Publisher*, International Yearbook number for 1926, January 30, 1926.

37. Lyons, *Newspaper Story*, 154.

38. *Chicago Tribune*, June 21, 1920, 8.

39. The objectives changed slightly over the course of the decade; these are drawn from Sunday papers in 1924.

40. From a reader's description printed in *Collier's Weekly*, August 19, 1911, 18.

41. Harold A. Williams, *The Baltimore Sun, 1837–1987* (Baltimore: Johns Hopkins University Press, 1987), 120.

42. James O'Donnell Bennett, "Chicagoland's Shrines," *Chicago Tribune*, July 27, 1926, front page.

43. *Chicago Herald*, April 29, 1917, Humor and City Life section.

44. All of these appeared in the *Philadelphia Public Ledger* in the 1910s and 1920s.

45. For example, one account by Alfred Lee in 1935 told of the *Philadelphia Inquirer*'s Sunday staff, which went from forty to sixty in the early 1900s and then shrank to only a handful by 1934. Lee, *The Daily Newspaper in America*, 404, 599.

46. Will Irwin, "Newspapers and Canned Thought," *Collier's Weekly*, June 21, 1924, 14.

47. *Collier's Weekly*, September 30, 1911, 34.

48. Information on 1930 chains comes from *Editor & Publisher*, International Yearbook number for 1930, January 25, 1930, 138–39.

49. Lee, *The Daily Newspaper in America*, 215, 217.

50. For "The Inquisitive Reporter," see the *Wisconsin News*, February 2, 1921, 2, and February 5, 1921, 2.

51. Gerald J. Baldasty, *E. W. Scripps and the Business of Newspapers* (Urbana: University of Illinois Press, 1999), 47–48.

52. These titles come from an anthology of this feature: William Ely Hill and Franklin Pierce Adams, eds., *Among Us Mortals; Pictures and Legends by W. E. Hill* (Boston: Houghton Mifflin, 1917), and from the *Philadelphia Inquirer*, June 5, 1919, magazine section, 8.

53. *Milwaukee Journal*, May 22, 1927, Section 8, 10.

54. *Milwaukee Sentinel*, November 6, 1910, 3.

55. This feature ran on the front page of the *American Weekly*; see the *Milwaukee Sentinel*, February 14, 1926, magazine section, 1.

56. Willard Grosvenor Bleyer, *How to Write Special Feature Articles* (Boston: Houghton Mifflin, 1919), 39. For a syndicate manager with the same message, see Moses Koenigsberg, *King News: An Autobiography* (Philadelphia: F. A. Stokes, 1941), 394.

3. The Ominous Clang

1. On Viereck, see Niel Johnson, *George Sylvester Viereck, German-American Propagandist* (Urbana: University of Illinois Press, 1972), with the quotation on page 22. On the atrocity tales, the early historiography focused on the exaggerations, whereas more recent scholarship has found some validity in them. On the early view, see James Morgan Read, *Atrocity Propaganda, 1914–1919* (New Haven, Conn.: Yale University Press, 1941), 201–4; and on the recent scholarship, see John Horne and Alan Kramer, *German Atrocities, 1914: A History of Denial* (New Haven, Conn.: Yale University Press, 2001), and Larry Zuckerman, *The Rape of Belgium: The Untold Story of World War I* (New York: New York University Press, 2004), 132–36. A longer discussion of this material can be found in my book *Republic of Spin: An Inside History of the American Presidency* (New York: W. W. Norton, 2016).

2. On the Albert affair, see William McAdoo, *Crowded Years: The Reminiscences of William G. McAdoo* (Port Washington, N.Y.: Kennikat Press, 1931), 324–30; and Arthur S. Link, *Wilson: The Struggle for Neutrality* (Princeton, N.J.: Princeton University Press, 1960), 554–56.

3. John Milton Cooper, *Woodrow Wilson: A Biography* (New York: Knopf, 2009), 286.

4. McAdoo, *Crowded Years*, 328; House to Wilson, August 10, 1915, in Arthur S. Link, ed., *The Papers of Woodrow Wilson*, vol. 34 (Princeton, N.J.: Princeton University Press, 1980), 158.

5. *New York World*, August 15, 1915, 1; and subsequent stories through August 23. On German sabotage and espionage see Henry Landau, *The Enemy Within: The Inside Story of German Sabotage in America* (New York: G. P. Putnam's Sons, 1937); Jules Witcover, *Sabotage at Black Tom: Imperial Germany's Secret War in America, 1914–1917* (New York: Algonquin Books, 1989); and Tracie Lynn Provost, "The Great Game: Imperial German Sabotage and Espionage Against the United States, 1914–1917" (Ph.D. diss., University of Toledo, 2003).

6. *Fatherland*, August 25, 1915, 48; *New York Times*, August 17, 1915, 2.

7. Erwin Fellows, "Propaganda: History of a Word," *American Speech* 34, no. 3 (October 1959): 182–89; Harold Lasswell, *Propaganda Techniques in the World War* (New York: Knopf, 1927), 2.

8. Steven Pinker, *The Blank Slate: The Modern Denial of Human Nature* (New York: Viking, 2002), 212–13.

9. Plato, *Gorgias*, translated with an introduction and notes by Robin Waterfield (New York: Oxford University Press, 1998); Aristotle, *Rhetoric*, translated by W. Rhys Roberts (Mineola, N.Y.: Dover Publications, 2004).

10. Douglass Cater, *The Fourth Branch of Government* (New York: Vintage Books, 1965 [1959]), 76.

11. On TR and publicity see George Juergens, "Theodore Roosevelt and the Press," *Daedalus* 114, no. 1 (Fall 1982): 113–33; Thaddeus Seymour Jr., "A Progressive Partnership: Theodore Roosevelt and the Reform Press—Riis, Steffens, Baker, and White" (Ph.D. diss., University of Wisconsin, 1985); Doris Kearns Goodwin, *The Bully Pulpit: Theodore Roosevelt, William Howard Taft, and the Golden Age of Journalism* (New York: Simon & Schuster, 2013); David Greenberg, "Theodore Roosevelt and the Image of Presidential Activism," *Social Research: An International Quarterly* 78, no. 4 (Winter 2011): 1057–88; and Stephen Ponder, "Executive Publicity and Congressional Resistance, 1905–1913: Congress and the Roosevelt Administration's PR Men," *Congress & the Presidency* 13, no. 2 (Autumn 1986): 177–86.

12. George C. Edwards III, *The Public Presidency: The Pursuit of Popular Support* (New York: St. Martin's Press, 1983). Edwards's concept of the "public presidency" resembles similar ideas proposed by other scholars. The idea is that the "modern" American presidency begins with Theodore Roosevelt or perhaps Woodrow Wilson, in large part because of the new focus on public opinion and mass communication. See, for example, Elmer E. Cornwell Jr., *Presidential Leadership of Public Opinion* (Bloomington: Indiana University Press, 1965); Samuel Kernell, *Going Public: New Strategies of Presidential Leadership* (Washington, D.C.: CQ Press, 1986); and Jeffrey Tulis, *The Rhetorical Presidency* (Princeton, N.J.: Princeton University Press, 1987). Historians who chronicle the presidency have seen TR's presidency as a natural starting point for this reason, giving some credit to William McKinley as well. See Lewis L. Gould, *The Modern American Presidency* (Lawrence: University Press of Kansas, 2003); William E. Leuchtenburg, *The American President: From Teddy Roosevelt to Bill Clinton* (New York: Oxford University Press, 2015).

13. *New York Times*, January 18, 1906, 1; *Washington Post*, January 18, 1906, 1.

14. Ibid. On the Tillman episode, see also James Creelman, "A Defender of the Senate," *Pearson's Magazine*, June 1906, 622–29.

15. Mordecai Lee, *Congress vs. the Bureaucracy: Muzzling Agency Public Relations* (Norman: University of Oklahoma Press, 2011), 32–48, quotation on page 37.

16. On the rise of executive publicity agents see, in addition to Lee, *Congress vs. the Bureaucracy*, James McCamy, *Government Publicity: Its Practice in Federal Administration* (Chicago: University of Chicago Press, 1939); and J. A. R. Pimlott, *Public Relations and American Democracy* (Princeton, N.J.: Princeton University Press, 1951).

17. Government publicity aides were of course hired but given titles such as "Director of Information" and "Editor-in-Chief." *New York Times*, August 20, 1913, 8.

18. Robert Hilderbrand, *The Complete Press Conferences, 1913–1919*, vol. 50 of *The Papers of Woodrow Wilson*, Arthur Link, ed. (Princeton, N.J.: Princeton University Press, 1985), 260–61.

19. Stephen Vaughn, *Holding Fast the Inner Lines: Democracy, Nationalism, and the Committee on Public Information* (Chapel Hill: University of North Carolina Press, 1980), 9.

20. U.S. Committee on Public Information, and George Creel, *The Creel Report: Complete Report of the Chairman of the Committee on Public Information* (Washington, D.C.: U.S. Government Printing Office, 1920), 1.

21. Vaughn, *Holding Fast the Inner Lines*, 18.

22. George Creel, *How We Advertised America: The First Telling of the Amazing Story of the Committee on Public Information That Carried the Gospel of Americanism to Every Corner of the Globe* (New York: Harper & Brothers, 1920), 444–46; Walton Bean, "George Creel and His Critics: A Study of the Attacks on the Committee on Public Information" (Ph.D. diss., University of California, 1941), 202, 205, 214, 253. Bean's unpublished dissertation remains the least tendentious study of Creel and the Committee on Public Information.

23. The notion that propaganda led the nation into not only World War I but also the Spanish-American War—specifically in the form of agitation by the yellow press—took root only after World War I bred a retroactive disillusionment with war in general. On the myth of the yellow press's responsibility for U.S. involvement in war of 1898, see Lewis Gould, *The Presidency of William McKinley* (Lawrence: University Press of Kansas, 1980), 62–63; George Herring, "William McKinley, the War of 1898, and the New Empire," in Kenneth Osgood and Andrew Frank, eds., *Selling War in a Media Age: The Presidency and Public Opinion in the American Century* (Gainesville: University Press of Florida, 2010), 26–28. On the argument that this myth gained currency only after World War I, see Mark Matthew Welter, "Minnesota Newspapers and the Cuban Crisis, 1895–1898: Minnesota as a Test Case for the 'Yellow Journalism' Theory" (Ph.D. diss., University of Minnesota, 1970).

24. Silas Bent, *Ballyhoo: The Voice of the Press* (New York: Boni and Liveright, 1927). On advertising in this period see Roland Marchand, *Advertising the American Dream: Making Way for Modernity* (Berkeley: University of California Press, 1985); and T. J. Jackson Lears, *Fables of Abundance: A Cultural History of Advertising in America* (New York: Basic Books, 1994).

25. Lears, *Fables of Abundance*, 225.

26. Bruce Barton, "Here Is the Lever, Archimedes," Bruce Barton Papers, State Historical Society of Wisconsin, Box 144.

27. On Barton see Richard Fried, *The Man Everybody Knew: Bruce Barton and the Making of Modern America* (Chicago: Ivan R. Dee, 2005); Leo Ribuffo, "Jesus Christ as Business Statesman: Bruce Barton and the Selling of Corporate Capitalism," *American Quarterly* 33, no. 2 (Summer 1981): 206–21; and T. J. Jackson Lears, "From Salvation to Self-Realization: Advertising and the Therapeutic Roots of Consumer Culture, 1880–1930," in Richard Wightman Fox and T. J. Jackson Lears, eds., *The Culture of Consumption: Critical Essays in American History, 1880–1980* (New York: Pantheon Books, 1983), 1–38.

28. Bruce Barton, *The Man Nobody Knows: A Discovery of the Real Jesus* (Indianapolis: Bobbs-Merrill, 1925).

29. Frank Cobb, "The Press and Public Opinion," *The New Republic*, December 31, 1919, 144.

30. On Bernays, see his memoir, *Biography of an Idea: Memoirs of Public Relations Counsel Edward Bernays* (New York: Simon and Schuster, 1965); and Larry Tye, *The Father of Spin: Edward Bernays and the Birth of Public Relations* (New York: Crown Publishers, 1998).

31. Henry Pringle, "Mass Psychologist," *American Mercury*, December 1930, 155–62; John Flynn, "Edward Bernays: The Science of Ballyhoo," *Atlantic Monthly*, May 1932, 562–71.

32. Edward Bernays, *Crystallizing Public Opinion* (New York: Boni and Liveright, 1923); Edward Bernays, *Propaganda*, with an introduction by Mark Crispin Miller (Brooklyn, N.Y.: Ig Publishing, 2005 [1928]), quotation on pages 37–38.

33. *New York Times*, May 20, 1928, 74.

34. Pearson quoted in Paul Martin Lester, *On Floods and Photo-Ops: How Herbert Hoover and George W. Bush Exploited Catastrophes* (Jackson: University Press of Mississippi, 2010), 48.

35. On Michelson, see Charles Michelson, *The Ghost Talks* (New York: G. P. Putnam's Sons, 1944); "Michelson: Rise of a Cynic," *News-Week*, August 7, 1937, 16–17; Frank Kent, "Charley Michelson," *Scribner's*, September 1930, 290–96; Alva Johnston, "Hundred-Tongued Charley, the Great Silent Orator," *Saturday Evening Post*, May 30, 1936, 5–7, 32, 37.

36. C. H. Hamlin, in *The War Myth in United States History* (New York: Vanguard Press, 1927), 92; Peter Odegard, *American Public Mind* (New York: Columbia University Press, 1930), 197.

37. George Sylvester Viereck, *Spreading Germs of Hate*, with an introduction by Edward House (New York: Horace Liveright, 1931), 168, 184, 210–11.

38. Ludwig Lore, "Nazi Politics in America," *Nation*, November 29, 1933, 615–17.

39. *New York Times*, May 18, 1934, 1, 3; *New York Times*, July 11, 1934, 11.

40. Kenneth Cmiel, "On Cynicism, Evil, and the Discovery of Communication in the 1940s," *Journal of Communication* 46, no. 3 (Summer 1996): 92.

41. Archibald MacLeish, "Post-War Writers and Pre-War Readers," *New Republic*, June 10, 1940, 789–90; Signi Linea Falk, *Archibald MacLeish* (New York: Twayne, 1966), 105–7.

42. Max Lerner, "Propaganda in Our Time," review of *War Propaganda and the United States*, by Harold Lavine and James Wechsler, *New Republic*, August 26, 1940, 282.

43. Allan Nevins, "Propaganda: An Explosive Word Analyzed," *New York Times Magazine*, October 29, 1939, SM2.

44. Lewis Mumford, "The Corruption of Liberalism," *New Republic*, April 29, 1940, 568–73; Lewis Mumford, *Values for Survival* (New York: Harcourt, Brace, and

Company, 1946), 39fn44. On Barnes, see Deborah E. Lipstadt, *Denying the Holocaust: The Growing Assault on Truth and Memory* (New York: Free Press, 1993), 67–83.

45. On brainwashing, see Matthew W. Dunne, *A Cold War State of Mind: Brainwashing and Postwar American Society* (Amherst, Mass.: University of Massachusetts Press, 2013). On Packard, see his *Hidden Persuaders* (Brooklyn, N.Y.: Ig Publishing, 2007 [1957]); and Daniel Horowitz, *Vance Packard and American Social Criticism* (Chapel Hill: University of North Carolina Press, 1994).

46. On the Moynihan statement, see Steven Weisman, ed., *Daniel Patrick Moynihan: A Portrait in Letters of an American Visionary* (New York: Public Affairs, 2012), 2. The version commonly attributed to Baruch is: "Everyone has a right to be wrong in his opinions. But no man has a right to be wrong in his facts." See Charles Clay Doyle, Wolfgang Mieder, and Fred R. Shapiro, eds., *The Dictionary of Modern Proverbs* (New Haven, Conn.: Yale University Press, 2012).

4. When the "Mainstream Media" Was Conservative

1. Rick Perlstein, *Nixonland: The Rise of a President and the Fracturing of America* (New York: Scribner, 2008), 430–39; Scott Donaldson, *Archibald MacLeish: An American Life* (Boston: Houghton Mifflin, 1992).

2. "Agnew Attacks Press as Unfair," *New York Times*, November 21, 1969, 1; "Agnew Criticizes TV News," *Boston Globe*, November 14, 1969, 19.

3. Archibald MacLeish, *A Time to Act: Selected Addresses* (Freeport, N.Y.: Books for Libraries Press, 1970), 9–31.

4. Archibald MacLeish, *Draft Commission on Freedom of the Press General Report*, January 21, 1946, 3–4, Box 4, Folder 2; Archibald MacLeish, *Commission on Freedom of the Press General Report (Revised Draft)*, February 26, 1946, 6, Box 4, Folder 8, both in Commission on Freedom of the Press Records, Special Collections Research Center, University of Chicago Library, Chicago, Ill.

5. Margaret A. Blanchard, "The Associated Press Antitrust Suit: A Philosophical Clash over Ownership of First Amendment Rights," *Business History Review* 61 (1987): 43–85; Sam Lebovic, *Free Speech and Unfree News: The Paradox of Press Freedom in America* (Cambridge, Mass.: Harvard University Press, 2016), 76–84.

6. David Greenberg, "The Idea of 'The Liberal Media' and Its Roots in the Civil Rights Movement," *The Sixties: A Journal of History, Politics and Culture* 1 (December 2008): 167–86; Mark Major, "Objective but Not Impartial: *Human Events*, Barry Goldwater, and the Development of the 'Liberal Media' in the Conservative Counter-Sphere," *New Political Science* 34 (December 2012): 455–68.

7. "Burch Supports Agnew," *New York Times*, November 15, 1969, 1.

8. "Text of Agnew Speech," *Boston Globe*, November 21, 1969, 23.

9. Leonard W. Levy, ed., *Freedom of the Press: From Zenger to Jefferson; Early American Libertarian Theories* (Indianapolis, Ind.: Bobbs-Merrill Company, 1966), 372–73.

10. Marion Tuttle Marzolf, *Civilizing Voices: American Press Criticism 1880–1950* (New York: Longman, 1991), 7–61.

11. Alfred McClung Lee, "Trends Affecting the Daily Newspapers," *Public Opinion Quarterly* 3 (1939): 497–502; Raymond B. Nixon, "Trends in Daily Newspaper Ownership Since 1945," *Journalism Quarterly* 31 (Winter 1954): 7; Gerald J. Baldasty, *The Commercialization of the News in the Nineteenth Century* (Madison: University of Wisconsin Press, 1992).

12. Hamilton Holt, *Commercialism and Journalism* (Boston: Houghton Mifflin Company, 1909), 34.

13. James T. Hamilton, *All the News That's Fit to Sell: How the Market Transforms Information into News* (Princeton, N.J.: Princeton University Press, 2004), 48.

14. Linda Lawson, *Truth in Publishing: Federal Regulation of the Press's Business Practices, 1880–1920* (Carbondale: Southern Illinois University Press, 1993), 69–70.

15. Henry George, *The Menace of Privilege* (New York: Grosset & Dunlap, 1906), excerpted in Robert McChesney and Ben Scott, eds., *Our Unfree Press: 100 Years of Radical Media Criticism* (New York: New Press, 2004), 88.

16. C. C. Regier, *The Era of the Muckrakers* (Gloucester, Mass.: Peter Smith, 1957), 165–79.

17. Oswald Garrison Villard, "Some Weaknesses of Modern Journalism," in Merle Thorpe, ed., *The Coming Newspaper* (New York: H. Holt and Company, 1915), 53; Margaret A. Blanchard, "Press Criticism and National Reform Movements: The Progressive Era and the New Deal," *Journalism History* (Summer 1978): 33–37, 54–55.

18. Will Irwin, *The American Newspaper*, commentary by Clifford F. Weigle and David G. Clark (Ames: Iowa State University Press, 1969), 15–16, 52, 71; Robert V. Hudson, *The Writing Game: A Biography of Will Irwin* (Ames: Iowa State University Press, 1982), 68–73.

19. Upton Sinclair, *The Brass Check: A Study of American Journalism* (Pasadena, Calif.: Author, 1920), 39; Kevin Mattson, *Upton Sinclair and the Other American Century* (Hoboken, N.J.: John Wiley and Sons, 2006), 128.

20. Marzolf, *Civilizing Voices*, 76–106, 119–32.

21. Alfred H. Lloyd, "Newspaper Conscience: A Study in Half-Truths," *American Journal of Sociology* 27 (September 1921): 201–3.

22. Oswald Garrison Villard, *Some Newspapers and Newspaper Men* (New York: A. A. Knopf, 1926), ix.

23. Richard L. Kaplan, "From Partisanship to Professionalism: The Transformation of the Daily Press," in Carl F. Kaestle and Janice A. Radway, eds., *A History of the Book in America*, vol. 4 (Chapel Hill: University of North Carolina Press, 2009), 136.

24. Silas Bent, *Ballyhoo: The Voice of the Press* (New York: Boni and Liveright, 1927).

25. James Boylan, "Publicity for the Great Depression: Newspaper Default and Literary Reportage," in Catherine L. Covert and John D. Stevens, eds., *Mass Media*

Between the Wars: Perceptions of Cultural Tension, 1918-1941 (Syracuse, N.Y.: Syracuse University Press, 1984), 160-66.

26. "Press Underemphasized the Slump, Journalism Students are Told," *Editor & Publisher*, April 8, 1933, 26.

27. John W. Perry, "Utilities Abandon Propaganda Work," *Editor & Publisher*, February 18, 1933, 7; George Seldes, *Freedom of the Press* (Indianapolis, Ind.: Bobbs-Merrill, 1935), 78, 85.

28. Philip M. Glende, "Labor Makes the News: Newspapers, Journalism and Organized Labor, 1933-1955" (Ph.D. diss., University of Wisconsin–Madison, 2010), quotation on page 108.

29. Ferdinand Lundberg, *America's Sixty Families* (New York: Citadel Press, 1937), 287-88.

30. *St. Louis Post-Dispatch Symposium on Freedom of the Press: Expressions by 120 Representative Americans*, reprinted from December 13 to December 25, 1938 issues, no publication details, 1938, p. 43.

31. Roper Commercial Survey, August 1938, retrieved April 4, 2015, from the iPOLL Databank, Roper Center for Public Opinion Research, University of Connecticut.

32. Michael Stamm, *Sound Business: Newspapers, Radio and the Politics of New Media* (Philadelphia: University of Pennsylvania Press, 2011), 60, 64-66; Eric Barnouw, *The Golden Web: A History of Broadcasting in the US*, vol. 2: *1933-1953* (New York: Oxford University Press, 1968), 17-22, 74-83; Eric Barnouw, *A Tower in Babel: A History of Broadcasting in the US*, vol. 1 (New York, Oxford University Press, 1966), 138, 278; Victor Pickard, *America's Battle for Media Democracy: The Triumph of Corporate Libertarianism and the Future of Media Reform* (New York: Cambridge University Press, 2015), 9-37.

33. Richard Norton Smith: *The Colonel: The Life and Legend of Robert T. McCormick, 1880-1955* (Boston: Houghton Mifflin, 1997), 342; David Nasaw, *The Chief: The Life of William Randolph Hearst* (Boston: Houghton Mifflin, 2000), 500; Richard Polenberg, *Reorganizing Roosevelt's Government: The Controversy over Executive Reorganization, 1936-1939* (Cambridge, Mass.: Harvard University Press, 1966), 64-65, 149; Betty Houchin Winfield, *FDR and the News Media* (Urbana: University of Illinois Press, 1990), 127-47.

34. Smith, *The Colonel*, 345-49; Nasaw, *The Chief*, 500-527; Michael Schudson, "The Persistence of Vision: Partisan Journalism in the Mainstream Press," in *A History of the Book in America*, vol. 4, 144; Winfield, *FDR and the News Media*, 128.

35. Villard, *The Disappearing Daily*, 9; "Editors' Afterthoughts," *Time*, November 16, 1936, 84.

36. Nasaw, *The Chief*, 515; Winfield, *FDR and the News Media*, 128, 130. Graham White has argued that the news was less biased than FDR claimed, but his statistics still show significant press opposition, particularly in the late 1930s. Graham J. White, *FDR and the Press* (Chicago: University of Chicago Press, 1979), 69-91, 109.

37. Brant, "The Press for Willkie Club," in Harold Ickes, ed., *Freedom of the Press Today* (New York: Vanguard, 1941), 59–60; Winfield, *FDR and the News Media*, 127–47.

38. This would soon become codified as the "limited effects" theory of media reception in Paul Lazarsfeld, Bernard Berelson, and Hazel Gaudet, *The People's Choice: How the Voter Makes Up His Mind in a President Campaign* (New York: Columbia University Press, 1944).

39. Smith, *The Colonel*, 351.

40. Nasaw, *The Chief*, 521.

41. "15,000 Here Object to Rift with Reds," *New York Times*, February 26, 1935, 8; "Educators Assail Hearst 'Influence,'" *New York Times*, February 25, 1935, 18; "Radicals Assail Hearst," *New York Times*, February 4, 1935, 9; Memorandum, re: communist mass meeting, Box 95, Folder: CPUSA, Record Group 233, National Archives and Records Administration, Washington, D.C.

42. Harold L. Ickes, *America's House of Lords: An Inquiry into Freedom of the Press* (New York: Harcourt, Brace and Company, 1939), x; George Seldes, *Lords of the Press* (New York: Blue Ribbon Books, 1938).

43. "Ickes and Gannett Debate Free Press," *New York Times*, January 13, 1939, 14.

44. Ickes, *Freedom of the Press Today*, 12; Stamm, *Sound Business*, 104.

45. "Newspaper Curb Bill Offered," *Los Angeles Times*, April 29, 1938, 2; "Minton Asks Bill Falsifying News Be Made Penalty," *Atlanta Constitution*, April 29, 1938, 9.

46. Winfield, *FDR and the News Media*, 144.

47. White, *FDR and the Press*, 91; Franklin D. Roosevelt, "Letter of Congratulations to the St. Louis Post-Dispatch," November 2, 1938. Online by Gerhard Peters and John T. Woolley, *The American Presidency Project*, http://www.presidency.ucsb.edu /ws/?pid=15566.

48. White, *FDR and the Press*, 50.

49. George H. Gallup, "The People and the Press," in Ickes, *Freedom of the Press Today*, 118.

50. Roper Commercial Survey, August 1938, retrieved April 4, 2015, from the iPOLL Databank, Roper Center for Public Opinion Research, University of Connecticut.

51. *St. Louis Post-Dispatch Symposium on Freedom of the Press*, 31.

52. James L. McCamy, *Government Publicity: Its Practice in Federal Administration* (Chicago: University of Chicago Press, 1939), 248.

53. Leon Svirsky, ed., *Your Newspaper: Blueprint for a Better Press* (New York: Macmillan, 1947), ix, 16–17.

54. George Marion, *"The Free Press": Portrait of a Monopoly* (New York: New Century, 1946), 11; Morris L. Ernst, *The First Freedom* (New York: MacMillan, 1946).

55. George Seldes Interview with Howard Zinn, n.d., Box 64, Folder 16, Howard Zinn Papers, Tamiment Library, New York University; Pamela A. Brown, "George

Seldes and the Winter Soldier Brigade: The Press Criticism of *In Fact*, 1940–1950," *American Journalism* 6 (1989): 85–102.

56. Ben Bagdikian, *The Media Monopoly* (Boston: Beacon Press, 1983); Noam Chomsky and Edward S. Herman, *Manufacturing Consent: The Political Economy of the Mass Media* (New York: Pantheon Books, 2002); Robert W. McChesney, *The Problem of the Media: U.S. Communication Politics in the Twenty-First Century* (New York: Monthly Review Press, 2004).

57. McChesney, *The Problem of the Media,* 113.

58. Michael Schudson, *Watergate in American Memory: How We Remember, Forget, and Reconstruct the Past* (New York: Basic Books, 1992), 107.

59. David Greenberg, "The Idea of 'The Liberal Media'"; Major, "Objective but Not Impartial"; Gene Roberts and Hank Klibanoff, *The Race Beat: The Press, The Civil Rights Struggle and the Awakening of a Nation* (New York: Knopf, 2006).

60. For an exploration of the tensions between free market economics and theories of liberal media bias, see Daniel Sutter, "Can the Media Be So Liberal? The Economics of Media Bias," *Cato Journal* 20 (Winter 2001): 431–51.

61. Major, "Objective but Not Impartial," 463.

62. "Agnew Criticizes TV News," *Boston Globe*, November 14, 1969, 19.

63. Edith Efron, *The News Twisters* (Los Angeles: Nash Publishing, 1971), 207.

64. See, for examples, J. David Stern, "The Newspaper Publisher Moves Across the Railroad," or Raymond Clapper, "A Free Press Needs Discriminating Public Criticism," both in Ickes, *Freedom of the Press Today*, 92, 245–46.

65. Irwin, *The American Newspaper*, 69.

66. Commission on Freedom of the Press, *A Free and Responsible Press: A General Report on Mass Communication: Newspapers, Radio, Motion Pictures, Magazines, and Books* (Chicago: University of Chicago Press, 1947), 15–16.

5. "We're All in This Thing Together"

1. Robert S. Allen diary entry, May 18, 1956, Box 23, Robert Sharon Allen Papers, Wisconsin Historical Society (WHS).

2. Schedule for April 11, 1953, Gridiron Dinner, Box 53, folder "Gridiron," James B. Reston papers, University of Illinois, Urbana (JBR).

3. Though he was closeted—and though he entered a marriage of convenience with his friend Susan Mary Patten in 1961—within Washington, Alsop's homosexuality was an open secret.

4. Script for April 11, 1953, Gridiron Dinner, folder "Gridiron," Box 53, JBR.

5. Press release, April 11, 1953, Box 44, folder "v. 56," Gridiron Club Papers, Library of Congress (LC).

6. See Donald A. Ritchie, *Reporting From Washington: The History of the Washington Press Corps* (New York: Oxford University Press, 2005).

7. Leo C. Rosten, *The Washington Correspondents* (New York: Arno Press, 1974 [1937]), 10.

8. Gridiron script for April 11, 1953, folder "Gridiron," Box 53, JBR.

9. Wendy Wall, *Inventing the American Way: The Politics of Consensus from the New Deal to the Civil Rights Movement* (Oxford: Oxford University Press, 2008).

10. Excavating the cultural life of Washington at mid-century has been an important project for historians of gender and sexuality. See especially Robert D. Dean, *Imperial Brotherhood: Gender and the Making of Cold War Foreign Policy* (Amherst: University of Massachusetts Press, 2001), and David K. Johnson, *The Lavender Scare: The Cold War Persecution of Gays and Lesbians in the Federal Government* (Chicago: University of Chicago Press, 2004).

11. Timothy Crouse, *The Boys on the Bus* (New York: Random House, 1973), 7.

12. To some extent, the social-professional insularity of Washington remains today; see, for example, Mark Leibovich, *This Town: Two Parties and a Funeral—Plus, Plenty of Valet Parking!—in America's Gilded Capital* (New York: Blue Rider Press, 2013).

13. Daniel C. Hallin, *The "Uncensored War": The Media and Vietnam* (Berkeley: University of California Press, 1986), 110–18 et seq. Hallin argues that the media were not as critical of Vietnam policy as is commonly remembered; rather, they mostly followed the government's line. When they were critical in the later years, it was after elite consensus on Vietnam had already broken down.

14. Ruth Gmeimer to Martha Strayer, February 2, 1954, folder "Professional file 1954," Box 1, WNPC President's Files, National Press Club Archives (NPC).

15. Bess Furman to Martha Strayer, February 4, 1954, WNPC President's files, Box 1, folder "Professional file, 1954," NPC. The Gridiron accepted its first woman member in 1975.

16. See Pamela Walker Laird, *Pull: Networking and Success Since Benjamin Franklin* (Cambridge, Mass.: Harvard University Press, 2006) for clubs as "buffers" in the business world, preventing the "wrong sort" from gaining access to social capital.

17. NPC Bar Committee Report for 1953, NPC Board of Governors papers, Box 1950–1954, NPC.

18. National Press Club, *"Shrdlu: An Affectionate Chronicle"* (Washington, D.C.: 1958), 5.

19. Carl Charlick, *The Metropolitan Club of Washington: The Story of Its Men and Its Place in City and Country* (Washington, D.C.: Judd & Detweiler, 1964), 275.

20. Ibid., 284–85.

21. Datebooks, Boxes 204–5, Eugene Meyer Papers, LC.

22. Crouse, *The Boys on the Bus*, 223.

23. Michael S. Sherry, *In the Shadow of War: The United States Since the 1930s* (New Haven, Conn.: Yale University Press, 1995), 89.

24. Barbara Matusow, *The Evening Stars: The Making of the Network News Anchor* (Boston: Houghton Mifflin, 1983), 53.

25. John. B. Oakes, interview by Kenneth Leish, February 17, 1961, "Reminiscences of John Bertram Oakes," vol. 1, 22, Columbia University Oral History Collection, Columbia University.

26. "Army to Release All Data on War," *New York Times*, November 19, 1947, 1.

27. Memo to Luther Huston, May 15, 1951, folder 5, Box 7, National Desk papers, New York Times Company Records, New York Public Library (NYPL).

28. Memo, October 25, 1947, by Felix Belair, Book 1, p. 184, Arthur Krock papers, Mudd Library, Princeton University (AK).

29. Memo, James Reston to Arthur Krock, September 28, 1948, Book 2, p. 212, AK.

30. Murrow to Collingwood, February 13, 1959, folder 291, Box 49, R. Murrow papers, Tufts University (ERM).

31. Script, August 19, 1950, folder 310, Box 51, ERM.

32. Typed producers' notes, "Background to Murrow 'Kill Order,'" folder 310, Box 51, ERM.

33. Script, August 19, 1950.

34. "Background to Murrow 'Kill Order.'"

35. For more on the circle rather than "flow" of information, see Bernard C. Cohen, *The Press and Foreign Policy* (Princeton, N.J.: Princeton University Press, 1963), 59, 89.

36. For "Blacksheeting," see Rosten, *The Washington Correspondents*, 88–89.

37. Transcript, interview of James B. Reston by Bernard Cohen, undated [cover letter from Cohen December 31, 1958], Box 97, JBR.

38. Cohen, *The Press and Foreign Policy*, 82.

39. James Reston, "New Red Divisions in Indochina Stir U.S.-French Alarm," *New York Times*, November 20, 1954, 1.

40. Memo, "Salary Statistics on 10 Highest Paid Members of the Staff," Box 35, JBR.

41. Joseph Alsop and Stewart Alsop, *The Reporter's Trade* (New York: Reynal and Company, 1958), 4.

42. Joseph Alsop's business entertainment expenses for May 1953, Box 115, The Papers of Joseph W. and Stewart J. Alsop, LC.

43. Memo, Pete Brandt to R. L. Crowley, June 22, 1951, Box 26, Marquis Childs Papers, WHS.

44. James Reston interview by Susan Dryfoos, March 14, 1984, Box 10, folder 5, New York Times Oral History Collection, NYPL.

45. Joe Kraft, "Washington's Most Powerful Reporter," *Esquire*, November 1958, 124.

46. Memo, May 21, 1947, Pete Brandt to Ben Reese, Box 24, Marquis Childs papers, WHS.

47. Diary entry, January 1, 1950, folder "Diary, 1947, 1950," Box 21, JBR.

48. Audiocassette, David Halberstam interview by John Stacks, Box 2, John F. Stacks papers, University of Illinois, Urbana.

49. Diary entry, January 1, 1950, folder "Diary, 1947, 1950," Box 21, JBR.

50. Ibid.

51. James Reston to Arthur Hays Sulzberger, March 28, 1951, Box 39, JBR.

52. Reston to Sulzberger, October 2, 1952, Box 35, JBR.

53. Memo, Peter Brandt to Ben Reese, July 20, 1950, Box 25, Marquis Childs Papers, WHS.

54. Memo, Ben Reese to Richard Stokes, May 26, 1947, Box 24, Marquis Childs Papers, WHS.

55. For more on objectivity as a barrier to accurate news reporting, see Hallin, *The "Uncensored War"* and Michael Schudson, *Discovering the News: A Social History of American Newspapers* (New York: Basic Books, 1967).

56. Cohen, *The Press and Foreign Policy*, 19.

57. Journal, April 6, 1953, Box 13, Wallace Deuel Papers, LC.

58. Memo, April 6, 1953, Wallace Deuel to Harold Meek, Box 26, Marquis Childs Papers, WHS.

59. State Department memo, April 9, 1953, folder 2, Box 6, Dwight D. Eisenhower Library files relating to John Foster Dulles, Mudd Library, Princeton University.

60. James Reston, "Split-Korea Policy Disavowed by U.S.," *New York Times*, April 10, 1953, 1.

61. Memo, Anthony Leviero to Arthur Krock, April 28, 1953, folder 2, Box 21, Arthur Hays Sulzberger Papers, NYPL.

62. James Reston to Turner Catledge, Box 39, April 30, 1953, JBR.

63. Lyle Wilson to James Reston, October 12, 1953, folder, "Gridiron" Box 53, JBR.

6. Objectivity and Its Discontents

1. Tim Rutten, interview with author, August 2, 2014; George Cotliar, interview with author, September 16, 2014. Rutten recalled that, as a young *Los Angeles Times* editor in the mid-1970s, he was scolded for booking himself a business-class flight to Washington. The assistant managing editor told him, "This is the *L.A. Times*. We fly first-class. Cancel the reservation. I've told the travel people to make you a first-class reservation."

2. Nick Williams to Stu Loory, July 23, 1971, Los Angeles Times Records, Box 454, folder 9, Huntington Library, San Marino, Calif. (hereafter THL).

3. Transcript of Otis Chandler speech to the Colorado Press Association Convention, February 21, 1969, Los Angeles Times Records, Box 231, folder 17, THL.

4. Bruce Schulman argues that Americans in the 1970s "developed a deeper, more thorough suspicion of the instruments of public life and a more profound disillusionment with the corruption and inefficiency of public institutions." According to Howard Brick, by the late 1960s, "Lost was the kind of intellectual authority and self-confidence of the early 60s that accompanied a stout belief in the maturity of modern disciplines and the virtue of serving public agencies." The challenge to established authority even extended to the spiritual realm; see Michael J. Lacey and Francis Oakley, eds., *The Crisis of Authority in Catholic Modernity* (New York: Oxford University Press, 2011); Bruce J. Schulman, *The Seventies: The Great Shift in American Culture, Society, and Politics* (New York: Free Press, 2001), xv; Howard Brick, *Age of Contradiction: American Thought and Culture in the 1960s* (New York: Twayne Publishers, 1998), xv.

5. Memorandum from Charles C. Guthrie to Ivan Veit, March 7, 1973, John B. Oakes Papers, Box 15, folder "Ivan Veit," Columbia University Library.

6. Several scholars have addressed the adoption of objectivity as a professional ideal in American journalism. See especially Stephen J. A. Ward, *The Invention of Journalism Ethics: The Path to Objectivity and Beyond* (Montreal: McGill-Queen's University Press, 2006), 214–16; Michael Schudson, *Discovering the News: A Social History of American Newspapers* (New York: Basic Books, 1978), 121–59. While Ward and Schudson argue that the press did not embrace objectivity until the early twentieth century, others believe the roots of objectivity can be found in the nineteenth century; see David T. Z. Mindich, *Just the Facts: How "Objectivity" Came to Define American Journalism* (New York: New York University Press, 1988), and Dan Schiller, *Objectivity and the News: The Public and the Rise of Commercial Journalism* (Philadelphia: University of Pennsylvania Press, 1981).

7. The Harris Survey, "Public Confidence in Institutions Remains Low," press release, November 13, 1972, www.harrisinteractive.com/vault/Harris-Interactive-Poll -Research-PUBLIC-CONFIDENCE-IN-INSTITUTIONS-REMAINS-LOW-1972-11 .pdf; Gallup Poll, July 1, 1973, "Confidence in Key American Institutions, *The Gallup Poll: Public Opinion 1972–1977*, vol. 1 (Wilmington, Del.: Scholarly Resources Inc., 1978), 131–32; Jonathan M. Ladd, *Why Americans Hate the Media and How It Matters* (Princeton, N.J.: Princeton University Press, 2012), 65, 88–89; John Hughes, "Why Doesn't Public Trust Press?" *Chicago Tribune*, May 25, 1979; Nicholas von Hoffman, "Media Losing Public's Trust," *Washington Post*, June 12, 1976; memo, Charles C. Guthrie to Ivan Veit, March 7, 1973, John B. Oakes Papers, Box 15, folder "Ivan Veit."

8. Nick Williams memo to Otis Chandler, August 24, 1966, Los Angeles Times Records, Box 230, folder 2.

9. Bill Thomas speech to Management Conference Installation Banquet, June 1972, Los Angeles Times Records, Box 408, folder 4, THL.

10. A. M. Rosenthal memo to the staff, October 7, 1969, New York Times Company Records, A. M. Rosenthal Papers, Box 70, folder 2, New York Public Library (hereafter NYPL).

11. A. M. Rosenthal, journal entry, March 13, 1971, A. M. Rosenthal Papers, Box 4, NYPL.

12. See, for example, A. M. Rosenthal to Gerald Gold, September 27, 1973, New York Times Company Records, A. M. Rosenthal Papers, Box 70, folder 1, NYPL.

13. Jules Witcover, *White Knight: The Rise of Spiro Agnew* (New York: Random House, 1972), 322.

14. Many authors have written about the *New York Times* under Ochs, most notably Susan Tifft and Alex S. Jones, *The Trust: The Private and Powerful Family Behind the New York Times* (Boston: Little, Brown, 1999), and Michael Schudson, *Discovering the News: A Social History of American Newspapers* (New York: Basic Books, 1978). Andrew Porwancher has shown that Ochs often disregarded his stated ideals about

objectivity: Andrew Porwancher, "Objectivity's Prophet: Adolph Ochs and the *New York Times*, 1896–1935," *Journalism History* 36, no. 4 (Winter 2011): 186–95.

15. The other two beliefs were "that every accused man or institution should have the immediate right of reply" and "that we should not use a typewriter to stick our fingers in people's eyes just because we have the power to do so." A. M. Rosenthal memo to the staff, October 7, 1969, New York Times Company Records, A. M. Rosenthal Papers, Box 70, folder 2, NYPL.

16. Ibid.

17. A. M. Rosenthal to James Reston, September 4, 1968, New York Times Company Records, A. M. Rosenthal Papers, Box 70, folder 2, NYPL.

18. Herbert Brucker, "What's Wrong with Objectivity?" *Saturday Review*, October 11, 1969, 77.

19. Transcript of remarks by John H. Colburn at the annual meeting of the Blue Pencil Club of Ohio, May 17, 1970, Los Angeles Times Records, Box 232, folder 14, THL.

20. "Attack on Objectivity Increases from Within," *Editor & Publisher*, June 13, 1970, 24.

21. Stanford Sesser, "Journalists: Objectivity and Activism," *Wall Street Journal*, October 21, 1969. Requests for the memo can be found in New York Times Company Records, A. M. Rosenthal Papers, Box 92, folders 12 and 13, NYPL.

22. "Attacked from within" quote: A. M. Rosenthal to Arthur Ochs Sulzberger, October 17, 1974, New York Times Company Records, A. M. Rosenthal Papers, Box 69, folder 13, NYPL.

23. Gay Talese, *The Kingdom and the Power: Behind the Scenes at the New York Times, the Institution That Influences the World* (New York: Random House, 1969).

24. Tom Wicker, "The Greening of the Press," *Columbia Journalism Review*, May/June 1971, 7–12.

25. Rosenthal to Sulzberger, May 26, 1971, New York Times Company Records, A. M. Rosenthal Papers, Box 70, folder 1, NYPL.

26. Steven V. Roberts, interview with author, October 3, 2014.

27. A. M. Rosenthal, "Combat and Compassion at Columbia," *New York Times*, May 1, 1968.

28. Prime examples include Tom Wicker, John Hess, and Anthony Lukas.

29. Daniel C. Hallin, *The "Uncensored War": The Media in Vietnam* (New York: Oxford University Press, 1986), 116–17.

30. C. Gerald Fraser, interview with author, October 24, 2014.

31. Ibid.; Earl Caldwell, interview with author, October 3, 2014.

32. Caldwell, interview with author.

33. Spiro Agnew speech to Alabama Chamber of Commerce, November 20, 1969, text in John Coyne Jr., *The Impudent Snobs: Agnew vs. the Intellectual Establishment* (New Rochelle, N.Y.: Arlington House, 1972), 272.

34. The *Times*, responding to Agnew's accusation, said that it had printed a story in that day's paper, but the story did not make it into the early edition that went to Washington; furthermore, it had carried essentially the same news on the front page on two other days. "Response to Vice President's Attack," *New York Times*, November 21, 1969.

35. David Greenberg, "The Idea of 'Liberal Bias' and Its Roots in the Civil Rights Movement," *The Sixties: A Journal of History, Politics and Culture* 1, no. 2 (December 2008): 167–86.

36. During the 1952 presidential campaign, Democratic candidate Adlai Stevenson complained that the United States had a "one-party press" biased in favor of Republicans; see "The Texts of the Addresses by Governor Stevenson at Portland and Seattle" and "Mr. Stevenson and the Press," *New York Times*, September 9, 1952.

37. Jack Smith, "L.A.'s No. 1 Red Finds U.S. Isn't All Bad," *Los Angeles Times*, February 16, 1969; George Putnam News, "One Reporter's Opinion," KTTV-Los Angeles, February 17, 1969, transcript in Los Angeles Times Records, Box 459, folder 5, THL.

38. Jack Nelson, "Negroes Further Alienated by Nixon's Cabinet Appointments," *Los Angeles Times*, December 16, 1968; Hernando Courtright to Nick Williams, December 19, 1968, Los Angeles Times Records, Box 448, folder 8, THL.

39. Bill Thomas, "The Press: Is It Biased Against the Establishment?" *Los Angeles Times*, March 30, 1975.

40. Bill Boyarsky, interview with author, July 31, 2014.

41. A. M. Rosenthal memo to Gene Roberts and Arthur Gelb, November 7, 1969, New York Times Company Records, A. M. Rosenthal Papers, Box 70, folder 2, NYPL.

42. See, for example, Katrina Vanden Heuvel, "The Distorting Reality of 'False Balance' in the Media," *Washington Post*, July 15, 2014; Margaret Sullivan, "He Said, She Said, and the Truth," *New York Times*, September 16, 2012. Similar debates about objectivity have taken place in other fields, including history; see Thomas Haskell, *Objectivity Is Not Neutrality: Explanatory Schemes in History* (Baltimore: Johns Hopkins University Press, 1998), and Peter Novick, *That Noble Dream: The "Objectivity Question" and the American Historical Profession* (New York: Cambridge University Press, 1988).

43. Text of Nick B. Williams speech to California Newspaper Publishers Association, June 20, 1961, Los Angeles Times Records, Box 468, folder 15, THL.

44. Irving Kristol, "The Underdeveloped Profession," *Public Interest* (Winter 1967): 50–51.

45. Leslie R. Collitt, "The Mask of Objectivity," *The Nation*, June 17, 1968, 789–90.

46. David Deitch, "The Case for Advocacy Journalism," *The Nation*, November 17, 1969, 531.

47. Edwin Diamond, "The Cabal at the New York Times: Which Way to the Revolution?" *New York Times*, May 5, 1970, 42–45; Joseph Lelyveld, interview with author, September 5, 2014.

48. J. Anthony Lukas, *The Barnyard Epithet and Other Obscenities: Notes on the Chicago Conspiracy Trial* (New York: Harper & Row, 1970), viii.

49. Edwin Diamond, "'Reporter Power' Takes Root," *Columbia Journalism Review* 9 (Summer 1970): 12–18.

50. Several prominent *New York Times* reporters left the paper—and left daily journalism—in the 1960s and '70s in order to have greater writerly freedom, including Gay Talese, David Halberstam, and J. Anthony Lukas.

51. Spiro Agnew speech to Midwest Regional Republican Committee, Des Moines, Iowa, November 13, 1969, text in Coyne, *The Impudent Snobs*, 267.

52. Tom Wicker, "The Reporter and His Story: How Far Should He Go?" *Nieman Reports*, June 1972.

53. Abraham Kalish, letter to the editor of *Nieman Reports*, September 23, 1972, New York Times Company Records, Tom Wicker Papers, Box 8, folder 15, NYPL.

54. See Kathryn McGarr's essay in this volume on journalism in 1950s Washington.

55. On the turn toward adversarialism in the late 1960s and '70s, see Schudson, *Discovering the News*, 176–91; Thomas E. Patterson, *Out of Order* (New York: Knopf, 1993), 79; Irving Kristol, "Is the Press Misusing Its Powers?" *Chicago Tribune*, January 11, 1975; Louis Banks, "Memo to the Press: They Hate You Out There," *The Atlantic*, April 1978, 35–42.

56. See Hemmer's essay in this volume.

57. Rosenthal expressed his desire for vivid, interpretive writing on many occasions. See, for example, A. M. Rosenthal to Clifton Daniel and James Reston, August 29, 1968, New York Times Company Records, A. M. Rosenthal Papers, Box 70, folder 2, NYPL; A. M. Rosenthal, journal entry, January 29, 1971, A. M. Rosenthal Papers (personal papers), Box 4, NYPL.

58. Nick Williams draft template for form letter, approved by Otis Chandler, circa 1964, Los Angeles Times Records, Box 448, folder 15, THL.

59. Nick Williams to Richard L. Bean, June 19, 1969, Los Angeles Times Records, Box 447, folder 9, THL.

60. Text of Nick Williams speech to Claremont University Club, circa 1970, Los Angeles Times Records, Box 469, folder 1, THL.

61. Transcript of "News Conference," May 13, 1972, KNBC-TV Los Angeles, Los Angeles Times Records, Box 409, folder 7, THL.

62. Chandler delivered the same remarks in other speeches as well. Transcript of Otis Chandler speech at UCLA, May 21, 1971, Los Angeles Times Records, Box 233, folder 8; transcript of Otis Chandler speech at Temple Beth Am, January 12, 1971, Los Angeles Times Records, Box 233, folder 1, THL.

63. A. M. Rosenthal, journal entry, January 29, 1971, A. M. Rosenthal Papers (personal papers), Box 4; A. M. Rosenthal to Punch Sulzberger, May 26, 1971, New York Times Company Records, A. M. Rosenthal Papers, Box 70, folder 1, NYPL.

64. Nick Williams to Frank Haven, Jim Bellows, and Jim Bassett, March 20, 1970, Los Angeles Times Records, Box 466, folder 6, THL.

65. Emphasis in original. Text of Nick Williams speech to Theta Sigma Phi, Denver, April 17, 1966, Los Angeles Times Records, Box 468, folder 20; text of

unlabeled Nick Williams speech, n.d., Los Angeles Times Records, Box 468, folder 19, THL.

66. Evidently Chandler's loathing for objectivity had not yet developed—or he put it aside when he wrote this letter. Otis Chandler to Louis Berke, September 13, 1968, Los Angeles Times Records, Box 220, folder 33, THL.

67. Harrison Salisbury to Earl J. Johnson, December 3, 1971, Harrison Salisbury Papers, Box 6, unlabeled folder, Columbia University Library.

68. Seymour Topping, interview with author, May 5, 2013.

69. George Gallup, "National Survey of Newspaper Readers," July 1976, Los Angeles Times Records, Box 222, folder 71, THL.

70. Otis Chandler to Nick Williams, December 7, 1966, Los Angeles Times Records, Box 228, folder 1, THL.

71. Text of Otis Chandler speech to Colorado Press Association, February 21, 1969, Los Angeles Times Records, Box 231, folder 17, THL; Daniel Yankelovich, "What They Believe," *Fortune*, January 1969.

72. Robert D. Nelson to Pat Reynolds, June 23, 1970, New York Times Company Records, Seymour Topping Papers, Box 23, folder 9, NYPL.

73. Seymour Topping to John M. Lee, David R. Jones, and Mitchel Levitas, September 16, 1976, New York Times Company Records, Seymour Topping Papers, Box 16, folder 3, NYPL.

74. Seymour Topping to Jones, Lee, Levitas, Peck, Tuite, and Whitman, January 6, 1977; Grace Lichtenstein to David R. Jones, September 19, 1976, New York Times Company Records, Seymour Topping Papers, Box 23, folder 9, NYPL.

75. Nick Williams to Gust W. George, March 3, 1970, Los Angeles Times Records, Box 466, folder 6, THL.

76. Bill Thomas to Otis Chandler and Robert D. Nelson, Los Angeles Times Records, Box 395, folder 9, THL.

77. The first of the reviews, the *Chicago Journalism Review*, ceased publication in 1975, and New York–based *MORE: A Journalism Review*, one of the most influential, folded in 1978. As Michael Schudson noted in 1978, most of the reviews "did not survive the decline of radical political activity in the early seventies" (Schudson, *Discovering the News*, 189).

78. Emphasis in original. Text of Bill Thomas speech before SPJ-SDX Conference, Costa Mesa, California, April 22, 1978, Los Angeles Times Records, Box 408, folder 7, THL.

79. A. M. Rosenthal to Arthur Ochs Sulzberger, January 23, 1978, New York Times Company Records, A. M. Rosenthal Papers, Box 92, folder 11, NYPL.

7. "No on 14"

1. Press release, "No on 14," September 4, 1964, folder 15, Box 5, Max Mont Collection, Special Collections and Archives, Oviatt Library, California State University–Northridge (hereafter cited as MM Collection).

2. Letter from William L. Becker to Gregory Peck, March 2, 1964; form letter for Stars for Freedom, June 1, 1964; and letter from Edmund G. Brown to Gregory Peck, May 29, 1964, folder "Proposition 14," Gregory Peck Papers, Special Collections (hereafter cited as Peck Papers), Margaret Herrick Library—Academy of Motion Pictures Arts and Sciences, Beverly Hills, Calif. (hereafter cited as MHL-AMPAS).

3. Donald Bogle, *Toms, Coons, Mulattoes, Mammies, and Bucks: An Interpretive History of Blacks in American Films* (New York: Continuum, 2001); Thomas Cripps, *Making Movies Black: The Hollywood Message Movie from World War II to the Civil Rights Era* (New York: Oxford University Press, 1993); Richard Iton, *Solidarity Blues: Race, Culture, and the American Left* (Chapel Hill: University of North Carolina Press, 2000).

4. Aniko Bodroghkozy, *Equal Time: Television and the Civil Rights Movement* (Urbana, Ill.: University of Chicago Press, 2012); Christine Acham, *Revolution Televised: Prime Time and the Struggle for Black Power* (Minneapolis: University of Minnesota Press, 2004); Steven D. Classen, *Watching Jim Crow: The Struggles over Mississippi TV, 1955–1969* (Durham, N.C.: Duke University Press, 2004).

5. Donald T. Critchlow, *When Hollywood Was Right: How Movie Stars, Studio Moguls, and Big Business Remade American Politics* (New York: Cambridge University Press, 2013); Kathryn Cramer Brownell, *Showbiz Politics: Hollywood in American Political Life* (Chapel Hill: University of North Carolina Press, 2014); and Steven J. Ross, *Hollywood Left and Right: How Movie Stars Shaped American Politics* (New York: Oxford University Press, 2011).

6. Mark Brilliant, *The Color of America Has Changed: How Racial Diversity Shaped Civil Rights Reform in California, 1941–1978* (Oxford: Oxford University Press, 2012); Daniel Martinez HoSang, "Racial Liberalism and the Rise of the Sunbelt West: The Defeat of Fair Housing on the 1964 California Ballot," in D. Dochuck and M. Nickerson, eds., *Sunbelt Rising: The Politics of Space, Place, and Region in the American South and Southwest* (Philadelphia: University of Pennsylvania Press), 188–213; Robert O. Self, *American Babylon: Race and the Struggle for Postwar Oakland* (Princeton, N.J.: Princeton University Press, 2003); Thomas W. Casstevens, *Politics, Housing, and Race Relations: California's Rumford Act and Proposition 14* (Berkeley: Institute of Governmental Studies, University of California, 1967); and Raymond E. Wolfinger and Fred I. Greenstein, "The Repeal of Fair Housing in California: An Analysis of Referendum Voting," *American Political Science Review* 62, no. 3 (September 1968): 753–69.

7. Bogle, *Toms, Coons, Mulattoes, Mammies, and Bucks*, 3–18; and Aram Goudsouzian, *Sidney Poitier: Man, Actor, Icon* (Chapel Hill: University of North Carolina Press, 2004), 67.

8. Douglas Flamming, *Bound for Freedom: Black Los Angeles in Jim Crow America* (Berkeley: University of California Press, 2005), 153, 175, 349–50.

9. Sammy Davis Jr., *Yes, I Can: The Story of Sammy Davis, Jr.* (New York: Farrar, Straus, and Giroux, 1965), 185, 278.

10. Jill Watts, *Hattie McDaniel: Black Ambition, White Hollywood* (New York: Amistad, 2005), 223, 227.

11. Murray Schumasch, "NAACP Scores Film Labor Units: Crafts Said to Bar Negroes—Gains for Actors Noted," *New York Times*, June 1, 1964, 33.

12. Dorothy Dandridge in *We Want to Be Free*, BB4745b, Pacifica Radio Archive.

13. Cripps, *Making Movies Black*, 215–20 and "$20,000 Box Office Payoff for H'Wood Negro—Tolerance Pix," *Variety*, November 30, 1949, 1, 18.

14. "Hearings Regarding Communist Infiltration of Minority Groups—Parts I and II," Hearings Before the Committee on Un-American Activities House of Representatives, 81st Cong., 1st sess., July 13, 14, and 18, 1949, 479–83 and 516.

15. Martha Biondi, *To Stand and Fight: The Struggle for Civil Rights in Postwar New York City* (Cambridge, Mass.: Harvard University Press, 2003), 67; Sidney Poitier in Goudsouzian, *Sidney Poitier*, 88; Ossie Davis and Ruby Dee, *With Ossie and Ruby: In This Life Together* (New York: William Morrow and Company, 1998), 232–33; *Counterattack* 8, no. 2 (January 8, 1954): 4; *Counterattack* 8, no. 7 (February 12, 1954): 4.

16. Adam Fairclough, *To Redeem the Soul of America: The Southern Christian Leadership Conference and Martin Luther King, Jr.* (Athens: University of Georgia Press, 1987), 31–32; FBI File, Sammy Davis Jr., 100-450712; Harry Belafonte, *My Song: A Memoir* (New York: Knopf, 2011), 189; "Mammoth L.A. Rights Rally Attracts 20,000, Raises $30,000," *Jet*, July 6, 1961, 58–59.

17. "Sammy Davis, Jr., Brought Friends to Chicago Jazz Bash," *Pittsburgh Courier*, September 10, 1960, 23; "$60,000 Worth of Fun!" *Pittsburgh Courier*, April 22, 1961, 2.

18. See F. "Martin Luther King Jr., Committee to Defend," Box 24, A. Philip Randolph Papers, Manuscripts Division, Library of Congress (hereafter cited as MD-LOC).

19. Ingrid Monson, *Freedom Sounds: Civil Rights Call Out to Jazz and Africa* (Oxford: Oxford University Press, 2007), 157.

20. Pamphlet, circa 1957, F. "Benefits, General, 1956–1963," General Office Files, III: A44, NAACP Papers, MD-LOC; letters between George Stevens, Harry Belafonte, and Sidney Poitier, folder "Charities #3522," George Stevens Papers, Special Collection, MHL-AMPAS; letter from James Forman to Ruby Dee and Ossie Davis, July 11, 1962, Student Nonviolent Coordinating Committee Papers, reel 6.

21. Emilie Raymond, *"From My Cold, Dead Hands": Charlton Heston and American Politics* (Lexington: University Press of Kentucky, 2006), 74; Theodore Bikel, interview with the author, Westwood, Calif., January 13, 2011.

22. Claude Sitton, "Mississippi Town Seizes 19 Negroes: Dick Gregory, Not Held, Leads Greenwood March," *New York Times*, April 4, 1963, 22; "Dick Gregory Accuses Police of Brutality in Alabama Jail," *New York Times*, May 10, 1963, 14; "Gregory Held in Arkansas," *New York Times*, February 18, 1964, 21.

23. Bill Lane, "Nat Cole Defends Stars Who Shun Dixie Racial Picket Lines," *Chicago Defender*, May 11, 1963, 10.

24. *We Want to Be Free*, Pacifica Radio; Louie Robinson, "50,000 Jam L.A. Ball Park for Biggest Civil Rights Rally," *Jet*, June 14, 1963, 58; Fairclough, *To Redeem the Soul of America*, 148.

25. Letter from Pauline Marshall (secretary, "Stars for Freedom"), November 4, 1963, folder "MCA Artists," Howard Fleming Papers, Special Collections, MHL-AMPAS; and "Stars for Freedom Benefit Performance—December 5, 1963, Santa Monica Civic Auditorium Statement of Income and Expenditures, September 27, 1963 to March 18, 1964," folder "Benefits, General, 1956–1963," General Office Files, III: A44, NAACP Papers, MD-LOC.

26. Marlon Brando in Louie Robinson, "Brando Fights for Civil Rights," *Ebony* 18 (October 1963): 61.

27. Thomas J. Sugrue, *Sweet Land of Liberty: The Forgotten Struggle for Civil Rights in the North* (New York: Random House, 2008), 284.

28. HoSang, "Racial Liberalism and the Rise of the Sunbelt West," 191; "Owner Agrees to Integrate Torrance Tract," *Los Angeles Times*, July 13, 1963; "Brando Fights for Civil Rights," 65–67; Malcolm Boyd, "Blind No More," *Pittsburgh Courier*, August 10, 1963, 11.

29. Sugrue, *Sweet Land of Liberty*, 200–250.

30. HoSang, "Racial Liberalism and the Rise of the Sunbelt West," 190–91.

31. Wolfinger and Greenstein, "The Repeal of Fair Housing in California," 753.

32. "Meeting Executive Committee, Californians Against Proposition 14," August 17, 1964, folder "Prop 14," Peck Papers, MHL-AMPAS.

33. "California: Proposition 14," *Time*, September 25, 1964, 23.

34. HoSang, "Racial Liberalism and the Rise of the Sunbelt West," 199.

35. Donald T. Critchlow and Emilie Raymond, eds., *Hollywood and Politics: A Sourcebook* (New York: Routledge, 2009), 17–23.

36. Ibid., 36.

37. Herbert Gold, "Nobody's Mad at Murphy," *New York Times*, December 13, 1964, SM42.

38. Press release, "Arts Division—Californians Against Proposition 14," n.d. (circa September 1964), Box 5, folder 15, MM Collection.

39. Army Archerd, "Just for Variety," *Variety*, September 4, 1964.

40. Minutes from First Meeting of the Arts Division Committee, August 8, 1964, folder "Proposition 14," Peck Papers, MHL-AMPAS.

41. "Meeting Executive Committee," 2; and press release "Hollywood Bowl October 4," n.d. (circa September 1964), Box 5, folder 15, MM Collection.

42. "Liz and Dick to Do Bowl Benefit to Defeat Prop. 14," *Variety*, September 11, 1964, 2; "Meeting Executive Committee," 2–3.

43. Letter from George Schlaff to Gregory Peck, November 3, 1964, folder "Prop. 14," Peck Papers, MHL-AMPAS; and Casstevens, *Politics, Housing, and Race Relations*, 66.

44. "An Open Letter," *Variety*, September 18, 1964; "Is There Time?" *Variety*, October 27, 1964.

45. "Meeting Executive Committee," 4–5.

46. "No on 14" newsletter, August 27, 1964, folder "Proposition 14," Peck Papers, MHL-AMPAS.

47. Notes for speech for "No on Prop 14"—Thousand Oaks Luncheon, n.d. (circa August 1964); Peck Speech, n.d. (circa August 1964); letter from Mrs. Dick Van Dyke to Gregory Peck, October 17, 1964, folder "Proposition 14," Peck Papers, MHL-AMPAS; report on operation of NAACP Headquarters, November 12, 1964, Box 5, folder 21, MM Collection.

48. Brilliant, *The Color of America Has Changed*, 194.

49. Ibid., 200–203.

50. HoSang, "Racial Liberalism and the Rise of the Sunbelt West," 205; and Brilliant, *The Color of America Has Changed*, 208.

51. Self, *American Babylon*, 265.

52. "NAACP Weighs Movie Job Suits," *New York Times*, July 9, 1965, 16; "Push Negro Employment in Movie Industry," *Chicago Defender*, April 25, 1966, 15.

53. Tom Wolfe, *Radical Chic and Mau-Mauing the Flak Catchers* (New York: Noonday Press, 1970); Ann Coulter, "Let Them Eat Tofu!" Universal Press Syndicate, February 28, 2007.

54. Memo from Jeffrey Donfeld for the President's File, "President's Meeting with Mr. Sammy Davis, Jr.," July 21, 1971, Box 9, folder "Celebrities 3 of 3," H. R. Haldeman Donated Papers, Subseries A Working Files, Richard Nixon Presidential Library, Yorba Linda, Calif.; Sammy Davis Jr., "Why I Went to the Troops," *Ebony* (June 1972): 141–47.

8. From "Faith in Facts" to "Fair and Balanced"

1. *Manion Forum* Broadcast No. 1,000, "A Manion Forum Milestone: Prominent Americans Pay Tribute to Dean Manion on 1000th Consecutive Weekly Broadcast," December 9, 1973.

2. Andrew Porwancher, "Objectivity's Prophet: Adolph S. Ochs and the *New York Times*, 1896–1935," *Journalism History* 36 (Winter 2011): 186–95.

3. Richard L. Kaplan, *Politics and the American Press: The Rise of Objectivity, 1865–1920* (New York: Cambridge University Press, 2002); Michael Schudson, *Discovering the News: A Social History of American Newspapers* (New York: Basic Books, 1978); David T. Z. Mindich, *Just the Facts: How Objectivity Came to Define American Journalism* (New York: New York University Press, 1998); Lynn D. Gordon, "Why Dorothy Thompson Lost Her Job: Political Columnists and the Press Wars of the 1930s and 1940s," *History of Education Quarterly* 34 (Autumn, 1994): 281–303.

4. Daniel Hallin, *The "Uncensored War": The Media and Vietnam* (Oxford: Oxford University Press, 1986).

5. David Greenberg, "The Idea of 'the Liberal Media' and Its Roots in the Civil Rights Movement," *The Sixties: A Journal of History, Politics, and Culture* 1 (December 2008): 167–86.

6. "How Accurate Is America's News?" *Facts Forum News*, April 1955, 28–29, 41, in Box 93, folder 13, Herbert A. Philbrick Papers, Library of Congress (hereafter LOC), Washington, D.C.

7. Regnery to Buckley, December 30, 1958, Box 56, folder 8, Regnery Papers, Hoover Institution (hereafter HI), Palo Alto, Calif.

8. Though the phrase "marketplace of ideas" was not coined until 1953, the concept traces back (in American jurisprudence) to Justice Oliver Wendell Holmes's dissent in *Abrams v. U.S.* (1919), where Holmes discussed "free trade in ideas," and in British thought to John Milton's *Areopagitica* (1644) and John Stuart Mills's *On Liberty* (1859). For a history of "the marketplace of ideas," see Gregory Brazeal, "How Much Does a Belief Cost? Revisiting the Marketplace of Ideas," *Southern California Interdisciplinary Law Journal* 21, no. 1 (2011–2012): 1–46.

9. "Re: A New Magazine," Box 10, folder 15, Regnery Papers, HI.

10. Ibid.

11. Ibid.

12. Felix Morley, "An Adventure in Journalism," in *A Year of Human Events: A Weekly Analysis for the American Citizen* (Chicago: Human Events, Inc., 1945), vii–ix.

13. "The Who, What, How and Why of Your Washington News Service," *Human Events*, April 21, 1961.

14. Letter to contributors, September 21, 1956, Box 97, folder 42, Manion Papers, Chicago History Museum (hereafter CHM), Chicago, Ill.

15. U.S. Congress, House, *Legislative History of the Fairness Doctrine* (Washington, D.C.: U.S. Government Printing Office, 1968).

16. On objectivity, see Kaplan, *Politics and the American Press*; Schudson, *Origins of the Ideal of Objectivity in the Professions*; Mindich, *Just the Facts*. On conservative attitudes toward balance, see for instance, *Manion Forum Newsletter* 4, no. 21 (October 21, 1964), in Box 85, folder 2, Manion Papers, CHM.

17. *Manion Forum* Broadcast No. 474, "Do You Really Want Federal Censorship for Your Local Radio?" October 27, 1963.

18. FCC 64-611 ("Applicability of the Fairness Doctrine in the Handling of Controversial Issues of Public Importance"), 29 Fed Reg. 10416–27 1964; Congress, *Legislative History*, 5; Ben Waple to Arthur I. Boreman, December 16, 1963, Box 66, folder 12, Manion Papers, CHM; G. H. Thompson to Manion, October 6, 1963, Box 11, folder 5, Manion Papers, CHM; Manion to H. R. Gross, October 15, 1963, Box 11, folder 6, Manion Papers, CHM.

19. Marjorie Hunter, "Agnew Says 'Effete Snobs' Incited War Moratorium," *New York Times*, October 20, 1969.

20. Robert B. Semple Jr., "Assent: Agnew Calls for Protest against TV," *New York Times*, November 16, 1969.

21. Max Frankel, "Agnew's Speech: Three in One," *New York Times*, November 15, 1969; Richard Harwood and Laurence Stern, "Sneers at Vice President Won't Dispel Doubts about Media's Performance," *Washington Post*, November 19, 1969; William Greider, "Public Backs Agnew Blast at Networks," *Washington Post*, November 15, 1969; Tom Wicker, "The Tradition of Objectivity in the American Press—and What's Wrong with It," *Proceedings of the Massachusetts Historical Society* 83 (1971): 83–100; Edward S. Herman and Noam Chomsky, *Manufacturing Consent: The Political Economy of the Mass Media* (New York: Pantheon Books, 1988).

22. *Manion Forum* Broadcast No. 795, "Hanky-Panky: Liberal News Manipulators Are Caught with Their Scripts Down," January 4, 1970; Manion to Clayton Kirkpatrick, January 1, 1970, Box 55, folder 3, Manion Papers, CHM; *Manion Forum* Broadcast No. 805, "We Shall Overcome: Free Flow of News and Good Sense of a Free People Will Insure Nation's Survival," March 15, 1970; Draft of Suggested Letter for Vig. List, n.d., Box 107, folder 2, Manion Papers, CHM.

23. David B. Frisk, *If Not Us, Who? William Rusher, National Review, and the Conservative Movement* (Wilmington, Del.: ISI Books), 244; *Human Events* insert card, "How Much News Is Being Withheld from You?" attached to Robert D. Kephart to Manion, March 22, 1971, Box 107, folder 2, Manion Papers, CHM; Stephen J. Ganslen to Rusher, November 6, 1972, Box 41, folder 9, Rusher Papers, LOC; Arlington House catalog, Fall 1970, Arlington House Publishers Ephemera, Wilcox Collection, University of Kansas (hereafter KU), Lawrence, Kans.

24. Thomas L. Winter to "Dear Fellow American," Committee to Combat Bias in Broadcasting Ephemera, Wilcox Collection, KU.

25. Edith Efron, "Why Speech on Television Is Not Really Free," *TV Guide*, April 11, 1964, clipping in Box 67, folder 1, Manion Papers, CHM; Edith Efron, "There Is a Network News Bias," *TV Guide*, February 28, 1970, reprinted in *Human Events*, March 14, 1970.

26. Edith Efron, *The News Twisters* (Los Angeles: Nash, 1971).

27. Efron to Buckley, June 4, 1971; Buckley memo to Frank Meyer, Priscilla Buckley, Warren Steibel, WAR, McCaffrey, James Buckley, June 17, 1971, Box 121, folder 4, Rusher Papers, LOC.

28. John Chamberlain, "TV Reporting on '72 Campaign Should Be Different," *Human Events*, September 18, 1971, 11. The Nixon administration's involvement in Efron's book is detailed in David Brocks, *The Republican Noise Machine: Right-Wing Media and How It Corrupts Democracy* (New York: Crown, 2004), 26–33.

29. Michael T. Kaufman, "Reed Irvine, 82, the Founder of a Media Criticism Group, Dies," *New York Times*, November 19, 2004; *Manion Forum* Broadcast No. 1099, "Monitoring the News: 'Accuracy in Media' Scores in Combating Inaccurate and Biased Reporting," November 2, 1975.

30. *Manion Forum* Broadcast No. 1,099, "Monitoring the News," November 2, 1975; Chad Raphael, *Investigated Reporting: Muckrakers, Regulators, and the Struggle over Television Documentary* (Urbana: University of Illinois Press, 2005), 214.

31. Raphael, *Investigated Reporting*, 90–98.

32. Ibid., 213–17.

33. Footnote 927, January 6, 1976, Box 86, folder 6; Footnote 1273, May 4, 1977, Box 86, folder 9, Manion Papers, CHM.

34. William B. Arthur, "The Winds Are Ablowin'," February 13, 1974, in Box 156, folder 8, Rusher Papers, LOC; Frisk, *If Not Us, Who?* 190–92.

35. Winter to Rusher, May 25, 1978, Box 101, folder 1, Rusher Papers, LOC.

36. Manion to Rusher, May 21, 1974, Box 61, folder 4, Manion Papers, CHM.

37. Lawrie Mifflin, "At the Fox News Channel, the Buzzword Is Fairness, Separating News from Bias," *New York Times*, October 7, 1996.

9. Abe Rosenthal's Project X

1. Daniel Ellsberg, *Secrets: A Memoir of Vietnam and the Pentagon Papers* (New York: Penguin, 2002).

2. Chris Daly, *Covering America: A Narrative History of a Nation's Journalism* (Amherst: University of Massachusetts Press, 2012), 369–70.

3. See David Rudenstine, *The Day the Presses Stopped: A History of the Pentagon Papers Case* (Berkeley: University of California Press, 1996).

4. Don R. Pember and Clay Calvert. *Mass Media Law*, 19th ed. (New York: McGraw-Hill, 2015), 80.

5. Harrison Salisbury, *Without Fear or Favor: An Uncompromising Look at the New York Times* (New York: Times Books, 1980), 89–93.

6. Ibid., 91.

7. Ibid.

8. Ibid., 92.

9. A. M. Rosenthal Papers, MssCol 17930, Box 4, New York Public Library Manuscripts and Archives Division, 1971 journal.

10. A. M. Rosenthal Journal, January 29, 1971, A. M. Rosenthal Papers, MssCol 17930, Box 4, New York Public Library Manuscripts and Archives Division.

11. James C. Goodale, *Fighting for the Press: The Inside Story of the Pentagon Papers and Other Battles* (New York: City University of New York Journalism Press, 2013), 21.

12. Daniel Ellsberg, *Papers on the War* (New York: Simon and Schuster, 1972), 39. See also David Rudenstine, *The Day the Presses Stopped: A History of the Pentagon Papers Case* (Berkeley: University of California, 1996), 47; Sanford J. Ungar, "The Papers Papers," *Esquire* 7, no. 5 (May 1972): 99–108; John Prados and Margaret Pratt Porter, eds., *Inside the Pentagon Papers* (Lawrence: University Press of Kansas, 2004); Ungar, *The Papers and The Papers: An Account of the Legal and Political Battle over the Pentagon Papers* (New York: Columbia University Press, 1989).

13. For details see Rudenstine, *The Day the Presses Stopped*; Goodale, *Fighting for the Press*; Ungar, "The Papers Papers."

14. Max Frankel, *The Times of My Life and My Life with the* Times (New York: Delta, 2000).

15. Ibid., 324.

16. A. M. Rosenthal Journal, July 13, 1971. A. M. Rosenthal Papers, MssCol 17930, Box 4, New York Public Library Manuscripts and Archives Division.

17. Memo from Seymour Topping to A. M. Rosenthal, April 16, 1971, New York Times Company Records, A. M. Rosenthal Papers, MssCol 17929, Box 100, folder 100.1, Pentagon Papers (General), April–June 1971.

18. A. M. Rosenthal Journal, July 13, 1971. A. M. Rosenthal Papers, MssCol 17930, Box 4, New York Public Library Manuscripts and Archives Division.

19. Goodale, *Fighting for the Press*, 5.

20. Journal entry, April 23, 1971. A. M. Rosenthal Papers, MssCol 17930, Box 4, New York Public Library Manuscripts and Archives Division, 1971 journal.

21. Journal entry, June 15, 1971. A. M. Rosenthal Papers, MssCol 17930, Box 4, New York Public Library Manuscripts and Archives Division, 1971 journal.

22. Journal entry, July 13, 1971. A. M. Rosenthal Papers, MssCol 17930, Box 4, New York Public Library Manuscripts and Archives Division, 1971 journal.

23. Ibid.

24. Ibid.

25. Ibid.

26. Memo from A. M. Rosenthal to Charlotte Curtis, August 25, 1975, New York Times Company Records, A. M. Rosenthal Papers, MssCol 17929, Box 99, folder 99.27, Pentagon Papers (General), 1971–80.

27. Journal entry, July 13, 1971. A. M. Rosenthal Papers, MssCol 17930, Box 4, New York Public Library Manuscripts and Archives Division, 1971 journal.

28. Ibid.

29. Ibid.

30. Journal entry, July 14, 1971. A. M. Rosenthal Papers, MssCol 17930, Box 4, New York Public Library Manuscripts and Archives Division, 1971 journal.

31. Journal entry, July 15, 1971. A. M. Rosenthal Papers, MssCol 17930, Box 4, New York Public Library Manuscripts and Archives Division, 1971 journal.

32. Ibid.

33. Ibid.

34. Ibid.

35. Memo from A. M. Rosenthal to A. O. Sulzberger, June 1, 1971, New York Times Company Records, A. M. Rosenthal Papers, MssCol 17929, Box 100, folder 100.1, Pentagon Papers (General), April–June 1971.

36. Journal entry, June 15, 1971. A. M. Rosenthal Papers, MssCol 17930, Box 4, New York Public Library Manuscripts and Archives Division, 1971 journal.

37. Memo from A. M. Rosenthal to A. O. Sulzberger, June 21, 1971. New York Times Company Records, A. M. Rosenthal Papers, MssCol 17929, Box 100, folder 100.1, Pentagon Papers (General), April–June 1971.

38. John L. Hess, *My Times: A Memoir of Dissent* (New York: Seven Stories, 2003).

39. Arthur Gelb, *City Room* (New York: Putnam, 2003), 559.

40. A. M. Rosenthal Journal, January 29, 1971. A. M. Rosenthal Papers, MssCol 17930, Box 4, New York Public Library Manuscripts and Archives Division.

10. "Ideological Plugola," "Elitist Gossip," and the Need for Cable Television

1. On Nixon's media innovations, see Kathryn Cramer Brownell, *Showbiz Politics: Hollywood in American Political Life* (Chapel Hill: University of North Carolina Press, 2014).

2. "The Polar Star of CATV," address of Frederick W. Ford, president, before the Seventeenth Annual Convention of the National Cable Television Association, Inc. Boston, Mass., July 2, 1968, folder Telecommunications Meetings with the National Cable Television Association, Box 22, Clay T. Whitehead Papers (CTWP), Library of Congress, Washington, D.C.

3. *On the Cable,* Report by the Alfred Sloan Commission on Cable Communications (New York: McGraw-Hill, 1972), 3.

4. Paul Starr, *The Creation of the Media: Political Origins of Modern Communications* (New York: Basic Books, 2004), 1–2.

5. These phrases commonly appear in Nixon's discussion of the press, especially after a speech delivered by his Office of Telecommunications director, Clay Whitehead; see Correspondence between Colson and Whitehead, December 7, 13, 14, Box 42, folder Speech—Indiana Broadcasters Association, December 18, 1972, CTWP.

6. William E. Porter, *Assault on the Media: The Nixon Years* (Ann Arbor: University of Michigan Press, 1976); Bruce J. Schulman, *The Seventies: The Great Shift in American Culture, Society, and Politics* (Cambridge, Mass.: Da Capo Press, 2002); Michael Schudson, *The Power of News* (Cambridge, Mass.: Harvard University Press, 1996); Mark Feldstein, *Poisoning the Press: Richard Nixon, Jack Anderson, and the Rise of Washington's Scandal Culture* (New York: Farrar, Straus and Giroux, 2010); David Greenberg, *Nixon's Shadow: A Cultural History of an Image* (New York: W. W. Norton, 2003); Kathryn Cramer Brownell, *Showbiz Politics: Hollywood in American Political Life* (Chapel Hill: University of North Carolina Press, 2014); Nicole Hemmer, *Messengers of the Right: The Origins of Conservative Media* (Philadelphia, University of Pennsylvania Press, 2016).

7. Task force membership is listed in White House Press Release, August 14, 1967, folder, Domestic Satellite and Telecommunications, 197-1969, Box 5, CTWP.

8. On differences between the Rostow Report and the Nixon administration's view, see "Rostow Task Force Recommendations," Box 27, folder CTW Nomination and Resignation to/from the OTP, CTWP.

9. Transcript, "Hearings Before the Committee on Commerce," U.S. Senate, June 30, 1970, Box 27, folder CTW Nomination and Resignation to-from the OTP, CTWP.

10. James Baughman, *Television's Guardians: The FCC and the Politics of Programming, 1958–1967* (Knoxville: University of Tennessee Press, 1985).

11. "Organizing and Staffing the OTP," n.d., Box 34, folder OTP Organization (2 of 2), CTWP.

12. Letter from Clay Whitehead to Charlie McWhorter, January 8, 1970, Box 34, folder OTP Organization, CTWP.

13. Transcript, "Hearings Before the Committee on Commerce," U.S. Senate, June 30, 1970, Box 27, folder CTW Nomination and Resignation to-from the OTP, CTWP.

14. Stephen M. Aug, "White House to Stress Communications Policy," *Evening Star*, September 24, 1970, Box 27, folder CTW OTP Senate Confirmation and miscellaneous materials, CTWP.

15. "Tentative Outline of History of Nixon Administration's Handling of Communications Issues, January 1969 to September 1970," Box 33, folder OTP History, 1 of 2, CTWP.

16. "Pastore Briefing on OTP Budget Points to Stress," n.d. [1970], Box 32, folder Organization of the OTP Office + CTW's Confirmation, CTWP.

17. Patrick Parsons, *Blue Skies: A History of Cable Television* (Philadelphia: Temple University Press, 2008), 1–3.

18. Ibid., 106–7.

19. Michele Hilmes, *Hollywood and Broadcasting: From Radio to Cable* (Urbana: University of Illinois Press, 1999).

20. Quoted in Parsons, *Blue Skies*, 238.

21. As Thomas Streeter shows in "Blue Skies and Strange Bedfellows," these studies frequently reinforced one another, creating a "common consensus" among this coalition. In *The Revolution Wasn't Televised: Sixties Television and Social Conflict*, ed. Lynn Spigel and Michael Curtin (New York: Routledge, 1997).

22. Remarks by Frederick W. Ford, President of National Cable Television Association Before the Telecommunications Symposium of the Broadcast Advertising Club of Chicago, Chicago, Ill., March 29, 1968, Box 22, folder Telecommunications Meetings with National Cable Television Association, CTWP.

23. Ralph Lee Smith, *The Wired Nation: Cable TV: The Electronic Communications Highway* (New York: Harper & Row), 1–2. The article "The Wired Nation" first appeared in *The Nation* on May 18, 1970.

24. Nixon also used this approach in other domestic policies areas, see Schulman, *The Seventies*, 24–30.

25. Letter to Robert Finch from Clay Whitehead, June 7, 1971, Box 2, folder Cable Trends, WHCF, FG 6-14, RNL.

26. "Cable Television Background Paper," Box 2, folder Cable Trends, WHCF, FG 6-14, RNL

27. "The Whitehead Years," news clipping, Box 36, folder Communications Reform- OTP, Domestic Policy Staff; Simon Lazarus's 1976 Campaign Transition Files, Jimmy Carter Presidential Library, Atlanta, Ga.

28. Parsons, *Blue Skies*, 266.

29. Statement by Clay T. Whitehead, director, Office of Telecommunications Policy Before the Subcommittee on Constitutional Rights, U.S. Senate, February 2, 1972, Box 33, folder Organization of the OTP (2 of 2), CTWP.

30. Memorandum: First Meeting of the Cable Television Committee, Box 3, folder White House Committee, Cable Television, WHCF, FG 6-14, RNL.

31. Ibid.

32. "General Policy: Cable Television," draft by Bruce Owen, April 12, 1970, Box 4, folder Cable Policy, 1970, CTWP.

33. Bruce Owen, "Project Bun: Background Paper," December 5, 1972, Box 36, folder Project BUN, CTWP.

34. Memorandum re: Broadcasting Policy and Network Power, addendum to the Owen's "Project Bun," Box 36, folder Project BUN, CTWP.

35. On the idea for "GOP News" see Gabriel Sherman, *The Loudest Voice in the Room: How the Brilliant, Bombastic Roger Ailes Built Fox News and Divided a Country* (New York: Random House, 2014), 60–78.

36. Memorandum from Clay Whitehead to John Ehrlichman, December 6, 1972, Box 27, folder CTW OTP Senate Confirmation and Miscellaneous materials, CTWP.

37. Hemmer, *Messengers of the Right.*

38. Memorandum from Clay Whitehead to John Ehrlichman, December 6, 1972, Box 27, folder CTW OTP Senate Confirmation and Miscellaneous materials, CTWP.

39. Remarks of Clay Whitehead, director of Office of Telecommunications Policy, at the Sigma Delta Chi Luncheon, Indianapolis, Ind., December 18, 1972, Box 42, folder Speech—Indiana Broadcasters Association, December 18, 1972, CTWP.

40. Reactions, interview requests, and news clippings in response to this speech are found in Box 42, folder Speech—Indiana Broadcasters Association, December 18, 1972, CTWP.

41. News clipping, James Kilpatrick, "Whitehead Off Base in Attack on TV Industry," *Evening Star and Daily News*, December 26, 1972, Box 42, folder Speech—Indiana Broadcasters Association, December 18, 1972, CTWP.

42. Letter from Clay Whitehead to Mark Evans, January 26, 1973, Box 42, folder Speech—Indiana Broadcasters Association, December 18, 1972, CTWP.

43. Correspondence between Colson and Whitehead, December 7, 13, 14, Box 42, folder Speech—Indiana Broadcasters Association, December 18, 1972, CTWP.

44. Ibid.

45. Memorandum re: Meeting the President, February 5, 1973, Box 47, folder Congressional Testimony and Meeting with Nixon, CTWP.

46. Transcript, *Firing Line* (taped February 1, 1973, and aired February 16) with guest Clay Whitehead. Southern Educational Communications Association, Hoover Institution Library and Archives, Stanford University, Stanford, Calif.

47. Cable: Report to the President by the Cabinet Committee on Cable Communications, 1974, Box 36, folder Report to the President, the Cabinet Committee on Cable Communication, CTWP.

48. Ibid., 9.

49. Sol Schildhause, "Memorandum on the Cabinet Committee on Cable Communications," January 16, 1974, Box 3, folder 10- Memorandum 1967–76, Sol Schildhause Collection, Barco Library, Denver, Co.

50. Les Brown, "Press Freedom for Cable TV Is Urged in Whitehead Report," *New York Times*, January 17, 1974, 1.

51. Ibid.

52. Thomas Whiteside, "Cable Television: Onward and Upward with the Arts, Part 1," *New Yorker*, May 20, 1984, 58–59.

53. Monroe E. Price, "Requiem for the Wired Nation: Cable Rulemaking at the FCC," *Virginia Law Review* 61, no. 3 (April 1974): 541–77.

54. The cable fable first emerged as a concept in a special issue devoted entirely to cable television, *Yale Review of Law and Social Action* 2, no. 3 (Spring 1972).

55. "Telecommunications Issues," September 11, 1979, http://www.c-span.org /video/?152194-1/telecommunications-issues.

56. "The Communications and Technology Legacy of Clay Whitehead," Library of Congress, http://claytwhitehead.com/about_the_papers/video/cspan.

11. How Washington Helped Create the Contemporary Media

1. Victor Pickard, *America's Battle for Media Democracy: The Triumph of Corporate Libertarianism and the Future of Media Reform* (New York: Cambridge University Press, 2015), 106–7.

2. Ibid.

3. Tona Hangen, *Redeeming the Dial: Radio, Religion, and Popular Culture in America* (Chapel Hill: University of North Carolina Press, 2002).

4. Myer Feldman, "Memorandum for the President: Right-Wing Groups," August 16, 1963, John F. Kennedy Library, Presidential Papers, President's Office Files, Box 106, folder Right Wing Movements, Part 1 (Boston, Mass.).

5. Fred J. Cook, "Hate Clubs of the Air," *The Nation*, 523–27.

6. Ibid.

7. Fred W. Friendly, *The Good Guys, The Bad Guys and the First Amendment: Free Speech vs. Fairness in Broadcasting* (New York: Random House, 1975).

8. Ibid.

9. Ibid.

10. *Red Lion v. FCC*, June 9, 1969.

11. Steve Rendall, "The Fairness Doctrine: How We Lost It and Why We Need it Back," *Common Dreams*, February 12, 2005.

12. Gary Bauer to Rhett Dawson, June 16, 1987, Ronald Reagan Presidential Library, Howard Baker Files, Box 2, folder Fairness Doctrine (Simi Valley, Calif.).

13. Clarence Brown to Assistant Attorney General Charles Cooper, 1987, Ronald Reagan Presidential Library, Howard Baker Files, Box 2, folder Fairness Doctrine (Simi Valley, Calif.).

14. Ibid.

15. Rendall, *The Fairness Doctrine*.

16. Ibid.

17. "Selling the Airwaves to the Highest Bidders," *Mother Jones* 8, no. 9 (November 1983): 9.

18. "Mark Fowler, FCC," *The Nader Page*, https://blog.nader.org/1989/08/05/mark-fowler-fcc/ (accessed May 13, 2016).

19. Bruce Fein to James Murr, February 24, 1984, Ronald Reagan Presidential Library, Howard Baker Files, Box 2, folder Fairness Doctrine (Simi Valley, Calif.).

20. Federal Communications Commission, "General Fairness Doctrine Obligations of Broadcast Licensees," *Federal Register*, August 30, 1985.

21. "Why the Fairness Doctrine Is Still Important," *New York Times*, September 15, 1985.

22. Stephen Chapman, "Let Ideas Compete on the Air," *Chicago Tribune*, February 17, 1985.

23. Joyce Tuomy to Ronald Reagan, November 22, 1986, Ronald Reagan Presidential Library, Howard Baker Files, Box 2, folder Fairness Doctrine (Simi Valley, Calif.).

24. "A Level Playing Field in the Marketplace of Ideas," *Boston Globe*, November 10, 1986.

25. "'Fairness Doctrine' Approved by House," *United Press International*, June 4, 1987; "How Fair Is the Fairness Doctrine?" *New York Times*, April 5, 1987.

26. Ibid.

27. Kenneth Cribb to Rhett Dawson, June 17, 1987, Ronald Reagan Presidential Library, Howard Baker Files, Box 2, folder Fairness Doctrine (Simi Valley, Calif.).

28. Ibid.

29. James Miller to the President, June 12, 1987, Ronald Reagan Library, Howard Baker Files, Box 2, folder Fairness Doctrine (Simi Valley, Calif.).

30. "'Fairness Doctrine' Calls for a Veto," *Washington Post*, June 10, 1987.

31. Ronald Reagan, *Message to the Senate Returning Without My Approval S. 742, the Fairness in Broadcasting Bill* (Washington, D.C.: U.S. Government Printing Office, 1987).

32. "The Fairness Doctrine May Rise Again," *Chicago Tribune*, August 9, 1987.

33. "F.C.C. Votes Down Fairness Doctrine in a 4-0 Decision," *New York Times*, August 5, 1987.

12. The Multiple Political Roles of American Journalism

1. David E. Pozen, "The Leaky Leviathan: Why the Government Condemns and Condones Unlawful Disclosures of Information," *Harvard Law Review* 127 (2013): 513–635.

2. Cited in David Carr, "Retreading Memories, from a Perch Too Public," *New York Times*, February 9, 2015, B1.

3. See Michael Schudson, "Persistence of Vision: Partisan Journalism in the Mainstream Press," in Carl F. Kaestle and Janice A. Radway, eds., *Print in Motion: A History of the Book in America*, vol. 4 (Chapel Hill: University of North Carolina Press, 2009), 140–51.

4. George P. Kennedy, "Advocates of Openness: The Freedom of Information Movement" (Ph.D. diss., University of Missouri, 1978), 67. (Kennedy relies here on a 1978 letter to him from Pope.)

5. Address to the Upper Midwest News Executives Conference, Minneapolis, Minnesota, May 3, 1957. John E. Moss Papers, Box 427, folder 3, Special Collections, California State University–Sacramento, Sacramento, Calif.

6. Kennedy, "Advocates of Openness," 20–30. Kennedy's information comes largely from ASNE and Sigma Delta Chi contemporaneous publications.

7. A footnote added that school boards barred the public from meetings also in Chicago, Ill.; Columbia, Mo.; Denver, Colo.; Roanoke, Va.; Providence, R.I.; Evansville, Ind.; Flint, Mich.; Baltimore, Md.; and elsewhere. "Access to Official Information: A Neglected Constitutional Right," *Indiana Law Journal* 27 (1951–52): 209–30.

8. Jacob Scher, "Access to Information: Recent Legal Problems," *Journalism Quarterly* 37 (1960): 41–52.

9. Robert O. Blanchard, "A Watchdog in Decline," *Columbia Journalism Review* 5 (Summer 1966): 17–21 at 18.

10. The early history of the Freedom of Information Act is recounted in more detail in my *The Rise of the Right to Know: Politics and the Culture of Transparency, 1945–1975* (Cambridge, Mass.: Harvard University Press, 2015).

11. James W. Carey, "A Short History of Journalism for Journalists: A Proposal and Essay," *Harvard International Journal of Press/Politics* 12, no. 1 (2007): 3–16 at 13.

12. Susan E. Tifft and Alex S. Jones, *The Trust: The Private and Powerful Family Behind the New York Times* (Boston: Little, Brown, 1999), 311–15. See also Max Frankel, *The Times of My Life and My Life at the Times* (New York: Random House, 1999), 209; and John F. Stacks, *Scotty: James B. Reston and the Rise and Fall of American Journalism* (Boston: Little, Brown, 2003), 192.

13. Bob Woodward, *Veil: The Secret Wars of the CIA, 1981–1987* (New York: Pocket Books, 1988), 516–35.

14. Marcus Brauchli, Third Annual Richard S. Salant Lecture, Joan Shorenstein Center on the Press, Politics and Public Policy, Kennedy School, Harvard University, Cambridge, Mass., 2010, 12.

15. See Norman J. Ornstein and David W. Rohde, "The Strategy of Reform: Recorded Teller Voting in the U.S. House of Representatives," typescript, paper prepared for 1974 Midwest Political Science Association convention, Chicago, Ill., April 25–27, 1974, 1; and Steven S. Smith, *Call to Order: Floor Politics in the House and Senate* (Washington, D.C.: Brookings Institution, 1989), 256.

16. Democratic Study Group, "Secrecy in the House of Representatives," June 24, 1970, 7. James O'Hara Papers, Bentley Historical Library, Box 12, folder "Congressional Reorganization 1." A fuller account of the passage of the Legislative Reorganization Act and the DSG's role in it can be found in Michael Schudson, *Rise of the Right to Know: Politics and the Culture of Transparency, 1945–1975* (Cambridge, Mass.: Harvard University Press).

17. Richard Conlon, interview, July 5, 1974. This is a typed transcript of an interview with Conlon in the DSG Papers, Part 2, Box 2, folder 13, LOC. There is no indication of who conducted the interview or for what purpose.

18. See the many press clippings in DSG Papers, II-129, folder 2.

19. DSG Papers, Box I-4, folder 7, "Special Report: Secrecy in the House of Representatives," June 24, 1970.

20. Thanks to Sam Lebovic and Nicholas Lemann for ideas on this category of political influence.

21. Timothy Besley and Robin Burgess, "Political Agency, Government Responsiveness and the Role of the Press," *European Economic Review* 45 (2001): 629–40.

22. Philip Shabecoff, "The Environment Beat's Rocky Terrain," *Nieman Reports*, December 15, 2002, available at http://niemanreports.org/articles/the-environment -beats-rocky-terrain.

23. Steven Clayman, Marc Elliott, John Heritage, and Megan Beckett, "A Watershed in White House Journalism: Explaining the Post-1968 Rise of Aggressive Presidential News," *Political Communication* 27 (2010): 229–47 at 229.

24. Larry Sabato, *Feeding Frenzy: How Attack Journalism Has Transformed American Politics* (New York: Free Press, 1983), 31.

25. Ibid.

26. Douglass Cater, *The Fourth Branch of Government* (Boston: Houghton Mifflin, 1959), 107.

27. Ibid., 111.

28. Katherine Fink and Michael Schudson, "The Rise of Contextual Journalism, 1950s–2000s," *Journalism: Theory, Practice, Criticism* 15 (2014): 3–20.

29. Frank Esser and Andrea Umbricht, "The Evolution of Objective and Interpretative Journalism in the Western Press: Comparing Six News Systems Since the 1960s," *Journalism and Mass Communication Quarterly* 9, no. 2 (2014): 229–49.

30. Charles Hockett, "Chinese vs. English: An Exploration of the Whorfian Hypothesis," in H. Hoijer, ed., *Language in Culture* (Chicago: University of Chicago Press, 1954), 122.

CONTRIBUTORS

Kathryn Cramer Brownell is assistant professor of history at Purdue University. She is the author of *Showbiz Politics: Hollywood in American Political Life* (2014).

David Greenberg is professor of history and of journalism and media studies at Rutgers University, New Brunswick, N.J., and the author of several books, most recently *Republic of Spin: An Inside History of the American Presidency* (2016). Formerly managing editor and acting editor of the *New Republic*, he has also written for the *Atlantic*, *Foreign Affairs*, the *New Yorker*, the *New York Times*, *Slate*, the *Washington Post*, and many other scholarly and popular publications, and now writes a column for Politico.

Julia Guarneri is university lecturer in history at the University of Cambridge. She is at work on a book that examines the impact of daily newspapers on urban culture and growth in late nineteenth-century and early twentieth-century United States.

Nicole Hemmer is assistant professor in presidential studies at the Miller Center of Public Affairs at the University of Virginia. She is the author of *Messengers of the Right: Conservative Media and the Transformation of American Politics* (2016).

Richard R. John is a professor of history and communications at Columbia University. His most recent book is *Network Nation: Inventing American Telecommunications* (2010).

Sam Lebovic is assistant professor of history at George Mason University and the author of *Free Speech and Unfree News: The Paradox of Press Freedom in America* (2016).

Kevin Lerner is assistant professor of communication at Marist College, where he teaches American journalism history and mass communication law among other topics. He is at work on a history of the antiestablishment journalism review [MORE].

Kathryn McGarr is a doctoral student in history at Princeton University and the author of *The Whole Damn Deal: Robert Strauss and the Art of Politics* (2011).

Matthew Pressman is assistant professor of journalism at Seton Hall University. Prior to pursuing an academic career, he was an assistant editor and online columnist at *Vanity Fair.*

Emilie Raymond is associate professor of history at Virginia Commonwealth University. She is the author of *Stars for Freedom: Hollywood, Black Celebrities, and the Civil Rights Movement* (2015).

Michael Schudson, a sociologist, is professor of journalism at the Columbia Graduate School of Journalism. He is the author of books on the history and sociology of news, including *Discovering the News* (1978) and, most recently, *The Rise of the Right to Know: Politics and the Culture of Transparency, 1945–1975* (2015).

Bruce J. Schulman is the William E. Huntington Professor of History at Boston University. The author and editor of eight books, he is currently at work on a volume for the Oxford History of the United States covering the years 1896–1929.

Julian E. Zelizer is the Malcolm Stevenson Forbes, Class of 1941 Professor of History and Public Affairs at Princeton University and a fellow at New America. He is the author and editor of seventeen books on American political history, and he has written over 600 op-eds. His most recent book is *The Fierce Urgency of Now: Lyndon Johnson, Congress, and the Battle for the Great Society* (2015). He writes a popular weekly column for CNN.com.

INDEX

ABC (American Broadcasting Corporation), 1, 138, 140
"Access to Official Information" (*Indiana Law Journal* article), 194
Accuracy in Media (AIM), 106–7, 139–41
Acham, Christine, 115
Ade, George, 48
advertising, 1; celebrity activism, 123; criticism of, 66, 67, 72; in local newspapers, 38, 44, 45, 47; objectivity and, 98; propaganda and, 56–58, 59, 62
Advocates, The (television program), 139, 142
African Americans: in film industry, 115, 116–17, 119, 124; as journalists, 101–2; political representation of, 103. *See also* celebrity activism; civil rights movement; race; segregation
age: generational conflict, 99–100, 101; newspaper readership, 110–11
Agnew, Spiro, media/objectivity criticism by, 8, 63–65, 73, 76, 98; Fairness Doctrine, 140; interpretive reporting, 106; journalists' cliques, 75, 136; mainstream agreement with, 98, 102, 112, 136, 137, 142; *New York Times* and, 102, 107, 109, 228n34. *See also* media criticism; objectivity
Agriculture Committee, 198
AIM (Accuracy in Media), 106–7, 139–41
AIM Report (newsletter), 141
Albert, Heinrich, 51
Alfred Sloan Foundation, 161, 166, 175
Allen, Steve, 118
Alsop, Joseph, 78, 88–89, 192, 222n3
Alsop, Stewart, 88–89
American Broadcasting Corporation (ABC), 1, 138, 140

American Civil Liberties Union (ACLU), 165, 186
American Defense Society, 56
American Negro Theatre, 116
Americans for Democratic Action (ADA), 165, 186
American Society of Newspaper Editors (ASNE), 68, 193–94
American Sugar Refining Company, 10
American Weekly (newspaper), 48
America's House of Lords (Ickes), 71
Answers for Americans (television program), 129–30
antiestablishment perspectives, 103–4, 110, 136, 225n4; Pentagon Papers and, 147, 158
antimonopoly movement, 10–35, 64–65; consolidationists, 14, 19–31, 32; farmers/laborers in, 5, 10–11, 13–14, 23, 30, 34; government regulations, 10–11, 13, 26, 34; merchants/proprietors in, 5, 11–12, 30, 33–35; moralism in, 12, 14, 19, 21–22, 27; National Anti-Monopoly League, 23; nationalists, 14, 15, 32–33; open-access antimonopolists, 14, 15–19; railroad corporations and, 11, 15–18, 22–24, 27, 34; Standard Oil, 10, 12, 19, 20, 27–29, 33; Thurber, 10–11, 13, 22–24, 26–27, 30, 34–35; Western Union, 15, 16, 19–20, 27. *See also* communications monopolies; newspapers, antimonopoly movement and; political cartoons
antisecrecy measures, 199–200
Archibald, Sam, 195
Aristotle, 53
Arlington House (conservative publisher), 137
Arthur, William B., 141

Arts Division of CAP, 114, 119, 120–21, 122–24
Associated Press, 20, 64–65, 67
Atlantic Monthly (magazine), 67

Bagdikian, Ben, 73
Baker, Ray Stannard, 67
Baker, Russell, 84
Baltimore Sun (newspaper), 37, 45, 86
Baquet, Dean, 196–97
Barnes, Harry Elmer, 61–62
Barton, Bruce, 57, 58, 59
Barton, Durstine and Osborn (BDO, advertising firm), 57
Baruch, Bernard, 62, 218n46
Bauer, Gary, 182
Beale, Bill, 194
Beard, Charles, 61
Belafonte, Harry, 116–18, 121
Bellamy, Edward, 22, 32
Bellew, Frank, 16–19, 27, 30; "Comparative Bigness"/"Upon What Meat," 24–25, 210n37; Uncle Sam rendering, 16, 17, 209n17. *See also* political cartoons
Bennett, James O'Donnell, 45
Bent, Silas, 56, 58
Bentham, Jeremy, 21
Berger, Marilyn, 83
Bernays, Edward, 58–59
"Best Kind of Monopoly, The" (Wales cartoon), 31, 32
Bethmann-Hollweg, Theobald von, 51
big business, 11–12, 208n5; depicted as octopus, 17–18, 27, 33; newspaper industry as, 67, 69–70, 76
Biltmore Agreement, 69
Bishop, Joseph Bucklin, 54, 122
Black, Hugo, 65
Black Perspective, 102
blacksheeting (reporter collaboration), 87
Bleyer, William G., 48
Block, Herbert ("Herblock"), 84
blue sky advocacy for cable industry, 165–66, 167, 175, 240n21
Bonnet, Henri, 90
Bork, Robert, 183
"Bosses of the Senate" (Keppler cartoon), 33
Boston Globe (newspaper), 38, 105
Boston Post (newspaper), 44
Boyarsky, Bill, 104

boys' clubs. *See* journalists, social functions/clubs
Boys on the Bus, The (Crouse), 80, 83
Bradlee, Ben, 196
Bradley, Omar, 85
Brando, Marlon, 119–20, 121, 125
Brandt, Peter, 89
Brant, Irving, 70
Brass Check, The (Sinclair), 67–68
Brauchli, Marcus, 196
broadcast television: ABC, 1, 138, 140; licensing, 177–178, 181, 186; NBC, 1, 138, 162–163, 191; OTP and, 169–71; triopoly of., 162–163, 165, 169–170. *See also* cable television; Columbia Broadcasting System (CBS)
Brown, Clarence, 182
Brown, Edmund "Pat," 114, 119, 121
Brownell, Kathryn Cramer, 8, 115
Brucker, Herbert, 100
Bruggmann, Charles, 90
Bryan, William Jennings, 67
Buckley, James, 139
Buckley, William F., Jr., 102, 129–30, 131–32, 138–39, 142, 173
bully pulpit, 53
Burger, Warren, 181
Burleson, Albert, 56
Burton, Richard, 120, 122
Bush administration, 158
Byoir, Carl, 60

"cablecasting," 165–66
Cable News Network (CNN), 182
cable television, 8, 160–75, 177; blue sky advocacy, 165–66, 167, 175, 240n21; election campaign coverage, 168–69; Fairness Doctrine and, 182–83; FCC and, 160, 162, 163, 165, 167, 168, 173–74, 175; government regulations, 160–62, 165, 167–74; OTP and, 161, 163–64, 167–74; Owen report to OTP, 169–70; policymaking and, 160–162, 163, 166–174; Presidential Cabinet Committee, 167–68, 170–71, 173, 174; Project BUN, 169–70, 172; size of audience, 184; Whitehead and, 161, 163–164, 167, 168, 170–174; Whitehead speeches, 172–73
Caldwell, Earl, 102
Caldwell, Lynton Keith, 203–4

Californians Against Prop 14 (CAP) Arts Division, 114, 119, 120–21, 122–24
California Real Estate Association (CREA), 120, 124
CAP (Californians Against Prop 14), 114, 119, 120–121, 122–124
capitalism, 6, 15, 74–75, 208n13. *See also* deregulation/free market promotion
Carey, Jim, 195
Carnegie, Andrew, 11
Carter, Jimmy, 175
Carter administration, 112
Castro, Fidel, 134
Cater, Douglass, 202
Catledge, Turner, 92
CBS. *See* Columbia Broadcasting System (CBS)
celebrity activism, 7, 114–15; benefit shows, 117–18, 119, 122–23, 124; CAP Arts Division, 114, 119, 120–121, 122–124; direct action, 118, 119–20; in electoral politics, 121–22; Leading Six, 117–19. *See also* civil rights movement
Central Press Association, 46
"Cephalopod, or Terrestrial Devil Fish—A Monster of Centralization, The" (Bellew cartoon), 18
Chamberlain, John, 138, 139
Chamberlain, O. H., 43
Chandler, Otis, 97, 102–3, 108, 109, 110, 230n66
Chapman, Stephen, 185
Charleston News and Courier, 41
Chester, Ed, 86
Chicago, Illinois, 45, 46
Chicago Daily News, 39, 44, 84
Chicago Herald (newspaper), 45
Chicago Times (newspaper), 40
Chicago Tribune (newspaper), 12, 20, 45, 47, 92; assaults to building of, 70; Fairness Doctrine and, 185; subscription cost, 44, 213n32; suburban readers, 43–44
Chomsky, Noam, 73, 136
Christian Crusade (radio program), 135
Church, Wells, 86
Cincinnati Post (newspaper), 44
cities, local newspapers and, 36–49; charities, 41–42; muckraking reporting, 40–41; size of city, 41; suburban readers, 43–45; urban readers/content, 39–43,

44–46, 47–49. *See also* newspapers, local; specific newspaper
Civil Rights Act (1964), 124
civil rights movement, 7, 74; CAP, 114, 119, 120–121, 122–124; conservative opinion during, 128; in film industry, 115, 116–17, 119, 124. *See also* celebrity activism
Clark, Kenneth, 102
Classen, Steven D., 115
Clayman, Steven, 201–2
Cleveland, Grover, 53
Cleveland News, 42
Cleveland Press (newspaper), 44
Cobb, Frank, 51, 58
Cohen, Bernard C., 87, 92
Cold War consensus, 7, 80–81, 82, 92, 194; blacksheeting, 87; Murrow and, 85–86; *New York Times* and, 86, 87, 88. *See also* journalists, social functions/clubs
Cole, Nat "King," 118, 120, 122
Collier's (magazine), 67
Collingwood, Charles, 83
Collitt, Leslie, 105
Colson, Charles, 139, 140–41, 172
Columbia Broadcasting System (CBS), 1–2, 136, 185; Fairness Doctrine and, 140; liberal bias, 138; Murrow at, 85–86; *Spectrum,* 142; WWII experiences, 83–84. *See also* broadcast television
Columbia Journalism Review, 100, 106
Columbia State (newspaper), 45
Combs, George Hamilton, 129–30
commercialism, 2, 127; of newspaper industry, 63–64, 65–68, 74–75. *See also* newspaper industry, commercialism of
Commission on Cable Communications (Alfred Sloan Foundation), 161
Committee on Advancement of Freedom of Information, 194
Committee on Public Information (Creel Committee), 52, 55–56, 58, 59
Committee on World Freedom of Information, 194
Committee to Combat Bias in Broadcasting, 137–38
Committee to Uphold Constitutional Government, 70
Common Cause, 186

Communications Act (1934), 162, 178, 184
communications monopolies, 12; broadcast
    television triopoly, 162–63, 165, 169–70;
    criticism of, 64–65, 66–70; radio networks,
    69–70; Supreme Court antitrust suit
    against Associated Press, 64–65. *See also*
    antimonopoly movement
Communist Party, 103, 116–17, 134–35,
    180
community antenna television (CATV)
    (later National Cable Television
    Association), 164–65, 174
Community for the Negro in the Arts
    (CAN), 116
"Comparative Bigness"/"Upon What Meat"
    (Bellew cartoon), 24–25, 210n37
Congress, 10, 54, 197–98; Communications
    Act and, 162; communications policy,
    162, 163, 168, 174; DSG, 198–200;
    Fairness Doctrine and, 177, 178, 181, 182,
    183, 184, 186; FOIA in, 193
Conlon, Richard, 197, 199
consensus-style reporting, 7, 80–81, 82–83,
    107
conservation (term), 204
Conservative Book Club, 139
conservative media, 126–43; after Fairness
    Doctrine elimination, 188–89; Agnew
    and, 135–36, 137, 138, 140, 142; creation
    of establishment, 7–8, 126–32; Fairness
    Doctrine and, 133–35, 138, 140, 142,
    179–80, 182, 185; Fox News, 142–43;
    Human Events, 75, 128, 132, 137, 138, 141,
    143; liberal media, 178, 185, 188–89;
    Manion Forum, 126–27, 133, 137, 139–40,
    179; Mayflower Doctrine and, 178; media
    watchdog groups, 139–41; *National
    Review*, 102, 130, 131–32, 137, 138–39,
    140; "No-Spin Zone," 62; statistics to
    prove liberal bias, 137–39. *See also* liberal
    bias; media criticism by conservatives;
    media criticism by liberals
Conservative Political Action Committee,
    186
"Consolidated" (Keppler cartoon), 27–29
contextual reporting, 202
Cook, Fred, 180
Cooley, Harold, 198
Coolidge, Calvin, 3, 59
Copley, Ira, 46

corporations: *vs.* government ownership, 32;
    vs. proprietorships, 11–12, 13–14. *See also*
    antimonopoly movement
Counterattack (Communist publication),
    117
Crane, Phil, 126
credibility gap, 97, 112. *See also* objectivity
Creel, George, 52, 55–56, 59; Committee on
    Public Information, 52, 55–56, 58, 59
Cribb, Kenneth, 186–87
Cronkite, Walter, 135, 176
Crouse, Timothy, 80, 83
Crowell, Benedict, 56
Crystallizing Public Opinion (Bernays), 58

Daily Graphic (newspaper), 16, 27
Daly, Chris, 3
Dan Smoot Report (newsletter), 134
Davis, Elmer, 84
Davis, Ossie, 116–18, 124
Davis, Rita Wade, 123
Davis, Sammy, Jr., 114, 115–16, 117–18, 119,
    120, 124–25
Dawson, Rhett, 186
D.C. Circuit of U.S. Court of Appeals, 183
D.C. reporters. *See* journalists, social
    functions/clubs
Dee, Ruby, 116–18
Deitch, David, 105
democracy, 36
Democratic National Committee, 180
Democratic National Convention, 71–72,
    139
Democratic Party: antimonopoly movement
    and, 30–31; DNC, 71–72, 139; DSG and,
    197–200; Fairness Doctrine and, 186;
    liberal media, 130; media criticism, 65,
    70–72; public relations, 59; same-sex
    marriage and, 200–201. *See also*
    Republican Party
Democratic Study Group (DSG), 197–200
Democrat's Dilemma, The (Crane), 126
deregulation/free market promotion,
    161–63, 169–75; Fairness Doctrine and,
    182, 183–84, 187, 188. *See also* govern-
    ment regulations
Des Moines Register and *Tribune* (news-
    papers), 44
Deuel, Wallace, 84, 89, 93, 94
Diamond, Edwin, 146

Dos Passos, John, 61, 68–69
Downie, Leonard, Jr., 192
"Drag Up the Slums" (*New York World* article), 40–41
Dreiser, Theodore, 39–40
Duke, Paul, 202
Dulles, Allen, 78
Dulles, John Foster, 81, 92–94
Durstine, Roy, 57

Eagle Forum, 186
economic consolidation, 14–15. *See also* antimonopoly movement
economies of scale, 14, 46
editorials section, 191–92
Editor & Publisher (journal), 100
Edwards, George C., III, 53, 215n12
Efron, Edith, 75, 138–39, 141
Ehrlichman, John, 170
Eisenhower, Dwight, 3, 94, 121, 122; Gridiron Club dinner, 77, 78, 79
Elliston, Herbert, 90
Ellsberg, Daniel, 144, 147–48, 154
employment discrimination, 119
Enemies He Has Made, The: The Media vs. Spiro Agnew (Arlington House), 137
energy monopolies, 12
environmental issues, 27–28, 201, 203–4
"Environment: A New Focus for Public Policy?" (Caldwell), 203–4
Environment as a Focus for Public Policy (Caldwell's collected papers), 203
Ernst, Morris, 73
espionage plans, 50–51. *See also* propaganda
Esquire magazine, 89
Evans, Stan, 141
Evening Star (newspaper), 86
events listings, 37, 39
executive power. *See* White House/executive branch

Face in the Crowd, A (film), 62
Fair Employment Practices Commission, 120
fair housing debate, 114–15, 119–20; CAP, 114, 119, 120–121, 122–124; Prop 14 passing, 123–24
Fairness Doctrine, 177–89; AIM and, 140; cable television, 167; conservative media and, 133–135, 138, 140, 142, 179–180, 182,

185; creation of, 178–79; "editorial rule" of, 179; Efron's criticism, 138; enforcement of, 179–81, 184–85; license granting/renewal, 177–78, 181; objectivity and, 9, 177, 181; open disregard of, 179–80; opposition to, 179–82; scarcity rationale, 181, 182, 183, 184, 185, 188, 189; Supreme Court decisions, 180–181, 182, 183, 184; Whitehead on, 173. *See also* Federal Communications Commission (FCC); objectivity
Fairness Doctrine, elimination of, 8–9, 135, 142, 179–89; conservative media proliferation after, 188–89; efforts to reinstate after, 189; FCC investigation, 183–85; First Amendment arguments, 181, 183, 184, 187; free market promotion, 182, 183–184, 187, 188; opposition to, 185–86, 187; Reagan and, 8, 177, 182, 183–84, 186–187; support for, 186–87. *See also* conservative media
farmers/laborers, antimonopoly movement and, 5, 10–11, 13–14, 23, 30, 34
Fatherland, The (propaganda publication), 50–51
FCC v. League of Women Voters (1984), 183
Federal Communications Commission (FCC), 133–35, 140–41; AIM and, 140; cable television and, 160, 162, 163, 165, 167, 168, 173–174, 175; CATV and, 165; Communications Act and, 162; creation of, 178; deregulation, 173–74; Fairness Doctrine elimination, 8–9, 177; Fairness Doctrine investigation, 183–85; Fowler as chair, 183, 188; net neutrality, 189; OTP and, 163; Patrick as chair, 188; *Red Lion* decision, 180–81, 183; Whitehead on, 173. *See also* Fairness Doctrine; Office of Telecommunications Policy (OTP)
Federal Trade Commission (FTC), 69
Fein, Bruce, 184
Feldman, Myer, 179
Field, Cyrus, 29, 30
Fink, Katherine, 202
Finnegan, James J., 137
Firing Line (television program), 139, 142, 173
First Amendment, 151, 173, 175; Fairness Doctrine and, 181, 183, 184, 187
Flynn, Edward, 71–72

Flynn, William, 51
FOIA (Freedom of Information Act), 193–95
Foley, Tom, 198
Ford, Frederick, 160
Ford, Gerald, 175
Ford Foundation, 165, 166
Foundation for Objective News Reporting (FONR, media watchdog group), 141–42
Fowler, Mark, 183, 188
Fox News Channel, 142–43
Franciosa, Judy, 120, 122
Frankel, Max, 146, 148–49, 151–52, 155–56
Frankenstein (Shelley), 17
Frankovich, M. J., 120, 122
Fraser, Donald, 199
Fraser, Gerald, 101–2
Freedom of Information Act (FOIA, 1966), 193–95
Freedom of Information Center (University of Missouri), 199
free market. *See* deregulation/free market promotion
Fresh Air Fund (newspaper charity), 41–42, 212n20
Freud, Sigmund, 58
Friedman, Milton, 173
Friendly, Fred, 1–2
Fritts, Edward, 185
Fulbright, J. William, 1, 90
Furman, Bess, 81

Gallup, George, 110
Gannett, Frank, 70, 71
Gannett Newspapers, 46
Gardner, George, 164
Garment, Len, 167
Gelb, Arthur, 158
gender: boys' clubs and, 77, 78, 81, 83, 87, 223n15; WHCA and, 81
George, Henry, 19–20, 22, 67
Germany, propaganda during World Wars, 50–52, 55, 59, 60, 61
Gingrich, Newt, 182
Goebbels, Josef, 60
Goering, Hermann, 60
Goldwater, Barry, 121–22, 126, 175
golf clubs, 79
Goodale, James, 147, 149, 154
Gorgias (Plato), 52

Gould, Jay, 15, 26, 27, 29, 32
government ownership, 32
government regulations: antimonopoly movement, 10–11, 13, 26, 34; cable television and, 160–63, 165, 167–74; conservative media and, 130; Rostow Report, 162, 166. *See also* deregulation/ free market promotion; Fairness Doctrine; policymaking
Graham, Kay, 90
Graham, Philip, 90
Great Depression, 68
Greenfield, James, 148, 153, 154
Gregory, Thomas, 56
Gridiron Club, 77–81, 83, 92–95. *See also* journalists, social functions/clubs
La Guardia, Fiorello, 69
Guarneri, Julia, 6, 115

Hagerty, James, 93–94
Halberstam, David, 90, 147
Hallin, Daniel C., 80, 101, 128, 223n13
Hamilton, Grant E., 33
Hand, Learned, 65
Hanighen, Frank, 132
Harding, Warren, 58–59
Hargis, Billy James, 134–35, 180
Harris, Walter M., 72
Hartford Courant (newspaper), 100
Hearst, William Randolph, 46–47, 48, 70, 71
Hearst Corporation, 111
Helms, Jesse, 185
Hemingway, Ernest, 61, 63
Hemmer, Nicole, 7–8, 107
Hentoff, Nat, 147
Herman, Edward S., 73, 136
Hess, John, 157
Heston, Charlton, 118, 119, 120, 121, 125
Hidden Persuaders, The (Packard), 62
Higgins, Marguerite, 83
Historical Research Fund, 138
Hitler, Adolf, 60, 61, 71
Hockett, Charles, 204
Hodges, Charles, 129
Hoffman, Nicholas von, 142
Hollywood, California, 115–16. *See also* celebrity activism
Holt, Hamilton, 66
Home of the Brave (film), 116
Hoover, Herbert, 59

House, Edward, 51, 59
House of Representatives, 197–200
House Un-American Activities Committee
  (HUAC), 60, 116–17
Hugo, Victor, 17, 18
Human Events (conservative newsletter), 75,
  128, 132, 137, 138, 141, 143
Humphrey, Hubert, 138
Hunt, H. L., 179
Hutchins Commission, 76

Ickes, Harold, 6, 69, 71, 73
Illustrated Sunday Magazine (newspaper), 48
immigrants/immigration, 39, 47
incorporation/corporations, 11–12, 13–14, 32
"In Danger" (Keppler cartoon), 29, 33
Indiana Law Journal, 194
In Fact (newsletter), 73
instant analysis, 135–36
Internet, 189
interpretive reporting, 96, 105–9, 128, 176,
  178, 202
Interstate Commerce Act (1887), 34
"In the Clutch of a Grasping Monopoly"
  (Hamilton cartoon), 33
Intruder in the Dust (film), 116
Investigated Reporting (Raphael), 140
investigative journalism, 161. *See also*
  muckraking journalism
Irvine, Reed, 139–40, 141
Irwin, Will, 46, 67, 75
"Ivy Bells" story, 195–96

Jackson, Andrew, 53
Jamieson, Kathleen Hall, 4
Jefferson, Thomas, 66
John, Richard R., 4, 5, 177
Johnson, Lyndon B., 1–2, 162, 166; election/
  campaign of, 121, 123; Pentagon Papers
  and, 145, 152
journalists, political participation by, 2,
  190–205; agenda advocacy, 200–201;
  changes brought about by, 201–3;
  education and, 203; FOIA, 193–95;
  government employment, 197–200;
  language and, 203–4; lobbying, 192–95;
  motives for, 191; national security issues,
  94, 195–97
journalists, social functions/clubs, 7, 75,
  77–95, 136, 202; blacksheeting, 87;

cocktail parties, 88–89; consensus, 82–83;
  gender and, 77, 78, 81, 83, 87, 223n15;
  Gridiron Club, 77–81, 83, 92–95;
  Metropolitan Club, 80, 81, 82, 87; NPC,
  81–82, 83, 87; personal/public life
  merging, 7, 88–92; race and, 78, 81, 83;
  during WWII, 83–85
Journal of Social Science, 10
Judge (humor magazine), 27, 32
Jungle, The (Sinclair), 68
Justice (National Anti-Monopoly League
  newspaper), 23–26, 210n37
J. Walter Thompson Agency, 57

Kansas City Star (newspaper), 41, 79
Keller, G. Frederick, 30
Kelly, John, 30
Kennedy, John F., 3, 74, 86, 121, 145, 162
Kenworthy, Elizabeth, 91
Kenworthy, Ned, 91
Keppler, Joseph, 27–30, 33
Keppler, Joseph, Jr. ("Udo"), 33, 211n60
Khrushchev, Nikita, 134
Kilpatrick, James J., 142
King, Martin Luther, Jr., 117, 119
Kiplinger Washington Letter (journal), 72
Kissinger, Henry, 146
Kittle, William, 67
Klein, Herb, 167
Knowland, William, 93
Korean War, 85–86, 93
Kraft, Joe, 89
Kristol, Irving, 105
Krock, Arthur, 82, 85, 88, 89, 90, 94
Kuhn, Delia, 91
Kuhn, Ferdinand, 84, 91

laborers: antimonopoly movement, 5, 10–11,
  13–14, 23, 30, 34; media criticism, 69,
  72–73
Lamb, Brian, 174
Lancaster, Burt, 119, 120, 122
Landon, Alf, 70, 71
language, importance of, 203–4
Lasker, Albert, 58
Lasswell, Harold, 52, 59
L.A. Times. See Los Angeles Times
law. *See* government regulations; policy-
  making; Supreme Court
Lazarsfeld, Paul, 60

Leading Six (celebrity activists), 117–19. *See also* celebrity activism; race

Lebovic, Sam, 6, 102

Legislative Restorative Act (1970), 198

Lend-Lease Act (1941), 192

Lerner, Kevin, 8

Lerner, Max, 61, 69

LeSueur, Larry, 83–84

Leviero, Anthony, 93–94

Lewis, Fulton, Jr., 129

liberal bias, 126–43; cable policy, 169; conservative media creation in opposition to, 126–32; conservatives' efforts to prove, 137–39; election coverage, 138; Fairness Doctrine and, 133–35, 140, 182; media watchdog groups and, 141–42. *See also* Agnew, Spiro, media/objectivity criticism by; media criticism by conservatives

liberal media: Fairness Doctrine and, 185, 188–89; Mayflower Doctrine and, 178. *See also* conservative media; media criticism by conservatives

licensing for broadcasters, 177–78, 181, 186. *See also* Fairness Doctrine

Lindley, Ernest K., 93

Lindley Rule, 93

Lindsay, John, 165

Lippmann, Helen, 90–91

Lippmann, Walter, 87, 90–91, 192

Lloyd, Alfred H., 58

Lloyd, Henry Demarest, 19, 20–22, 26–27, 32

local newspapers. *See* newspapers, local

Looking Backward (Bellamy), 22

Lord, Day & Lord, 149, 154

Los Angeles Herald Examiner (newspaper), 111

Los Angeles Times, 96–97, 225n1; objectivity and, 7, 98, 102–4, 107–12; reader demographics, 110, 111

Lost Boundaries (film), 116

Lott, Trent, 182

Lovett, Bob, 85

Lukas, J. Anthony, 106

Lundberg, Ferdinand, 69

Mackin, Cassie, 83

MacLeish, Archibald, 60–61, 63, 64–65, 76

mainstream media criticism. *See* media criticism

managerial capitalism, 15, 208n13

Manion, Clarence, 133, 134, 137, 179; AIM and, 141; Irvine and, 139–40; on *Spectrum*, 142

Manion Forum (radio program), 126–27, 133, 137, 139–40, 179

Man Nobody Knows, The (Barton), 57, 58

Manufacturing Consent (Herman and Chomsky), 136

March on Washington (1963), 119, 120, 121

Marion, George, 73

marketplace of ideas, 131, 185, 235n8

Martin, Dean, 114, 118, 119

Mayflower Doctrine (1941), 178, 179

McAdoo, William, 51

McCarthy, Eugene, 199

McCarthy, Joseph, 105

McCarthyism, 128

McChesney, Robert, 4, 73

McChrystal, Stanley, 196

McCormick, Anne O'Hare, 83

McCormick, Robert, 70–71, 92

McDaniel, Hattie, 115

McGarr, Kathryn, 6–7

McGrory, Mary, 83

McIntire, Carl, 179

McKinley, William, 3, 54, 215n12

McLendon, Sarah, 83

McNamara, Robert, 152

McNaught Syndicate, 46

media criticism, 63–76; advertising, 66, 67, 72; by both conservatives and liberals, 6, 109–10, 136–37; commercialism arguments, 63–68, 74–75; consolidation arguments, 66–70, 73; early history of, 66; by government, 71–72, 75–76, 160–61, 220n36; by MacLeish, 63, 64–65, 76; by muckrakers, 65–66, 67, 68, 69; of newspaper industry, 63–69, 74–75; of radio, 69; by Sinclair, 67–68. *See also* Agnew, Spiro, media/objectivity criticism by; newspaper industry, criticism of

media criticism by conservatives, 63–65, 66, 73–76, 97, 112; cable television, 8, 169–72; efforts to prove liberal bias, 137–39; emergence of, 73–74; of Fairness Doctrine, 179–80, 182; interpretive reporting, 106–7, 108; of *L.A. Times*, 107–8, 109, 111; liberal media, 178, 185, 188–189; *News Twisters*, 138–39; Nixon,

160, 161, 170; objectivity, 98, 102, 127–29; OTP and, 170–71. *See also* Agnew, Spiro, media/objectivity criticism by; conservative media; liberal bias

media criticism by liberals, 63–73, 97, 112; commercialism arguments, 64, 65–68; consolidation arguments, 66–70, 73; Efron's interview with Smith, 138; by government administration, 71–72; of *L.A. Times,* 109; by New Left, 136–37; of *New York Times,* 146; objectivity, 98, 101; presidential elections, 70–72; of radio, 69–70. *See also* conservative media; liberal bias

media monopolization. *See* communications monopolies

media studies/media scholarship, 3–5

media watchdog groups, 129; AIM, 106–7, 139–42; FONR, 141–42; NNC, 141

men. *See* journalists, social functions/clubs

Mendès-France, Pierre, 87

merchants/proprietors, 5, 11–12, 30, 33–35

Merton, Robert, 60

message movies, 116

Metropolitan Club, 80, 81, 82, 87

Metropolitan Newspaper Service, 46

Meyer, Eugene, 82, 87

Miami Herald Publishing Co. v. Tornillo (1974), 181

Michelson, Charlie, 59

Middleton, Drew, 84

Milwaukee Free Press (newspaper), 39

Milwaukee Journal (newspaper), 202

Minton, Sherman, 71

Mitchell, John, 156

"Modern Laocoön" (Bellew cartoon), 17

Le Monde (newspaper), 105

"Monster Monopoly, The" (Keppler cartoon), 29

moralism: antimonopoly movement, 12, 14, 19, 21–22, 27; CAP activism, 123–24

Morality in the Media in Massachusetts, 185

Morley, Felix, 132

Moss, Frank E., 165–66

Moss, John, 193–95, 197

Mother Jones magazine, 183

Motley, Red, 137

Moynihan, Daniel Patrick, 62, 218n46

muckraking journalism, 21; in local newspapers, 40–41; media criticism,

65–66, 67, 68, 69; *vs.* objectivity, 127, 136; propaganda and, 52, 55; Watergate and, 161

multiple service operators (MSOs), 165

Mumford, Lewis, 61

Murphy, George, 121, 122

Murrow, Edward R., 83–84, 85–86

Nader, Ralph, 73, 184, 186

Nation, The, 105, 128, 166, 180

National Anti-Monopoly League, 23

National Association for the Advancement of Colored People (NAACP), 116, 117, 118, 119, 121, 124

National Association of Broadcasters, 185, 187

National Broadcasting Corporation (NBC), 1, 138, 162–63, 191. *See also* broadcast television

National Cable Television Association (formerly CATV), 160, 165

National News Council (NNC, media watchdog group), 141

National Press Club (NPC), 81–82, 83, 87

National Recovery Act, 70

National Review (journal), 102, 130, 131–32, 137, 140; advertising of *News Twisters,* 138–39

National Security Agency (NSA), 158, 195

National Security League, 56

"Natural History of the Newspaper, The" (Park), 36

Nazis, 60, 61

NBC (National Broadcasting Corporation), 1, 138, 162–163, 191. *See also* broadcast television

Nelson, Nell, 40

Nerone, John, 3–4

net neutrality, 189

network television. *See* broadcast television; cable television

Nevins, Allan, 61

New Deal, 64–65, 66, 166–67; media criticism, 68–69, 70, 71, 76; Nixon and, 167

Newfield, Jack, 147

New Left, 101, 110, 136–37

Newman, Paul, 119

New Republic, The (journal), 128

newspaper industry, commercialism of:
  conservative criticism, 63–64, 75; liberal
  criticism, 64, 65–68, 74–75
newspaper industry, criticism of: commercialization arguments, 63–64, 65–68,
  74–75; consolidation arguments, 64–65,
  66–69; sociological arguments, 75. *See
  also* media criticism
newspapers, antimonopoly movement and,
  5, 30; big-city press, 13–14; *Chicago
  Tribune,* 12, 20; *Daily Graphic,* 16, 27;
  George and Lloyd, 19–21; *Justice,* 23–26,
  210n37. *See also* antimonopoly movement; political cartoons
newspapers, local, 36–49; advertising, 38,
  44, 45, 47; charities, 41–42, 212n20;
  circulation, 37, 43–44, 47; city problems
  reports, 39–43; events listings, 37, 39;
  expansion of print space, 38; local
  reporting decline, 46–49; muckraking
  reports, 40–41; political content, 44–45,
  47; Progressive politics, 6, 37, 41, 46,
  48–49; purchase of, by newspaper chains,
  46–47; region-specific editions, 44–45;
  suburban readers and content, 43–49;
  Sunday edition, 44; syndicated content,
  46–49; technological advancements in
  production, 38; travelogues and human
  interest features, 39–40; urban readers
  and content, 39–43, 44–46, 47–49. *See
  also* cities, local newspapers and
newspapers, national, 37, 87; syndicated
  news, 37, 46–49
News Twisters, The (Efron), 138–39
New York City, New York, 23, 40–41
New Yorker (magazine), 174
New York Evening Globe (newspaper), 41
New York Evening Mail (newspaper), 51
New York Herald Tribune (newspaper), 42,
  43, 75, 83, 86, 111
New York Journal (newspaper), 42
New York magazine, 146
New York Post (newspaper), 146
New York Times, 40, 96; Agnew's criticism
  of, 102, 107, 109, 228n34; Baquet at, 196–97;
  charities, 42; Cold War consensus, 86,
  87, 88; conservative history of, 145–47,
  158; contextual reporting in, 202; on
  Coolidge, 59; environmental news, 201;
  Hearst interview in, 70; Krock, Arthur,

and, 82, 85, 88, 89, 90, 94; national security,
  195; *News Twisters* on best-seller list, 139;
  NNC and, 141; objectivity and, 7, 98–102,
  104–6, 107–12, 127, 136, 228n34; reader
  demographics, 110–11; social functions/
  clubs, 81, 82, 84, 93–94; Sulzberger,
  Arthur Hays and, 90, 91–92; Vandenberg
  speech, 192; women on staff, 83. *See also*
  Reston, James B. "Scotty"; Rosenthal,
  A. M. (Abe); Rosenthal, A. M. (Abe),
  Pentagon Papers and; Sulzberger, Arthur
  Ochs ("Punch")
New York Times, Pentagon Papers and, 8,
  144–59; editorial decisions, 150–55,
  156–57; initial meetings, 148–53, 155;
  injunction, 150, 154, 155, 156, 158; legal
  ramifications of publishing, 149, 151,
  155–56, 158; naming of story, 157; risk to
  newspaper, 150–51, 153; source for,
  147–48; space allotment for story, 154,
  157. *See also* Pentagon Papers (Project X);
  Rosenthal, A. M. (Abe), Pentagon Papers
  and
New York Times Company v. United States
  (1971), 144–45. *See also* Pentagon Papers
  (Project X)
New York Tribune (newspaper), 41–42
New York World (newspaper), 12, 37, 39,
  40–41; charities funded by, 42; German
  propaganda exposé, 51–52; regional
  readers, 44
"Night of Stars" benefit (CAP Arts
  Division), 122–23
Nixon, Richard, 74, 135, 160–75; AIM and,
  140–41; all-white cabinet of, 103; celebrity
  activism on campaign of, 124–25;
  deregulation of media, 8, 160–63, 165,
  167–74; FCC and, 140–41, 160, 162, 163;
  instant analysis criticism, 135–36; liberal
  bias in election coverage, 138, 139; *News
  Twisters* and, 139; OTP and, 161, 163–64,
  167–74; Pentagon Papers and, 145, 150,
  157–58; Project BUN, 172; resignation of,
  175; Rostow Report findings, 166;
  televised election coverage, 168–69;
  Watergate scandal, 89, 158, 161, 174, 175,
  202; Whitehead speeches, 172–73
Nixon, Tricia, 156
NNC (National News Council),
  141

"No-Spin Zone" (television show), 62
NPC (National Press Club), 81–82

Oakes, John, 84
objectivity, 169, 176, 191, 226n6; conserva-
    tive media backlash, 126–31; credibility
    gap, 97, 112; definition, 107, 108; Fairness
    Doctrine and, 9, 177, 181; FCC and,
    134–35; Fox News, 143; generational
    conflict, 99–100, 101; vs. interpretive
    reporting, 105–9; at L.A. Times, 7, 98,
    102–104, 107–112; media watchdog
    groups, 139–42; at New York Times, 7,
    98–102, 104–106, 107–112, 127, 136,
    228n34; Rosenthal and, 98, 99, 100–101,
    104–5, 107–108, 112, 227n15; tension
    between ideology and, 130, 132–33;
    Wicker and, 100–101, 106–7. See also
    Agnew, Spiro, media/objectivity
    criticism by; conservative media;
    Fairness Doctrine; liberal bias; media
    criticism by conservatives
Ochs, Adolph, 98–99, 127
O'Connell, James D., 162
Odom, William, 195–96
Office of Telecommunications Policy (OTP),
    167–74; Owen report, 169–70; Presiden-
    tial Committee report, 173–74; White-
    head as head of, 161, 163–164, 167, 168,
    170–174. See also Federal Communica-
    tions Commission (FCC)
Office of War Information (OWI), 84, 91
O'Reilly, Bill, 62, 176
Osborn, Alex, 57
Owen, Bruce, 169–70

Packard, Vance, 62
Packwood, Robert, 187
Page, Clarence, 187–88
Paley, William, 86
Panama Canal, 54
Panic of 1893, 12, 13
Parade magazine, 137
Park, Robert, 36, 37, 49
partisan press, 127–28, 191. See also
    conservative media; journalists, political
    participation by
Pastore, John, 164
Patrick, Dennis, 188
Pearson, Drew, 59

Peck, Gregory, 121, 122, 123
Pelton, Jack, 195–96
Pennsylvania Christian Crusade Radio
    Hour, 179–80
Pentagon Papers (Project X), 8, 144–59;
    authenticity doubts, 151; editorial
    decisions, 150–55, 156–57; initial
    meetings about, 148–53, 155; legal
    ramifications of publishing, 149, 151,
    155–56, 158; naming of, 157; source for,
    147–48; space allotment for story, 154,
    157. See also New York Times, Pentagon
    Papers and; Rosenthal, A. M. (Abe),
    Pentagon Papers and
Pershing, John J., 192
Pew, Howard, 179
Philadelphia Inquirer (newspaper), 43
Philadelphia North American (newspaper),
    42
Philadelphia Public Ledger (newspaper), 45
Pinker, Steven, 52
Pinky (film), 116
Plato, 52–53
Poitier, Sidney, 116–18, 120, 124
polarized news, 9, 176, 177, 189. See also
    Fairness Doctrine
policymaking, 2–3; cable television and,
    160–62, 163, 166–74; environmental
    issues, 203–4; OTP and, 161, 163–64,
    167–74; Roosevelt and, 53–54. See also
    Fairness Doctrine; government regulations
political cartoons, 5, 24–26; Bellew's, 16–19,
    24–25, 27, 30, 209n17, 210n37; in Daily
    Graphic, 16, 27; Hamilton's, 33; in Justice,
    24–25, 210n37; Keller's, 30; Keppler's,
    27–30, 33; octopus imagery in, 16–18, 27,
    33; Uncle Sam in, 16, 17, 29, 32, 209n17;
    Wales's, 31, 32. See also antimonopoly
    movement
political rhetoric, 53–54, 61, 62
Pope, James S., 193
Popular Front, 65, 66, 69
populists, 67, 75–76
Postel, Charles, 14
postmodernism, 4
Post Office, 32, 44
poverty, 39–41, 104
Powledge, Fred, 147
Pozen, David, 190
Prelude to Victory (Reston), 90

Presidential Cabinet Committee on Cable Television, 167–68, 170–71, 173, 174
presidential campaigns/elections, 80, 204; cable news coverage, 168–69; FDR, 72; Johnson, 121, 123; Kennedy, 74; liberal bias, 74, 109, 138, 139; Nixon, 74, 109; partisan media bias, 70–72, 220n36, 228n36; Reagan, 121–22, 182
presidential press strategies, 3, 121–22; "public"/"modern" presidency, 6, 53–54, 55, 215n12; public relations office, 54–55, 58–59, 215n12; Roosevelt, 53–54, 55, 215n12
Press and Foreign Policy, The (Cohen), 87
press corps, 79, 83
Pressman, Matthew, 7
Price, Monroe, 175
print journalism. *See also under newspapers*
print journalism, Fairness Doctrine and, 181, 182, 184, 188, 189
professionalism. *See* objectivity
Progress and Poverty (George), 22
Progressive politics: advertising, 57; local news, 6, 37, 41, 46, 48–49; media criticism, 67
Project B.U.N., 169–70, 172
Project X. *See New York Times,* Pentagon Papers and; Pentagon Papers (Project X); Rosenthal, A. M. (Abe), Pentagon Papers and
propaganda, 50–62; advertising industry, 56–58, 59, 62; conservative media accused of, 71; Creel and, 52, 55–56, 59; cynicism about, 59–62; Fairness Doctrine and, 134; by and about Germany, 50–52, 55, 59, 60, 61; during interwar period, 56–60; origin of term, 52; public relations, 6, 54–59, 215n12; rhetoric and, 52–54, 61, 62; Roosevelt's mobilization of public opinion, 53–54, 55; Viereck and, 50–52, 60; during WWI, 6, 50–56, 216n23; during WWII, 60–62
Propaganda (Bernays), 58
Proposition 14, 114–15, 119, 120–21, 122–24. *See also* celebrity activism
proprietorships, 11–15, 19, 33–35. *See also* antimonopoly movement
Public Administration Review, 203
Public Broadcasting System (PBS), 140

public relations, 3, 6, 54–59, 215n12; cable legislation, 174; Fairness Doctrine and, 185; *Selling of the Pentagon* documentary, 140; White House office of, 54–55, 58–59, 215n12
Puck (humor magazine), 26, 27, 29, 30, 33
Pulitzer, Joseph, 44, 92
Punch (magazine), 17, 30
Putnam, George, 103

race: boys' clubs, 78, 81, 83; *L.A. Times,* 103–4; Leading Six, 117–19; military desegregation, 91; objectivity and, 101–2, 103. *See also* African Americans; celebrity activism; civil rights movement; segregation
"Radical Chic" (Wolfe), 124
Radio Act (1927), 178
radio networks, 69, 133–35, 177–78
"Radio Right: Hate Clubs on the Air" (Cook), 180
Radio-Television News Directors Association, 187
railroad corporations: antimonopoly movement and, 11, 15–18, 22–24, 27, 34; newspaper delivery costs/Post Office, 44; propaganda by, 54
Raphael, Chad, 140
Raymond, Emilie, 7
Reagan, Ronald, 3, 121–22; Fairness Doctrine elimination, 8, 177, 182, 183–84, 186–87
real estate industry, 39, 114
Ream, Joe, 86
Red Lion Broadcast Company, 179–80
Red Lion Broadcasting Co., Inc. v. Federal Communications Commission (1969), 180–81, 183
Reese, Ben, 92
Regnery, Henry, 126, 130–31
regulations. *See* government regulations
religious broadcasting, 179. *See also* conservative media
reporters, local news, 37–38, 39–40, 46–49. *See also* journalists, political participation by; journalists, social functions/clubs
reporters, Washington D.C. *See* journalists, social functions/clubs
Reporter's Trade, The (Alsop, Joseph and Stewart), 88

Republican Party: conservative media, 129–30; Fairness Doctrine and, 182, 184, 186; media criticism, 70, 74; public relations, 58–59. *See also* Democratic Party

Reston, James B. "Scotty," 81, 84, 85; on blacksheeting, 87; conservative politics of, 146; Gridiron Club membership, 94–95; Lippmann and, 192; objectivity and, 99; Pentagon Papers meeting, 148–53, 155; Rosenthal and, 147, 148–50; social journalism, 89–92. *See also New York Times*

Reston, Sally, 90

Reuther, Walter, 180

rhetoric, 52–54, 61, 62

Richardson, Eliot, 167

Riis, Jacob, 40, 41

Risen, James, 158

Roberts, Steve, 101

Robeson, Paul, 116–17

Robinson, Elihu, 42

Rockefeller, John D., 19, 20, 27, 33

Rogers, Henry H., 33

Romney, George, 167

Roosevelt, Franklin D., 3, 60; media criticism, 63, 64–65, 70, 72, 220n36

Roosevelt, Theodore, 11, 33; public opinion mobilization by, 53–54, 54, 215n12

Rosenthal, A. M. (Abe): conservative politics of, 146–47; objectivity and, 98, 99, 100–101, 104–5, 107–8, 112; Sulzberger ("Punch") and, 147

Rosenthal, A. M. (Abe), Pentagon Papers and, 8, 144–59; authenticity doubts, 151; editorial decisions, 150–55, 156–57; initial meetings, 148–53, 155; journal of, 144–45, 146–47, 148, 149, 150, 154, 159; legal ramifications of publishing, 149, 151, 155–56; loyalty and, 150–51; naming of story, 157; Reston and, 147, 148–50; Sulzberger ("Punch") and, 153–56, 157

Rosten, Leo, 79

Rostow, Eugene V., 162

Rostow Report, 162, 166

Rumford Fair Housing Act (1963), 114, 120, 121

Rusher, Bill, 137, 139, 141, 142

Sabato, Larry, 202

Salisbury, Harrison, 109–10, 146

same-sex marriage, 200–201

San Francisco Call (newspaper), 37

Saturday Evening Post (newspaper), 59

Scalia, Antonin, 174, 183

scarcity rationale, 181, 182, 183, 184, 185, 188, 189. *See also* Fairness Doctrine

"Scenes of the Subway" *(Boston Globe)*, 38

Schildhouse, Sol, 174

Schlafly, Phyllis, 182

Schneider, John, 2

Schudson, Michael, 3, 9, 181, 202

Schwarzenneger, Arnold, 196

Screen Actors Guild, 116

Scripps, E. W., 44, 47

segregation, 115, 118, 119–20; CAP activism for integrated housing, 114, 119, 120–121, 122–124

Seldes, George, 6, 69, 71, 73

selfishness/self-interest, 21–22

Selling of the Pentagon, The (CBS documentary), 140

Senate, U.S., Fairness Doctrine and, 184

sexual orientation, 78, 222n3

Shabecoff, Philip, 201

Sheehan, Neil, 144, 148–53, 154, 156, 157

Shelley, Mary, 17

Shelley v. Kramer (1948), 120

Sherman Act (1890), 10–11, 13

Sherry, Michael, 83

Shoop, Duke, 79

Sigma Delta Chi, 194

Silent Majority, 63, 98, 124

Sinatra, Frank, 114, 118, 119

Sinclair, Upton, 6, 67–68

60 Minutes (television program), 142

Smith, Howard K., 138

Smith, Ralph Lee, 166

Smoot, Dan, 134

Southern Christian Leadership Conference (SCLC), 117, 124

Soviet Union, 195–96

Spectrum (television program), 142

spheres of consensus, legitimate controversy, and deviance, 80–81, 101, 128

spin, 52, 62

Spirit of Maryland (collection of *Baltimore Sun* articles), 45

Spreading Germs of Hate (Viereck), 59–60

Standard Oil, 10, 12, 19, 20, 27–29, 33

Stans, Maurice, 167

Stanton, Frank, 1–2, 86
Starr, Paul, 161
Stars and Stripes (military newspaper), 191
Stars for Freedom committee, 119
Stevens, George, 118, 120
Stevenson, Adlai, 121
St. Louis Post-Dispatch, 89, 92, 93
Stokes, Richard, 92
Stone, I. F., 73
Student Nonviolent Coordinating Committee
     (SNCC), 118, 124
suburbs, 43–49
Sulzberger, Arthur Hays, 90, 91–92
Sulzberger, Arthur Ochs ("Punch"), 100,
     112, 147; Pentagon Papers and, 145, 149,
     151, 153–156, 157
Supreme Court, 150; antitrust suit against
     Associated Press, 64–65; Fairness
     Doctrine decisions, 180–81, 182, 183,
     184; *FCC v. League of Women Voters,* 183;
     FDR plans to pack, 70; *Miami Herald
     Publishing Co. v. Tornillo,* 181; *New York
     Times Company v. United States,* 144–45,
     156; Prop 14, 124; *Red Lion Broadcasting
     Co., Inc. v. Federal Communications
     Commission,* 180–81, 183; *Shelley v.
     Kramer,* 120
Synar, Mike, 186
syndicated news, 37, 46–49
Syracuse Peace Council, 188

tabloid-style journalism, 127
Tacoma Ledger and *News* (newspapers), 42
Tammany Hall, 29–30
Tarbell, Ida M., 19, 20
Tarchiani, Alberto, 90
Task Force on Telecommunications Policy,
     162
Tauke, Tom, 186
Taylor, Elizabeth, 119, 120, 122
technological advancements, 56, 176–77;
     electricity/steam power, 23–24; Fairness
     Doctrine and, 182–83, 184; in newspaper
     production, 38. *See also* cable television
telegraph, 14, 15, 16, 22–24
television news. *See* broadcast television;
     cable television; conservative media
Television/Radio Age (magazine), 164
Texas Law Review, 183
"There *Is* Network News Bias" (Efron), 138

Thomas, Bill, 97, 103, 108–9, 111, 112
Thomas, Helen, 83
Thurber, Francis B., 10–11, 13, 22–24, 26–27,
     30, 34–35
Tillman, "Pitchfork Ben," 53–54
Time magazine, 121, 204
Times Books publishing, 148
"Today, by Arthur Brisbane" (column), 47
Toilers of the Sea (Hugo), 17
Topping, Seymour, 110, 111, 148, 149
transportation monopolies, 12
Truman, Harry S., 91, 93
TV Guide, 138, 141
Twentieth Century Reformation Hour (radio
     program), 179

Uncle Sam, 16, 17, 29, 32, 209n17
U.S. Court of Appeals, 183
United States Information Agency, 86
U.S. Secret Service, 51
United War Work Campaign, 57
Urban League, 117
USA Today, 184
utilitarianism, 21

Vandenberg, Arthur, 192
Vanderbilt, William H., 24–25, 27, 29, 30,
     210n37
Van Dyke, Dick, 121, 122
Variety magazine, 122, 123
Veit, Ivan, 148
Viereck, George Sylvester, 50–52, 60
Vietnam War, 89, 223n13. *See also* Pentagon
     Papers (Project X)
Vietnam War, television coverage, 1–2, 63,
     135–36
Villard, Oswald Garrison, 58, 67, 70

Waggoner, Walter, 93
Wales, James A., 31, 32
Wall, Wendy, 80
Wallen, James, 57
Wall Street Journal, 100, 184
Washington, D. C., 88
Washington, D. C. reporters. *See* journal-
     ists, social functions/clubs
Washington Correspondents, The (Rosten), 79
Washington Globe (newspaper), 53
Washington Post (newspaper), 82, 187, 202;
     Cold War consensus, 86, 87; editorials in,

192; FOIA and, 194; "Ivy Bells" story, 195–96; objectivity, 136; Reston and, 90; WWII correspondence, 84
Wasp (satirical magazine), 30
Watergate scandal, 89, 158, 161, 174, 175, 202
Watson, John, 57
Wealth Against Commonwealth (Lloyd), 20, 21–22, 26
Welliver, Judson, 58–59
Western Union, 15, 16, 19–20, 27
White, Walter, 116
Whitehead, Clay "Tom," 161, 163–64, 167, 168, 170–74
White House Correspondents' Association (WHCA), 81
White House/executive branch, 1–2; AIM and, 140–41; Communications Act and, 162; *News Twisters,* 139; OTP, 161, 163–164, 167–174; public relations, 54, 58–59
Whiteside, Thomas, 174
Wichita Eagle (newspaper), 100
Wicker, Tom, 100–101, 106–7, 136
Wiggins, James Russell, 194
Wikileaks, 158
Williams, Brian, 191
Williams, Nick, 96–97, 103, 105, 107–9, 112; reader demographics and, 110, 111

Willkie, Wendell, 70, 192
Wilson, Edmund, 69
Wilson, Lyle C., 94, 194
Wilson, Woodrow, 51, 52, 54–55, 56, 59, 215n12
Winter, Tom, 138, 141
Wisconsin News, 47
Wolfe, Tom, 124
women, exclusion from journalists' social realm, 77, 78, 81, 83, 88, 223n15
Women's National Press Club (WNPC), 81
Woodward, Bob, 196
World War I: cynicism about propaganda surrounding, 59, 60; isolationism following, 60, 61; propaganda after, 56–60; propaganda during, 6, 50–56, 216n23. *See also* propaganda
World War II: boys' clubs during, 83–85; conservative opinion during, 128; propaganda during, 60–62. *See also* propaganda

Yankelovich, Daniel, 110

Zelizer, Julian E., 8–9
Zinn, Howard, 73